Preparing Students to Engage
in Equitable Community Partnerships

Elizabeth A. Tryon, Haley C. Madden,
and Cory Sprinkel

Preparing Students to Engage in Equitable Community Partnerships

A Handbook

TEMPLE UNIVERSITY PRESS
Philadelphia • *Rome* • *Tokyo*

TEMPLE UNIVERSITY PRESS
Philadelphia, Pennsylvania 19122
tupress.temple.edu

Library of Congress Cataloging-in-Publication Data

Names: Tryon, Elizabeth A., author. | Madden, Haley C., 1987– author. |
Sprinkel, Cory, 1994– author.
Title: Preparing students to engage in equitable community partnerships : a
handbook / Elizabeth A. Tryon, Haley C. Madden, and Cory Sprinkel.
Description: Philadelphia : Temple University Press, 2023. | Includes
bibliographical references and index. | Summary: "A guidebook to help
faculty, staff, and graduate students who develop, maintain, and support
community-university partnerships to prepare students and themselves for
community engagement from a perspective of cultural and intellectual
humility"— Provided by publisher.
Identifiers: LCCN 2023010719 (print) | LCCN 2023010720 (ebook) | ISBN
9781439922736 (cloth) | ISBN 9781439922743 (paperback) | ISBN
9781439922750 (pdf)
Subjects: LCSH: Community and college—United States. | Universities and
colleges—United States—Public services. | Universities and
colleges—Public relations—United States. | Service learning—Study and
teaching (Higher)—United States. | Education, Higher—Social
aspects—United States.
Classification: LCC LC238 .T79 2023 (print) | LCC LC238 (ebook) | DDC
378.1/03—dc23/eng/20230607
LC record available at https://lccn.loc.gov/2023010719
LC ebook record available at https://lccn.loc.gov/2023010720

Printed in the United States of America

9 8 7 6 5 4 3 2 1

Contents

Illustrations and Tables

Figures

Tables

Preface

The pedagogy and practice of community engagement in its many forms have become fairly ubiquitous in higher education in the United States (Bringle & Hatcher, 2000; Dipadova-Stocks, 2005; Hartley, 2009; Jacoby, 1996; Peterson, 2009), with roots going back to the work of Dewey, Freire, and Kolb in further decades past. Community engagement's benefits to student learning are myriad: students report community-engaged courses are more meaningful than traditional classroom courses (Astin & Sax, 1998; Eyler & Giles, 2014; Mabry, 1998), and when done with deliberate attention to equity and good design, community engagement (we use "CE" for brevity) can create value in helping communities build self-capacity (Swords & Kiely, 2010). In sum, CE *can be* transformational for all those involved.

While the student learning outcomes of this practice are well documented (Association of American Colleges and Universities 2007; Kilgo et al., 2015; Kuh, 2008), the effects of CE on communities have been less examined. There is some literature on the unintended consequences of the academy entering communities haphazardly or, worse, with arrogance and assumptions (Sandy & Holland, 2006; Stoecker et al., 2010; Stoecker & Tryon, 2009; Chupp & Joseph, 2010; Tryon et al., 2015). Until recently, most other studies about the community mainly focused on the academic partner's perspective of the relationship. Beginning to emerge is a trend of attuning to community voices (Cronley et al., 2015; Padmanabha, 2018; Racin & Gordon, 2018); other research around the United States has begun to focus on the ethical implications of academic engagement (Van Stekelenburg et al., 2021) and finally, as we share in the following, a new attention to racial injustice.

We coauthors have all served as staff in the University of Wisconsin–Madison's Morgridge Center for Public Service and have collectively been working with students, instructors, and community partners in all these areas of community engagement for over twenty years. We have heard the good, the bad, and the ugly. Despite the potential pitfalls, we believe the practice can have value for *all* stakeholders when done properly. As well as advising on CE's nuts-and-bolts issues of timing, logistics, and other practical considerations, we help instructors and community engagement professionals prepare students (and themselves) for engagement in a "win-win-win" situation: (1) student learning experiences are more authentic and hence more useful, (2) faculty and staff add new knowledge to the field and their own tool belts, and (3) communities feel their investment of time and energy in supervising students has brought them a useful deliverable or even a long-term partnership. This authenticity only comes about in an atmosphere of mutual respect, self-awareness, and, we argue, cultural and intellectual humility.

We wish to note that we are three white authors writing from the landscape of a public service center within a primarily white, research-intensive university, and therefore we acknowledge the power, privilege, and positionality from which we speak and the need to include other voices in this book. Throughout, we have incorporated contributions from a diverse group of practitioners among community colleges, private colleges, historically Black colleges and universities (HBCUs), and minority-serving institutions (MSIs). We have made conscious and persistent efforts to include perspectives of people unlike ourselves and from environments unlike our own, and we are on a continuous, lifelong path to improve our own cultural humility practice. Here are our "identity statements":

CORY is an early career professional with a master's in higher education and student affairs. He has five years of combined professional and paraprofessional experiences supporting community-based learning practices and social justice education. He is a white, cis, able-bodied gay man who grew up in rural Wisconsin. He is also affiliated with a local abolitionist books-to-prisoners organization.

ELIZABETH (Beth) is an emeritus academic staff with almost twenty years as a community engagement professional after a career in jazz performing morphed into a nonprofit organization teaching music improvisation to youth in community settings. She is a child of the anti-war, civil, and women's rights movements of the 1960s and has retained that activist orientation throughout her work in academia.

HALEY is an early career community engagement professional with nine years of experience supporting community-engaged scholarship and conducting community-based research. She is a white, cis, able-bodied straight woman who grew up in Wisconsin and holds a Ph.D. in communications.

We also wish to note that our experiences as facilitators of the lessons and ideas in this book are deeply informed by an intricate weaving of wisdom we are beholden to from a diverse array of scholars, activists, and neighbors committed to this work. This work is not new, and yet it remains urgent. Indeed, for most, these past few years have presented ample challenges and in turn emphasized the necessity of more just and equitable concepts of community and the need for systems, students, and scholarship that rapidly actualize such realities. We have been fortunate to find ourselves in community with change-makers and visionaries, and this book is an attempt to further disseminate these learnings to others.

One book that centers on preparing students for community engagement was recently published—*Preparing Students for Community-Engaged Scholarship in Higher Education* (Zimmerman, 2020). This book contains excellent material from a variety of perspectives, and several chapters include some discussion of cultural sensitivity or cultural competency—but none had been solicited on preparing students with cultural humility or an equity lens per se and as the chapter's focus. Consequently, two of us suggested we coauthor a chapter with colleagues at UW-Madison, dedicated to delving into "Cultural Factors in Preparing Students for Community-Engaged Scholarship." Although the editors gave us a generous fifteen pages, we felt that we had only scratched the issue's surface and that an entire volume might be useful in expanding all the topics that go into this preparation to give them the space they need.

Much of this work to prepare students for CE intersects, but is not identical to, the efforts in student affairs to facilitate institutional diversity and inclusion efforts. While the two portfolios share curricula around interpersonal dynamics and structural oppression, CE adds a layer of complexity: the inherent power imbalance between the educational institution and the off-campus community, which has, by its nature, different priorities than college students and faculty/staff on any particular campus. Also, by instituting courses that require CE at many higher education institutions (HEIs), we are linking CE to a set of course learning objectives while "forcing" students to interact off campus, making it our responsibility to train them properly. This handbook will be centered primarily on American HEIs and U.S. societal issues, but many other countries have similar social issues (e.g., housing and food insecurity, unemployment, immigration, racial tension), albeit manifested in different ways depending on the culture (see the discussion of Science Shops in Chapter 9).

If you are teaching a community-based learning (CBL) course or facilitating a civic engagement program, this book is for you. If you are advising undergraduates or graduate students doing community-based research, this book is for you. If you are engaged in any form of community engagement as a scholar, this book is for you! No matter where you are in terms of experience, you will be able to use this book in the ways that most benefit your situation. For those of you who have taught CBL courses for years but are always looking for ways to tweak your content for new topics you want to address, each chapter is laid out with a discussion of topic areas followed by practical strategies, activities or links to them, and appendices of resource material to inform your curriculum development that are easy to find and tailor to your current knowledge base and needs.

Note: If you are brand new to the concept of CE in your teaching or practice, you will want to supplement this reading with a few foundational resources. There are many of these, and some we reach for and recommend time and time again. You will find a short list of these in Appendix B.

Rationale

Why is doing this cultural preparation work with students so important for quality community engagement, equity, and authentic partnerships? We summarize our reasons in the following:

- The community is asking for academia to do a better job.
- Volunteering and CBL seem here to stay in higher education, and student energy and enthusiasm are renewable and almost unlimited. Instead of charity, why not move toward supporting change to solve underlying issues together?
- The current cultural and political climate in the United States and the lack of dialogue across difference make this work even trickier but also crucial.

The Community Is Asking Us to Do a Better Job

This is not a recent surprise request but rather is coming from a community voice that had largely been unheeded in academic research until it began growing in volume in recent years.

In 2006, Beth participated in a graduate research methodologies course project that interviewed sixty-seven staff members of small-to-medium-sized local nonprofits and grassroots organizations on their perceptions of college students who came to them as "service learners." The answers were so provocative that it turned into a book project, published by Temple University Press: *The Unheard Voices* (Stoecker & Tryon, 2009). That book led to several years of traveling around the United States spreading the news about what that community had said about their experiences hosting college students and working with faculty. Since little had been written before that time from the community's perspective, it became widely circulated and cited in the field, along with a few similar studies, notably Marie Sandy and Barbara Holland's Campus Compact study that was conducted nearly simultaneously (2006).

The folks who participated in the *Unheard Voices* study suggested developing a list of "Community Standards for Service Learning," created in collaboration with about thirty of the partners from the original study (Stoecker & Tryon, 2007; view these at https://scholarshare.temple.edu/handle /20.500.12613/8178). The idea for a brochure came out of a group-think activity after the graduate students in the *Unheard Voices* project presented their draft findings at a charette-style planning event. The community partners suggested that their recommendations be published as a one-page pamphlet for organization staff to keep in their top drawers whenever they received a call from a student or professor. *The Unheard Voices* devotes a full chapter to unpack every recommendation and explain the process in detail. We distributed the standards among our community partners, and despite the challenges of frequent organization staff turnover, students graduating, and changing faculty course responsibilities, we have seen them used often as a resource, as well as a teaching tool in student orientations. Our center took on as much of the work contained in the recommendations as we possibly could, some of it requiring long-term planning and collaborations across campus aimed at better institutionalizing CE—a space in which many HEI engagement offices find themselves in these days.

One of the unanticipated findings through grounded theory analysis in the 2006 study was a recurring plea from the community to examine the issue of "diversity" in CE—a topic the project's community steering committee had not identified (one reason may have been a lack of diversity in organization staff, also pointed out in the interviews). One of the five planks of the platform of the standards became "promoting diversity." In this area, we heard the community's message that we needed to improve quickly, and we wanted to make learning about cultural issues accessible to instructors as soon as possible. We got to work on collecting and sifting through all the content we could find or gather from our peers. We also began collecting resources from outside academia, many of which you will see referenced in this volume. A tenet of community engagement is that we all have valuable expertise that should be recognized. Indeed, nonacademic resources can often be more relatable and useful than their academic counterparts.

By 2016, our staff had amassed a large collection of materials and resources on cultural issues and began to put them into annotated "buckets" on our website. We also started presenting some of that material at conferences. Every session we led with a title referring to "cultural humility" or "cultural awareness" became a standing-room-only space. HEI staff and faculty approached us afterward, telling us how much this kind of work was needed and how little experience and capacity they themselves, and many others at their institution, had to deliver it to students. (We also heard a bit of pushback; when doing a workshop at a national meeting of community engagement professionals, or CEPs, one attendee complained, "Why are you talking about 'equity?' I just coordinate service learning; I don't need to learn about all that stuff.")

Supporting Change within the Existing Academic Structure

Some of our colleagues maintain that students really should have a full semester of prep work before they are allowed to go out into community organizations to do service or project work, saying things like, "You wouldn't send a student out to do nursing without any nursing training." Of course not, but even in less acute circumstances, should we send students who know little about the job they might be performing in the community? We ourselves would love for a semester devoted entirely to preparation to be a prerequisite to any CE experience. Currently, however, it does not seem many HEIs are going to require or make space for that amount of training in the face of "time to degree" pressure and the packed, sequentially rigid semester course plans entailed by many majors. Indeed, faculty objected vociferously at a national meeting in 2012 where we suggested this, saying that students barely had time to take an elective CBL course, much less an entire semester's training course prior to that. There was an underappreciation of the urgency around mitigating bad outcomes of unintended harm to underresourced communities, and there was no community representation in that room. We have seen courses of study where a CE approach is scaffolded with plenty of preparation as a prerequisite (e.g., nursing, pharmacy, and social work practicums), but we recognize that not all departments can build in that structure. What can we do in the face of those limits?

Our center decided to take up the challenge in that question and began to organize the materials we had been collecting into training modules, shaped substantially by faculty who were good at preparing their students and our own CBL interns (undergraduates hired specifically because they had experience with engagement and, for many, backgrounds in dialogue facilitation; they supported CBL classes with various tasks, including student preparation and reflection). We have witnessed these peer mentors doing a magnificent job of leading sometimes very sensitive discussions with students, helping and guiding them to be more culturally aware with gentleness and skill, not by shaming them. Later chapters talk more about the different starting points that students come from and other issues in facilitating critical classroom conversations. One of these interns, Bertha Gonzalez, has provided a contribution in Chapter 6 about her valuable experience in the role.

We offered the services of these interns to instructors who would allow them an hour of class time to work with the students prior to service work. As busy instructors know, it is asking a lot for someone to give up a chunk of class time already packed with disciplinary content, so the effect is limited. We also can only cover so much ground with the human resources we have. We started thinking about online content that could be assigned as homework and other strategies to scale up and preserve class time for other content, since UW–Madison typically offers over a hundred CBL courses each year.

At that time, we were in the process of doing a follow-up to *The Unheard Voices* as a community-based research study in a UW class taught by Carolina Sarmiento. The students completed interviews and focus groups, and we prepared a report that was sent back to the participants (view this report at https://scholarshare.temple.edu/handle/20.500.12613/8178).

An oft-mentioned finding was that of "preparation" for students to serve:

> Community partners continue to invest a significant amount of their time in training—and then supervising—students. *Partners want the UW to do a better job of training students to work in the community, including helping students develop self and cultural awareness and understand social identity.* (Tryon et al., 2016; italics in the original)

The Civic Action Plan

In a parallel timeline, Campus Compact, an organization committed to advancing CE within higher education, called for HEIs to develop a Civic Action Plan or recommitment to the public purpose of education. In 2015, UW–Madison took up the call, and our center's faculty director, Kathy Cramer, was tapped to lead the campus-wide creation of a plan at the request of Chancellor Rebecca Blank (University of Wisconsin–Madison, Office of the Chancellor, 2018). These findings echoed those of the Sarmiento study (Tryon et al., 2016). One sentiment in particular from community partners in both studies boiled down to: "We're tired of shouldering the burden of teaching your students not to be culturally clueless. Stop bringing your white nonsense!"

With this report, we finally had enough leverage to create actionable steps. The Civic Action Plan was officially adopted, and our chancellor funded a position for a community engagement preparation specialist (Cory first filled this role) in our center for three years, with a budget to hire a few undergrad interns and graduate hourlies. In late 2019, Cory met again with community partners and faculty in focus groups to solicit insights to best shape this curriculum, which took the form of a tiered workshop, as well as online module curriculum—both of which, once drafted, were also reviewed by a small number of paid community consultants. With a small team and a large campus, the distribution of the online training modules has helped us still meet a large number of CBL students while also facilitating a substantial number of workshops each semester. The modules, which exist on UW's online learning platform, Canvas, can easily be added to instructor or program course pages.

Note: If your institution utilizes Canvas, you can access the modules through Canvas Commons under the title "Community Engagement Preparation Series—Academic Courses." If you do not have access to Canvas, we have also included material in the online modules as a collection in the Temple University Press Books: Supplemental Material online community, available at this link: https://scholarshare.temple.edu/handle/20.500.126 13/8178. Another use for the modules and the process of creating the content

Online Module Overviews

1. **Introduction to Community Engagement:** This introductory module explores our individual and collective motivations for engaging with community and the impact those motivations can have on our experience. This module also provides some general considerations and guidance regarding community engagement.

2. **Contextualizing Community:** The second module focuses on three key areas that affect our interactions with community: how we understand community, how we understand ourselves, and how we understand the big picture.

3. **Engaging with Community:** This module is focused on building skills and considerations crucial to engaging with community. From active listening to relationship building and building equitable partnerships, this module aims to ready you for engagement.

would be as a model that your institution can tailor to your own demographics and setting.

Cultural and Political Climate in the United States

We had already noticed a shift in American political dialogue in those years, and that divisiveness seemed to create an urgency to help students talk across difference. Then, in 2020, as anyone alive then knows, the entire platform shifted. We were first faced with a global pandemic that has impacted marginalized communities disproportionately, followed by a boiling-over point in a much-needed foregrounding of our country's inattention to racial justice, followed by an incredibly divisive presidential election and aftermath that resulted in real threats to American democracy. The higher education community needed to pivot, learn, respond, counsel, and advocate nimbly, as never before. Even in the "before times," we coauthors and our colleagues believed that colleges and universities have a moral responsibility to do as much work for equity as we humanly can, and we had started to draft this book. In 2020 it became even more urgent to ramp up the work, in the face of the huge challenges confronted by those who do not have the luxury of "work from home" jobs, as a small contribution to the goal of equitable partnership. As the front page of the Campus Compact national conference website stated in early 2022, "If we get back to normal, we will have failed. We come together to imagine a better way forward, mobilizing the power of higher education to drive innovation, build connections, and create a new normal centered in equity and justice" (Campus Compact, 2022).

Therefore, this book and our online modules are the modest tools we have to offer others seeking help with preparing students for this better way forward. We write this in hopes that instructors will find it helpful. We do not claim to have created a one-size-fits-all approach, but hopefully this book is a starting place, a jumping-off point along the way in this fast-changing social and political landscape. Please know that we in no way consider ourselves to be the final authority that community engagement professionals could ever need, but rather, we are eager to share what we have learned and gathered and to hear from you about what you know. We have included links and references to the sources and activities we have gleaned along the way. Also, please check out the annotated list of activities and recommended resources in the appendices. We encourage you to tailor these materials to your context and teaching style. Before you can impart ideas of identity, privilege, oppression, bias, or power dynamics to your students, you will want to become familiar and facile with these concepts yourself. Please take time with these before beginning to integrate them into your curriculum. Perhaps most importantly, realize this work can be delicate and fraught with potentially strong or inappropriate reactions from students, for which we will help you prepare.

Reflect deeply on what resources are available to you and what learning, relearning, or unlearning you may need to do in order to best support students and community. As authors, we have collectively attended an innumerable number of workshops and conferences and have actively sought feedback from our colleagues and partners, and we are still learning, making mistakes, and adjusting our practice. Consider potential partners in this work, perhaps in the form of graduate students, peer mentorship opportunities, or accountability partners, so you are creating opportunities to receive honest feedback and support. As we say repeatedly throughout this book, relationships are the bedrock, and this work cannot be done in isolation.

Organization of This Guidebook

This book is structured into three broad parts. The first part introduces essential topics and acts as a broad overview. The second part explores the core topics and strategies essential to student preparation for CE. This includes material about how to define and approach concepts like power and culture, develop student understanding of community context, and address issues such as saviorism. The concepts are structured with a developmental lens in mind, starting with understanding students' expectations and assumptions of CE and building toward engaging students with more complex understandings of social identity and systems of oppression. Ultimately, we aim to provide students with the grounding and skills necessary to actualize and appreciate the role of humility within community engagement. This middle part loosely follows the outline of the virtual training modules and workshop curriculum we have developed at our institution.

The third part of the book aims to provide instructors and staff with additional skills, considerations, and contexts useful to approaching CE in higher education. Throughout this book, but especially in Part III, you will find interspersed contributions from some of our colleagues and innovators in higher education who share their ideas, stories, and lessons about these concepts and practices. We are humbled and grateful to be able to showcase their perspectives through this book.

Each chapter begins with discussion and background on the main topic(s) and moves to specific, concrete strategies and tools for you to tailor for your classrooms or discussion groups. You may notice some overlap and intersections of some of the main concepts between chapters. We have come back to certain things intentionally to illustrate the interconnectivity and codependence of these concepts depending on what lens they are being viewed through, be it student, instructor, or community member.

Please accept our most heartfelt gratitude that you have picked up this book and our hopes that it will further develop your ability to prepare students to do equitable, authentic community engagement that is meaningful to them and more useful to the communities they engage with. Enjoy!

Acknowledgments

All of our outside contributors to this book—thank you so much for your thoughtful and informative pieces.

Thanks also go to the following:

Aaron Javsicas, Will Forrest, and Gary Kramer at Temple University Press for their constant guidance and support.

Campus Compact: Clayton Hurd and Marisol Morales for referring us to CEPs at all types of colleges and universities to gain their perspectives and contributions.

Dr. Earlise Ward, Professor Kathy Cramer, Lisa Chambers, and all the dedicated professional staff at the Morgridge Center for Public Service who have encouraged and supported the work over the years to develop this content and build infrastructure for equitable community engagement at the University of Wisconsin–Madison.

Michelle Hennings and Carolyn Daughtry Krill of DoIT Technology for helping us actualize our content digitally.

The national network of the Engagement Scholarship Consortium for being responsive thought partners and helping keep our community of scholars current with knowledge of the field's evolution, especially Dr. Lorilee Sandmann and Burton Bargerstock for their advice, support, and mentorship.

Andy Furco for helpfully sharing knowledge about University of Minnesota's policies on community engagement as well as facilitating our learning about their Urban Research and Outreach-Engagement Center.

And all our teachers, mentors, family, and friends in this work.

Beth: Thanks especially to Randy Stoecker, my graduate advisor and coeditor on *The Unheard Voices*, for his constant support and guidance through the years. Also to my husband, Ted, for being a sounding board and for his patience when I disappeared into the manuscript. And to coauthors Haley and Cory, you are a pleasure to write with!

Haley: I would like to thank my coauthors for being wonderful colleagues, mentors, cowriters, and friends! I would also like to thank my partner and my family for their steadfast support of me and my writing abilities.

Cory: Thank you to all those who have shaped me and engaged me further in this work. And a special thank you to my amazing coauthors, it has been a joy to create this with you.

Preparing Students to Engage
in Equitable Community Partnerships

Part I

Introduction and Theory

Introduction to Community Engagement

This introduction to community engagement includes ways of using this chapter, along with some definitions of terms that we use, and briefly touches on the topics that are important to cover in preparing students for CE done with humility.

The material in this chapter can be considered a Community Engagement Preparation 101 overview, which can be front-loaded into a student's CE experience at the beginning of a term or project, especially if time and course content constraints preclude integrating this material more deeply throughout the semester. This training should occur *before* students begin engaging with community partners, in order to give them an initial foundation in good practice and increase the odds that they get off on the right foot in building relationships. This chapter can be used by instructors, program managers, and mentors in at least four ways:

Condensed basic training: In some courses of study where extremely strict degree program requirements make more extensive training challenging, a CE 101 presentation based on the content of this chapter may be the only preparation material for which instructors can make space. We do not recommend this approach, but we recognize that logistical constraints may limit preparation to these basics. For instance, in cocurricular situations (e.g., a student volunteer organization), the time allotted to training may be short because of the minimal time expectation for cocurricular activities. Students may have agreed only to attend a ninety-minute orientation before embarking on a once-a-week tutoring program with middle school youth. As we discuss throughout this handbook, it is entirely possible to do harm to communities by sending students (or faculty) to do CE without adequate training and reflection (Doran et al., 2021). While some training is better than none at all, we maintain that it is better when students enter communities more fully prepared to respectfully engage with community members and be useful in the community setting. However, this introductory material can at least begin to address the concept of "do no harm."

Using the concepts as an integrated piece of a course or program: This book seeks to provide instructors with the tools, outside resources, and considerations necessary to develop sincere and civic-minded students, and we highly recommend this approach to prepare students as fully as possible both prior to and during engagement. We hope that the integration of these topics into the classroom allows you to better honor the humanity of your students and yourself. These are heavy yet ever-present topics in the minds of students, especially those who are most vulnerable because of the inequities in today's world. We encourage instructors to meaningfully reflect on their roles as educators and consider how they can foster a more equitable institution. We recognize that change is slow and hard, but we hope instructors and advisors might use this "primer" chapter to consider changes to their curriculum, begin a conversation with students, and spark curiosity in students' thought processes to motivate them to seek out more opportunities for learning on their own.

Introduction to more in-depth material: The best use for the material in this chapter would be to introduce students to all these concepts broadly in the very early days of a course or research project and explain that more content will unfold, linked to course content, as the weeks of the term progress. In this case, it is important that students' questions about the overview material can be saved in a "parking lot" (or bike rack!) in an online instructional platform, through student journaling, or in an email to the instructor. This introductory content scratches the surface of many complex, deep issues, and it is helpful for students to know they will have continued opportunities to learn and reflect as the semester goes on. Concepts introduced in this chapter are all unpacked in much deeper detail in subsequent chapters, which will be referred to by number for easy reference.

Because this overview can in no way do justice to some of the most complex issues of social and racial equity, framing the conversation by keeping the door open to further learning is key. Starting to talk about, for example, the topic of saviorism can be a stepping stone to understanding cultural humility (defined in this chapter and the subject of Chapter 7) and a relevant way to introduce the concept in the context of the campus–community partner power dynamic. Educators can set students up for more learning about cultural and intellectual humility in community interactions by encouraging them to focus on relationships and how and why to work with others. Also bear in mind that this collaborative approach to learning may be unfamiliar to a number of students who have become accustomed to being passively lectured at and adhering to strict curricular checklists. Building students' capacity to understand themselves as stakeholders in their own education is a process in its own right.

Baseline curriculum for instructors who have experience with this content: A final way that we recommend using this intro material is as a baseline for instructors who have knowledge and experience in some pieces of this curriculum but would like additional support in other areas. For instance, an instructor may feel comfortable discussing active listening or institutional power dynamics but may feel unprepared to teach on implicit bias or social identity. This chapter outlines foundational material and practices, with referrals to more in-depth resources in later chapters on topics to zero in on, while leaving space for instructors to include their own areas of expertise. Instructors can then use the following chapters on an as-needed basis to supplement their own materials.

Online Modules

As we mentioned in the previous chapter, we have developed several online modules for use at our institution that may be used in conjunction with this book. These interactive modules are designed to be self-guided so that instructors can assign them to students to complete outside of class. Using our institution's virtual learning platform (Instructure, n.d.), the modules are designed so that instructors can have access and grading permissions on the activities, such as reflections and reading checks. These modules include place markers that allow instructors to assign certain pieces of content to fill gaps while giving them flexibility to dig deeper in the areas they are skilled at teaching to augment those assignments. Any campus with a Canvas subscription is able to access our modules via Canvas Commons, with the caveat that some of the material is geared to UW–Madison students and the hyperlocal climate specifically, so not all may be as relevant at your institution. An ideal way to approach these modules at other institutions would be to use them as examples of what can be created and tailored to each campus' context, demographics, and setting and then create your own.

If your institution utilizes Canvas, you can access the modules through Canvas Commons under the title, "Community Engagement Preparation Series—Academic Courses."

Definitions

Before embarking on this curriculum, we feel it is important to ground the work in a common understanding of basic terms. It is easy to get myopic about jargon when you are steeped in it, but one piece of critical reflection that runs through the practice of cultural and intellectual humility is to be constantly vigilant in dialing back on assumptions and focus on creating shared understanding. Sharing definitions and terminology like this with students is also useful to ensure classroom discussions are grounded in a shared language. Because you are reading a book to help you prepare students for CE, you may know a lot of these terms already, but there are a lot of different ways of naming similar concepts, and we would like to introduce readers to this standard set of our mutually agreed-upon definitions for this book's purposes. As we stated in the preface, if this is the first experience you have ever had with the idea of teaching or researching in a community-engaged pedagogy, the list of resources in the appendixes will get you more familiar with the theory and practice of CE in general. Here, we operate on the assumption that you may know a bit about what these practices are and the basics of how they work.

The following is a list of the terms we feel are most important related to engagement. You may also have others to add to your own list.

Community: Wow. This is the biggest bucket and the most easily misinterpreted word in this field of practice! The term is thrown around loosely and with little context in different settings to the point that it is easily diluted and so vague as to be almost meaningless. For our shared understanding as part of a higher education institution, in an office that supports engagement, we use "community" with "engagement" in the context of working off campus, locally or globally, in a broad sense—but we make sure that class discussions, partnership ideas, and learning outcomes are grounded in how the term can shift in meaning depending on the audience and activity:

- "Community" can describe a group that is demographically similar ("college students at your institution" would be a student's own internal community). Externally it can refer to people bundled by circumstance (e.g., nonprofit organizations, grassroots groups, senior living communities, or K–12 schools).
- It can mean a group of people with shared interests (religion, job sector, environmental).
- "Community" can also describe a shared identity (race or ethnicity, sexual orientation, ability, age, religion). These identities may intersect and may also be socially constructed, which can signal fluidity in their interpretation and salience.

- "Community" may also be used to describe an area and the people in it bound solely by a geographic location, regardless of demographic characteristics or interests.

Instructors should attempt to be as clear as possible when conceptualizing their context-specific definitions of "community" with students. For example, working with youth in a community center is one thing, but if we get more specific, it might be middle school boys at a community center within a neighborhood community that is primarily low income and people of color.

Community-based organization (CBO): We use this term to define both nonprofit agencies and grassroots organizations, as well as loosely referring to public schools and their sanctioned afterschool and summer activities. Sometimes we use "community partners" when they have an established relationship with a campus or instructor/students. The acronym NGO (nongovernmental organization) is sometimes used. In the EU and other places, the common term is "Civil Society Organization" or CSO.

Community engagement (CE): This term is more prevalent in higher education than outside it, but it is gaining traction in industry sectors that have public service as part of their mission. To some people outside higher education institutions (HEIs) who have not had much interaction with students or faculty, it can seem rather nebulous or needlessly mystifying (e.g., Schechner, 1995). For the purposes of student preparation, we denote community engagement (CE for brevity) as any activity in which college students interact with community organizations for mutual benefit. Stanford developed a set of terms called the Pathways of Service Model (Haas Center for Public Service, n.d.) that helps categorize the different ways that CE happens from the perspective of the college student, and these may be useful to share with them, especially in entry-level courses:

- **Community-based learning (CBL) and community-based research (CBR):** Connecting coursework and academic research to community-identified concerns to enrich knowledge and inform action on social issues. Community-based research is academic research done in collaboration with community partners. There are a few different forms of CBR; other names or methodologies include community-based participatory research (CBPR; see more in Chapter 9), participatory action research (PAR), action research, and cooperative inquiry.
- **Community organizing and activism:** Involving, educating, and mobilizing individual or collective action to influence or persuade others.

- **Direct service:** Working to address the immediate needs of individuals or a community, often involving contact with the people or places being served.
- **Philanthropy:** Donating or using private funds or charitable contributions from individuals or institutions to contribute to the public good.
- **Policy and governance:** Participating in political processes, policy making, and public governance.
- **Social entrepreneurship and corporate social responsibility:** Using ethical business or private sector approaches to create or expand market-oriented responses to social or environmental problems.

Community-engaged scholarship (CES): The field of research on, as well as the scholarly practice of the credit-based or academic CE activities prior, can be referred to by the umbrella term "community-engaged scholarship," or CES. The Campus Compact (2022) website states:

Community engaged scholarship can be found in teaching, research and/or service. It is academically relevant work that simultaneously addresses disciplinary concerns and fulfills campus and community objectives. It involves sharing authority with community partners in the development of goals and approaches, as well as the conduct of work and its dissemination.

Community engagement professional (CEP): This is a relatively new term and a new way of defining the broad swath of people who are involved with this field, emerging from research done by Dr. Lina Dostilio for Campus Compact in 2017. For brevity, we (following Dostilio's lead) abbreviate this term to CEP. CEPs are "those whose formal administrative responsibilities are to support community engagement at post-secondary institutions" (Dostilio & Welch, 2019, p. 1). When you peel back the curtain of our institutions, it becomes clear that many people are involved in community-engaged work. From coordinators for a science, technology, engineering, and math (STEM) outreach program to advisors of community-engaged student organizations or university extension staff and faculty, as well as high-level leadership positions such as vice provosts for outreach or directors of community-engaged programs and offices, community engagement can show up in many places across a university, but not until recently have we begun to think of these disparate roles within a more centralized professional umbrella relating to community engagement.

Nowadays it is becoming more common for recent graduates to seek out training and work in this field after having taken CBL courses, served as

VISTAs (Volunteers in Service to America), or completed internships that made them aware of the possibilities that now exist to follow their passions for engaging with communities for mutual learning and progress (Mitchell & Rost-Banik, 2019). At several schools, including UW–Milwaukee, University of Colorado Boulder, and Merrimack College, actual degree programs have been established at both the undergraduate and graduate level with a specific emphasis on CES, and students are formally trained to take on a CEP job. Campus Compact (n.d.) has begun a certification for CEPs that includes a rigorous set of competencies.

Throughout this book we often use the term "CEP" interchangeably with "faculty" or "instructor." Although there are important distinctions between positions that lean administrative/program management and positions that lean strictly teaching (and those can be blurred), both CEPs and faculty/instructors often find themselves responsible for directing student CE and can make use of this material in similar ways.

Critical service learning: According to Tania Mitchell (2008), "Critical service-learning programs encourage students to see themselves as agents of social change, and use the experience of service to address and respond to injustice in communities" (p. 51). Critical service learning is explicit in its goal of social justice, and all activities in the course or CE experience work toward that goal.

Cultural humility: Cultural humility asks us to recognize that we will never know everything about another person's culture, but we can remain open to learning. Specifically, cultural humility asks us to recognize the many different ways of living in, experiencing, and understanding the world and not assign value to those different methods (Tervalon & Murray-Garcia, 1998). Chapter 7 is devoted to delving deep into this concept, as we believe that it is the foundation for authentic, equitable community partnership work and arguably the most important characteristic of good practice from which much of the rest flows.

Equity: Equity is just and fair inclusion. An equitable society is one in which all can participate and prosper (Natural Resources Defense Council, 2019). Distinct from equality, which posits that everyone be treated exactly the same, equity aims to ensure that everyone is granted the resources or conditions necessary to reach their full potential. Much more has been written about this in the last few years, pertaining to academia and beyond.

Equitable engagement (and, hence, partnership): This refers to a combination of processes that support the participation of those with marginalized identities (e.g., people of color, immigrant and refugee communities, and low-income people in neighborhood groups' outreach and public engagement processes). This type of engagement is about building strong and sustainable relationships and partnerships (Seattle Neighborhoods, n.d.).

Note that these activities can all fall into the two basic categories of credit based and cocurricular. We believe most of this material is relevant to either category—some will pertain more to credit-based learning than volunteering, but if we use the word "instructors," that does not mean we are excluding student organization advisors or any other category of CEPs.

Besides defining these terms specific to CE, academics need to be careful when they throw out current buzzwords or other sweepingly general terms that can be interpreted in a number of ways. Here are a couple examples of what we mean:

Reciprocal: HEIs typically interpret the term "reciprocal" as meaning that people on campus feel a mutual respect and an understanding of trying to listen to community partners' ideas instead of just swooping in with their own or boilerplate solutions to wicked problems of which they may not know the local context. With some partners, though, we have heard the interpretation of the word as, "Wait—you want us to *reciprocate*? *You* have all the resources of stuff, money, and the luxury of time your students can spend on unpaid projects . . . we don't have any resources we can reciprocate with that would benefit your institution!"

Service: The broad term, of course, refers to an "contribution to the welfare of others" (Merriam-Webster, n.d.). At our institution, we have moved from using the term "service learning" to "community-based learning" in response to community feedback in early research by our center at UW–Madison. When researchers asked community organization staff who worked with service learners what the term "service learning" meant, a number answered with some version of one of these responses (paraphrased):

a. "Oh, that's where we do you the service of educating your unskilled undergrads for free, while you go have a latte!"
b. "We think what you mean is that your students are doing us the service of giving us their time. . . . We know they mean well, but if they are unskilled and unprepared, it really isn't a net gain." Many community partners said the word was loaded with patriarchal meaning (indeed, the term "service" can have many meanings if not given context) and implied that HEIs only regarded communities through a deficit model that perpetuated an unequal power dynamic.

The word "service" can also have implications for how students understand the course experience; they may perceive their engagement as a "gift" to or for the organization, rather than framing the experience as a collaborative, reciprocal process in which, indeed, they have given their best effort at being useful while being grateful to the community partner's gift of knowledge to them. This is described in further detail in a case study by Sophie Oldfield (2008).

Thus, it is crucial to apply a critical lens to the language used when not in the academic "playground," where jargon is commonly understood, and to clearly spell out what actions lie behind the rhetoric. Once these definitions have been introduced and discussed, the fundamentals of preparing students to work with communities start with a basic understanding of the particular community in which they will engage, their motivations to be engaged there, and the potential impact of that engagement.

Essential Preparation Concepts

This section introduces specific topics educators should address with students prior to their engagement with communities. This is a brief overview to acquaint instructors with the basic concepts of preparing for community engagement, with more detailed "deep dives" in the following chapters.

Learning about the Community

How often, in higher education settings, do we hear the phrase "town-gown" and not stop to unpack the nuances of this campus-community dynamic? "The ivory tower" is a concept that has origins as far back as 1355, when a tavern brawl between Oxford students who insulted the quality of the wine and the "townies" who came to the aid of the offended innkeeper escalated into what became known as the St. Scholastica Day Riot. Over ninety people died and hundreds more were injured in a pitched battle with bows and arrows (Droucopoulos, 2021; Skoda, 2017; Taylor, n.d.). Adding insult to literal injury, because of Oxford's elevated place in the Catholic hierarchy at the time, King Edward III punished the townspeople of Oxford with an annual ritual humiliation that continued for almost five hundred years: every St. Scholastica's Day thereafter, the "mayor and leading citizens had to walk bareheaded through the town and attend a [Mass for the Dead to] pray for the souls of the slain students" (Droucopoulos, 2021, p. 4) and then swear an annual oath to observe the university's now expanded privileges.

That level of formalized elite status may be a thing of the past, but in many college towns, the attitude of superiority and elite status is still alive and well (Ratnatunga, 2012; Warren, 1976), with a resulting disconnect between campus and community. Students may be picking up perceptions that just by being at a respected university, they are better than those who do not have that privilege. At our institution, the campus is so self-contained (even though it is in the middle of a city) that students, while technically (albeit temporary) citizens of the city, do not have to venture very far out into it to meet their basic needs. As in many college towns, there is a "campustown" adjacent or even interwoven into the university's boundaries. Often, the twenty-first-century campus is marketed as having every imaginable amenity from faddish clothing to books to climbing walls, all onsite, to attract students who have choices on where to spend their tuition dollars (Koch, 2018; McClure, 2019). This means students can choose to self-isolate from the surrounding community, its people, and its priorities. This issue is compounded by the fact that for many students, whether from rural towns or outside the state (or even country), this may be their first time living somewhere new or encountering people with lived experiences or identities different than their own. This generally means they are bringing with them their own assumptions and biases, which may manifest in a myriad of ways (i.e., microaggressions, stereotyping, or fear of people different from them) that negatively impact other students on campus and the broader community.

Thus, students must either have the curiosity to discover what is beyond the boundaries of campus and their relation to it or be incentivized by instructors or mentors to seek out broader opportunities for enriching experience and understanding. The university has power and influence over the messaging around this dynamic (Barnhardt et al., 2015), and it can encourage exploration done in a culturally humble way or perpetuate the mentality of academic superiority (discussed in Chapters 5 and 7) that has been well documented as being unhelpful.

Over the years at our institution, we have heard that many students who did traverse beyond the campus bubble as part of a community-engaged program were flabbergasted that our city had such richness and diversity in businesses, natural attractions, and community members. We have heard students say, after a tour of a diverse area only a mile from campus, "I had no idea all this [ethnic restaurants and groceries, community centers, parks, nonprofit agencies serving diverse ethnic groups] was here!" Students of color have said, "I had no idea I could get a decent haircut/style here instead of having to travel to Chicago!" (M. Nellis, personal conversation, 2010). Elevating the assets and strengths of the communities that students engage with is essential to ensuring an impactful project and developing students' holistic understanding of community (more about asset-based approaches to CE can be found in Chapter 9).

Every town and campus situation is unique, but HEIs often have major differences in relationship to the communities they are in by the nature of who can afford to attend college, faculty education and income levels, and the fact that many students come from outside the community, state, or even country in which they attend college (Standifer, 2021; Warren, 1976). We discuss how these resource and power dynamics play out more fully in

Chapter 5. In terms of bridging the gaps created by this culture divide, there are many internet resources for familiarizing students with the community that surrounds their campus. A good first assignment in a CBL class would be to look up and summarize the community's makeup, as this is a great way to get a sense of the landscape and cut down on unnecessary questions students sometimes ask of community organization staff if they have not done this legwork. Some good sources for this may include these:

- Local government and census sites have economic, education, and housing statistics.
- Public health websites are extremely sophisticated, especially since the COVID-19 pandemic, and have rich information on community health and health disparities.
- Local archives or history museums may shed light on specific events or stories that can deepen students' understanding of the local community.
- Individual nonprofit websites generally have information on mission and vision, programs, and audience. No student should ever need to ask busy organization staff for this basic information.

Additionally, students need to be aware of their particular college or university's history with its own community (including Indigenous communities), as well as the relationship between higher education and the public generally (e.g., Tuskegee) that we describe at length in later chapters. At our university, we begin every facilitation opportunity with a land acknowledgment statement (see more in Chapter 3 and Appendix B.1) to center participants in a reflective, open, and empathetic mindset that is grounded in and attuned to place. Investigating and reflecting on these pieces of information within a course context allows students to think more critically about how the project or community relates to course content and why community context is a crucial consideration.

Framing the Community Engagement

Prior to much study about CE that took the community's perceptions into account, sources on "service learning" focused on the one-way direction of student energy being used to "help" community members (Cruz & Giles, 2000). To establish a more authentic, robust learning context for students and to ensure partners gain something impactful, instructors should frame CE as a collaborative process in which students and community members learn and gain from each other, rather than students believing their only role is to help or teach community members. Regardless of the interaction, students are guaranteed to learn *something* while they are in the community; community members have no such guarantee. While many partners answer end-of-semester surveys with high reviews and remarks of gratitude and satisfaction, these often reflect straightforward projects in which students are filling a gap in resources that the partner cannot fill (e.g., pulling invasive weeds or trimming bushes in front of a nonprofit building). As well, many partners report that there are lots of things to love about college students, including their youthful idealism and exuberance, which are often very appealing when they are working with K–12 students (Stoecker & Tryon, 2009). Beginning a class discussion with these basic reactions and motives of community partners is a good way to set the context for CE as a multifaceted, complex endeavor with a lot of nuance, not a straight-up binary of "good" or "bad." As laid out earlier, discussing with students why HEIs are starting to evolve in their more sophisticated understanding of CE and problematizing the assumptions inherent to different terminology, such as "service learning," can set the tone for an approach that centers cultural and intellectual humility.

When we facilitate these community engagement trainings with students at every level of training, we elevate three core values that we hope guide students' approach to CE: contributing to equitable partnerships, focusing on relationships, and considering root causes. Although there is a great deal of nuance and complexity within each one of those values that we explore throughout each training, we conceptualize much of the *how* of community engagement (e.g., to act with cultural humility, to think critically about the nature of your engagement, to engage respectfully with others) as falling under these three core ideas. As such, they become a useful way to provide students with a framework for understanding why preparing for community engagement is so important.

Contributing to Equitable Partnerships

This is essentially the goal of our approach to preparing students for CE, as our title suggests. Centering the value of partnership early in the preparation discussion can orient students toward more thoughtful approaches to relationships throughout their CE. Some helpful reflection questions include the following:

- What are characteristics of good partnerships?
- What are you committing to through this project?
- Who gets to call the shots or make decisions in the relationship?

- What values would ground students in creating equity in this relationship, despite the inherent power differential between HEIs and the communities in which they want to partner?

Community-engaged scholars are finding more evidence that supports better community *and* student learning outcomes in a move toward equitable collaboration through shared decision-making and power, equity in resource allocation, and ownership of data (Grande et al., 2014; Israel et al., 2001; Mathews, 2014; Mitchell, 2014). This means explicitly acknowledging the disparate power relationships between communities and HEIs and working to mitigate them within the scope of a partnership.

One aspect of this attention to power differentials involves being able to recognize and evaluate the capacity of the particular organization or group participating and then developing partnerships to support those community priorities. For instance, a small nonprofit with one paid staff member may want to work with *one* student to analyze some publicly available data and write a summary report, rather than working with *a class or team* of students or researchers. Or they may ask for a product, meet twice to design the process, and then turn the student team loose until near completion, maybe checking in on them occasionally. These partnerships are not "less" engaged than a more participatory project, they are just less hands on and can still actively work to integrate community voice in the end result. We go into detail in Chapter 3 about the spectrum of approaches to engagement.

Focusing on Relationships

Although social change may be a motivator for some students who participate in CE activities, within the scope of a semester (as most CE experiences are structured), large-scale change is almost impossible. We emphasize the importance of students building authentic and meaningful relationships with members of the community, however, as a foundational aspect of social change. An orientation toward relationships affirms their role in actualizing the interdisciplinary, multisector, and civically minded solutions demanded of our world. Building relationships that are grounded in the values of humility and authenticity means honoring different kinds of knowledge and ensuring community voice is fully integrated into HEI efforts at all times. Our engagement with community partners should focus on working as collaborators to address their concerns, issues, and opinions on what will work to build self-capacity, rather than well-intentioned citizens from outside the affected population approaching with preconceived ideas about the issues in a community, brushing aside work already being done, or not considering what would actually "stick." We illustrate some of these outdated practices in later chapters, including using a humorous TED Talk with Ernesto Sirolli (see Chapter 3).

It should also be noted that relationships are not just with community partners. Students as well as instructors may often struggle with approaching their own personal and professional relationships with equity and authenticity. However, these relationships are especially important in the classroom, where many of these sensitive issues may be discussed. Recent literature has pointed to the beneficial role of relationships, both with peers and instructors, in supporting student learning outcomes (Ingraham et al., 2018). Classroom components such as collaborative learning and interactive engagement, as well as rapport with the instructor, are credited to successful relationship formation.

Understanding the Sustainability and Trajectory of Relationships

There is also an ebb and flow to some relationships in this work. College students graduate and move away, grad students get (maybe!) academic positions elsewhere, and faculty sometimes are recruited to other institutions. Grants end, and projects dissipate. People in power transition and staffing shifts, and turnover in many nonprofits is high. All these moving parts mean there are many barriers that can impact relationship building in CE. Relationships take time, which is a very limited resource in today's high-speed economy. However, communicating with community partners about these potential challenges up front can ward off challenges that might arise later. We feel that having infrastructure that takes all these factors into account is crucial, as do many community partners we have heard from (Stoecker & Tryon, 2007). Developing structures to sustain CE work across semesters and student transitions can also support this sustainability. For example, students may cycle in and out of different parts of a longer project, taking on semester-sized chunks of work to support the development of a larger project. Campus engagement centers can also be helpful aspects of that infrastructure, which we delve into in later chapters. Communicating about partnerships to relevant offices allows for increased awareness of existing relationships across campus.

Instructors can support students' ability to navigate relationships with the community by being explicit about time constraints and intended outcomes. Perhaps students do not feel like their one semester of work is impactful, but if they can understand their place in an ongoing and evolving collaboration, they may see more value in it. Especially in contexts in which an instructor is supporting a long-term partnership, students should be reminded of their roles as stewards of the instructor-partner relationship and that their output and behavior impact its quality. Sometimes a relationship comes to a close due to projects going as far as they can, or both partners shifting focus in their work–a completely normal trajectory.

Considering Root Causes in CE Efforts

While there is value in—and, for the present, an urgent need for—direct service in the form of tutoring, stocking food pantries, and so forth, educators can frame it within larger frameworks of root causes and social systems. As numerous community-engaged scholars have suggested, failing to consider the systemic nature of social issues, one's own assumptions, and the complexities of change can ultimately do a disservice to students and communities by perpetuating colonial and unequal approaches to CE (Butin, 2006; Lund, 2016; Mitchell, 2008). Beginning this conversation might include reflection questions such as these:

- Why might certain groups experience disparities?
- Why do these inequities persist?
- What would need to happen for these services to become obsolete?
- What systems exacerbate injustice?
- What would more just systems look like?
- What policies or histories impact this community/topic?

Considering these broader questions allows students to think deeply on the conditions that necessitate service organizations and analyze the systems that the organizations exist within. This orientation toward engagement focuses more on conceptualizing change and building better systems, rather than expecting inequities to be a constant (see more in Chapters 4 and 6).

Student Self-Examination of Motivations, Assumptions, and Expectations

Once students have learned about the community they want to work with and the CE has been appropriately framed, it is time to start examining the standard practices of engagement. This begins with encouraging the students to reflect on their motivations for participating in CE (Chapter 3 takes a deep dive into these), beyond "it is required for my major" or "to put on my résumé." Some reflection questions can include the following:

- What does community engagement mean to you?
- What are you hoping to gain from this experience?

- What can you offer the community/organization?
- Why is this partnership between this class and the community useful?
- What are community members or students gaining from this partnership?
- What values will guide your approach to engaging with the community?

Often, students bring with them ideas about what CE is and what they are hoping to gain from the experience, even if they have not explicitly understood or stated these intentions previously. Encouraging them to critically reflect on these motivations or assumptions can unearth intentions that require further investigation, such as dehumanizing values, savior mentalities, or assumptions about CE. During these conversations and during a student's CE experience, educators must mindfully meet students where they are and encourage curiosity, reflection, introspection, and discovery. Students will likely start with a wide range of experiences, knowledge, and ideas around engaging with communities they are not part of. Some may not have been exposed to other views or had the opportunity to think deeply about CE and its impacts. Some may not have the language to discuss complex issues, such as the intersection of race or social identity with CE. An educator's role is to bring students into the conversation without shame while encouraging students to stretch by continuously engaging in self-reflection, and instructors should hold students accountable for the impact of their words and actions (as Chapter 8 discusses in detail).

Aside from those students who openly admit they took a CBL course because "it looks good on my résumé" or those who feel railroaded into it because of a degree requirement (more on this later), we know that most students who want to participate in CE do so from a truly altruistic motivation. They might belong to a church youth group in their hometown and have put in service hours at a local soup kitchen. They might have heard that public service is a civic duty they should participate in to be a good citizen. However, unless critical reflection practices are integrated into these activities, unintended harm for both the community and the student can and does occur by perpetuating unchecked stereotypes or unequal power dynamics (Peterson, 2009). Additionally, when courses lack a critical lens, they are more likely to enable short-term, "band-aid solutions" while ignoring the larger systems that may be impacting a given community. Students rarely examine the assumptions behind their motives. These reflection questions may be useful to start that conversation:

- Why is this project/service needed?

- What would alternative, structural solutions to this problem look like?
- What assumptions might you have about the people in this community or the clients of this organization?
- How might your life experiences or social identity impact your understanding of this community?
- What is your experience with or understanding of the community or issue at hand?

Intent versus Impact

As students begin to interrogate their own motivations for community engagement, educators can make connections between students' well-intended actions and the potential for suboptimal experiences and outcomes. You may notice that some of the following topics for discussion arise, as explored fully in later chapters.

The Savior Complex

The savior complex (Al-Atiyat et al., 2017; Cole, 2012; Donahue et al., 2015) is a phenomenon that positions those doing CE (often upper-class, educated, white people) as saviors to the (typically poor and/or racially marginalized) communities or individuals they work with. This is exemplified through movies like *Freedom Writers* (2007) or *The Blind Side* (2009), where a white person is positioned as a sort of hero to "disadvantaged" youth of color for simply providing the youth encouragement, all while failing to understand the broader challenges (such as racism, poverty, etc.) that created these circumstances for the youth. In this approach to CE, which has been incredibly common in academia, a group of scholars or students enters a community with preconceived ideas of an issue and ill-informed plans to address it that are rarely based on experience or a personal understanding of the community (Illich, 1968; Sirolli, 2012). Whole social media accounts exist to point out and address this trope (i.e., on Instagram, @barbiesavior and @nowhite-saviors). We have frequently pulled quotes and images from these accounts to spark reflection.

This savior orientation toward CE is inherently "othering" and separates the student from the community member by framing the interaction as unidirectional and transactional, with the student or university occupying a higher moral or intellectual ground. Some of the material we present in later chapters, including discussions of race and how it interacts with CE, can seem jarring to young students whose worldviews have never been called into question. Much time for classroom reflection is needed to process new viewpoints, and educators should be prepared to navigate challenging conversations with patience and empathy, which is discussed further in Chapter 8.

Unrealistic Student Expectations

Students may have unrealistic expectations about the impact of their CE. Many students enter college with ambitious goals for social change. Educators can keep the excitement for social change alive while encouraging students to critically reflect on their motivations and knowledge of issues. This will help students enter communities respectfully and in a way that is supportive of community priorities. Educators can encourage students to just get to know people and deepen their individual understandings of a social issue or community rather than single-handedly trying to "save the world" within the span of the semester. It can also be helpful for students to contextualize their experience and consider how it fits into larger goals for the community or change efforts. More on conceptualizing social change is included in Chapter 6.

Doing Good Better

It is not uncommon for students engaging in this sort of learning to become defensive. Often some students cling to their conceptions of what "good" is and struggle to understand how trying to "help" can be harmful. One potential way to orient students toward this learning is to emphasize the idea of consistent improvement and growth or the value of lifelong learning. We have found success in building the expectation of "doing good better." For example, while collecting canned food for a local pantry is certainly a good action, it is highly likely a community organization that focuses on food access could also put that student's time and energy to better use if students first inquire about what else the organization could use from them to build community capacity so that, over time, fewer people need to access the food pantry.

Building Student Self-Awareness

Perhaps one of the most important aspects of supporting student learning within CE requires educators to support students in actively developing their own self-awareness. Self-awareness is an essential personal and professional skill. However, within educational systems that often promote individualized outcomes, attention to how one understands and engages with others can be infrequent. In the following we outline some core components of self-awareness that impact CE.

Socialization and Social Identity

There are a variety of terms relating to social identity and the process of socialization that can give students the language to talk about what they are learning and experiencing in the community, as well as a more holistic understanding of social structures and systems. The following terms and descriptions are especially useful in building a foundational language and understanding of these ideas. It is important that these concepts are consistently considered within the course to allow for more robust discussion and informed action. Care must be taken in a short overview module to warn students that an overview gives only a taste of these concepts, reiterating that it will be in the content they receive later or that they might want to explore it on their own to attain a fuller understanding of cultural humility. In the remainder of this book, particularly Chapter 4, we expand upon these topics and discuss strategies and frameworks that can be utilized in CE work to engage with these ideas.

Socialization

Socialization is defined broadly in social psychology as the process by which an individual develops their own behavior in accordance with messages and expectations of what is deemed acceptable by the group standards (Child, 1954). Throughout our lives, we encounter a number of different institutions, such as our schools, families, or religions, that influence how we understand the world and others. Harro (2013) suggests that the norms and expectations we hold about the world are perpetuated by the messages internalized through said institutions, as depicted in Harro's Cycle of Socialization. It is not until we recognize the patterns and norms shaping us that we are able to actively disrupt such patterns or assumptions that no longer serve us or that uphold oppression. Discussing the role of socialization can help students consider how or why they understand things in a certain way and thus why others might see things differently.

Social Identity

Our identities shape how we experience and view the world. Social identity groups are based on the physical, social, and mental characteristics of individuals. They are sometimes obvious and clear, sometimes not; often self-claimed, but frequently ascribed by others. Some identities may give us power or privilege, such as college students who have access to educational resources and certain career opportunities. Other identities, such as being a trans woman, are at an increased risk of experiencing discrimination and oppression—for example, in hiring processes or being barred from certain restrooms or public spaces.

The important thing to note about social identities is that they are socially constructed. That is, our identities may give us power and privilege or put us at a disadvantage, simply because we exist in a social system that has categorized people based on perceived or constructed identities. We have done this throughout history. Even though our identities are socially constructed, they still have real impacts on our lives. That is why it is important for us to work to understand our own and others' identities and the ways our social systems and institutions privilege and oppress different people. For examples of common identity categories, see Figure 4.3.

The intention behind reflection on one's identities is not to assign blame or guilt to anyone for their affiliation with any group (more on this in Chapter 8), regardless of what contemporary attacks on critical race theory might suggest. Such information also should not be used to fuel stereotypes or inform generalizations about different groups. Rather, we argue that in order for us to best understand others and the social systems that construct our collective world, it is important that we strive to understand our own identities and the way they shape our reality, as well as how others experience the world differently as a result of their identities.

Implicit Bias and Microaggressions

The next two ideas are largely by-products of our socialization that can frequently show up when individuals engage with communities different than their own. Students need to be mindful about the assumptions they are bringing into community spaces and consider how those assumptions may impact communities.

Implicit Bias

Implicit bias is defined as the "attitudes or stereotypes that affect our understanding, actions, and decisions in an unconscious manner. These biases, which encompass both favorable and unfavorable assessments, are activated involuntarily and without an individual's awareness or intentional control" (Kirwan Institute, 2015). Whether we like to admit it or not, we all have implicit biases about ourselves and each other. Because we are socialized beings, we internalize different messages about others that can unconsciously shape our behavior. These messages can come to us from a number of different sources—the media, schooling, religion, and our peer groups. They often inform our preferences, beliefs about others, and understanding of what is "normal" (Harro, 2000).

Microaggressions

"Microaggressions are the everyday verbal, nonverbal, and environmental slights, snubs, or insults, whether intentional or unintentional, which communicate hostile, derogatory, or negative messages to target persons based solely upon their marginalized group membership. In many cases, these hidden messages may invalidate the group identity or experiential reality of target persons, demean them on a personal or group level, communicate they are lesser human beings, suggest they do not belong with the majority group, threaten and intimidate, or relegate them to inferior status and treatment" (Sue, 2010).

Systems of Power and Privilege

Power and privilege are dynamics and systems that can play out at an individual and institutional level, meaning that they can impact our interpersonal relationships, as well as how groups of people are treated by systems or institutions. Here are some very basic definitions of those terms:

- **Power:** The ability or authority to decide what is best for others, who has access to resources, or what is perceived as normal.
- **Privilege:** A set of unearned or earned advantages, rights, freedoms, or benefits given to a group of people based on group membership.
  - Privileged groups are *considered* to be the normative groups, while everyone else is minoritized and othered.
  - Privileged group membership is not a choice, and individuals often are not aware of how these advantages benefit them (definitions adapted from University of Wisconsin–Madison, Office of Inclusion Education, 2019).
- **Oppression:** The combination of prejudice and institutional power that creates systems that discriminate against some groups (often called "target groups") and benefit other groups (often called "dominant groups"). Examples include racism, sexism, and anti-Semitism.
- **Intersectionality:** Originally a legal framework (Crenshaw, 1989), intersectionality examines the ways multiple forms of oppression (i.e., racism, sexism, homophobia, etc.) can overlap to inform an individuals' experience of social systems and institutions. As an example, a Black gay man experiences oppression uniquely through the interactions of racism and homophobia.

These are inherently complex and uncomfortable topics that students should be given time to process. However, they are concepts that are abundant in our histories and consistently shaping our world, and as such, they must be grappled with. In Chapter 4 we discuss redlining as an example of systemic oppression and link to an NPR video that traces the impacts of those historic policies into today. These examples can be useful to help students reflect more critically on their CE experience.

Educational Privilege

An important aspect of privilege that is useful to share with students is educational privilege. All of us who are affiliated with an HEI in one way or another benefit from educational privilege, reaping the rewards (and burdens) that come from this institutional affiliation. Students have the relative luxury of time to spend in the pursuit of learning, complete with a reward system untethered from community outcomes, knowledge resources at their fingertips, and privileges such as free transportation that community members do not have access to. Upon graduation, students will receive a credential that is almost universally respected. No matter the financial or life challenges they have, the fact remains that they are perceived as privileged to be in school and may be associated with any negative feelings communities have about the institution simply through affiliation because of the history of harms perpetuated by academia. As an example of how this dynamic plays out, regardless of other aspects of a person's identity, let us imagine a Ph.D. holder who is a person of color with a background in community development. In many situations, that person is going to be given more intellectual credibility than a community organizer, even if their dissertation is not about or from the community being discussed in a CE relationship.

A sometimes overlooked element of this topic is that not all students actually have the same privilege in all ways, which affects their ability to participate in CE. As Mitchell et al. (2012) write:

> As service learning courses most often enroll white, middle-class, traditional age, college students who are not also juggling jobs, debt, and family responsibilities, Butin (2006) notes that "there is a distinct possibility that service-learning may ultimately come to be viewed as the 'Whitest of the White' enclave of postsecondary education . . . a luxury available only to the privileged few" (p. 620).

Acknowledging these differences and how educational privilege may operate to disadvantage those without degrees is essential to ensuring equitable partnership.

Positionality

Separate from our previous discussions on social identity and power, positionality is the culmination of these two realms. Positionality is defined as "the stance or positioning of the researcher in relation to the social and political context of the study—the community, the organization or the participant group" (Coghlan & Brydon-Miller, 2014). Fundamentally, it means the ways our identities, both personal and professional, impact our relationship to the group we are working with.

Cultural Humility

We view cultural humility as the joining of all these aforementioned topics. Cultural humility asks us to embrace a certain level of complexity, recognizing that we will never know everything. Rather, we can learn to expect and be open to difference and understand that there are many different ways of living in, experiencing, and understanding the world, none inherently superior to another. Cultural humility exists in contrast to the term we might be more familiar with, "cultural competency," which can frame learning about others as having an endpoint, rather than being a lifelong process. Chapter 7 is devoted to this concept.

The following chapters cover each of these factors more fully. These topics often require extensive unpacking, and there may not always be adequate course time to address them in depth, but any class-time capacity to engage with these ideas should be considered. Instructors can also encourage students to pursue further exploration and provide resources to follow up on.

Summary

Collaborative, mutually beneficial work between students and community partners is more likely to occur when students are prepared to enter the community, where "prepared" means more self-aware, humble, reflective, and educated about the community context and social justice topics. This chapter outlines how an educator can begin that conversation, with the anticipation of training continuing throughout a CE experience. This chapter could be used as a stand-alone resource to train students, although that approach does not provide nearly enough exposure and deep learning.

Prior to beginning CE, students should learn about community context, examine their own motivations, and learn about the aforementioned dispositions that ground our discussions throughout the book. That can be followed by delving into relevant topics in greater detail over the course of the semester in class discussion and written reflection. We hope this sets the stage for deeper learning for students and a better experience for the community partners they work with.

2

Theoretical Background
of Student Preparation

In this chapter, we explore the limited literature on preparing students for community engagement. Critical community engagement has noted the need for student preparation, and social justice education provides a rich well of resources for beginning topic exploration. More often, CE itself is seen as preparation for the "real world." Community-based organizations have mainly been carrying the burden of preparing students prior to engagement, yet their capacity is often limited, and they have expressed that it is the HEI's job to prepare students prior to sending them into communities.

The academic literature on preparing students for community engagement is sparse. We have written several articles on the subject (Tryon & Madden, 2019; Zastoupil et al., 2020) but have found limited study elsewhere. Lin et al. (2009) argued that attending to issues of diversity with service learners was an important part of building positive community relationships in CE contexts, but at that time partners could only hope for students to receive a cursory "cultural competence" workshop before entering CE. In terms of actual curriculum, Lawrence University has just developed an Intro to CBL course, a two-credit overview of theoretical and practical aspects of ethical and responsible community engagement. Some of the topics we cover in this book are mentioned in their course description, but the curriculum is not available to the public.

Other universities with some type of material include the University of Michigan, which has a set of massive open online courses (MOOCs) about CE that cover similar ideas but lack much capacity for instructor/learner interaction. Donahue and Plaxton-Moore (2018) also produced a companion reader geared for students that seeks to provide proper framing and emphasize the purpose of community-engaged learning. Michigan State University's doctoral certificate program in community engagement has a goal that "learners should be able to describe their own positionality, acknowledge power asymmetries present in their community partnerships, identify structural and cross-cultural differences they encounter, and describe how they navigated through those differences" (Doberneck et al., 2017, p. 131). However, these examples still lack some depth in their descriptions of humility and related concepts, as well as specific topics to focus on.

There is a fair amount of literature extolling the benefits of CE to prepare students for potential careers, although some scholars have noted the challenges with traditional CE models, including that students can be burdensome and can do more harm than good. These issues are sometimes addressed by volunteer training programs, yet these tend to focus on technical skills rather than overall approaches to CE. More frequently, the topics addressed in community engagement preparation (cultural humility, self-awareness, positionality) have been addressed in separate spaces, such as social justice workshops. This chapter reviews the existing offerings around preparation, looks into the history of community engagement as career preparation, and shares insights from the preparation training that does exist.

Social Justice Education

Going back to the characteristics of a well-prepared student in Chapter 1, it is clear that other training and educational resources exist that can be tailored to support some of these goals for the specifics of CE and are fairly widespread in academic spaces (e.g., Adams et al., 2007). For instance, many HEIs with multicultural centers or diversity and inclusion offices offer trainings around the topics of privilege, power, and oppression. These educational spaces often base their teachings on foundational theories such as the following:

- **Critical race theory:** Using the lens of race to examine, understand, and explain social, political, and legal structures (Delgado & Stefancic, 2017)
- **Feminist theory:** Better understanding the role and construction of gender and gender inequality (hooks, 2000)
- **Marxism:** Using materialism to understand societal class and social structure (Wolff & Resnick, 1987)
- **Disability justice:** Understanding the intersection of ableism and other forms of oppression (Piepzna-Samarasinha, 2018)

Some institutions, such as UW–Madison, make at least some of these topics mandatory at different times in students' educational careers, such as an introductory diversity workshop for incoming students. Other institutions may think an "ethnic studies" credit suffices. These programs typically cannot do more than scratch the surface and are often derided for being overly simplistic or run by administrators who are not well versed in this content (Devine & Ash, 2022; Vianden, 2018). Additionally, these programs are usually short in duration and occur only once over the course of the student's education.

However, depending on the institution, course, and/or program, students may or may not access these educational resources, and they are often optional rather than mandatory. In addition, social justice and diversity educational resources do not specifically focus on the field of community engagement and likely do not touch on those more specialized topics, including community-university power dynamics, the history of CE, the history of the institution in that community, academia's role in developing community mistrust of research and other institutions, and intellectual humility. While social justice education is indeed a bedrock of community engagement preparation (Mitchell, 2007; Mitchell et al., 2012; Santiago-Ortiz, 2019), the material in this book expands on these topics to create a more robust student preparation portfolio. Additionally, the framing of community engagement preparation (rather than social justice education) provides space for those CEPs who (wrongly, we argue) do not see social justice education as intersecting with their work. In other words, social justice education is a crucial piece of CE preparation and cannot be extricated, but it is just one piece of preparation.

Critical Community-Engaged Scholarship

In the last decade or so, a growing body of literature and practice by scholars in the community engagement field has begun to emerge, supporting and utilizing critical scholarship to address some preparation issues and reframe the goals of CE. Mitchell (2008) defines critical service learning as "working to redistribute power amongst all participants in the service-learning relationship, developing authentic relationships in the classroom and in the community, and working from a social change perspective" (p. 50). Utilizing critical race theory as a lens for viewing, understanding, and improving CE can additionally foreground race and racism in students' understandings of disparity and the roots of inequality and injustice. Santiago-Ortiz (2019) adds to critical engagement by asking the question of decolonization or undoing colonialism (Tuhiwai Smith, 2012) in service learning, advocating for an anticolonial practice in service learning: "This stance requires (a) the acknowledgment of settler colonialism as a distinct and continuing structure in academic spaces and beyond, (b) incorporating anticolonial and decolonizing methodologies that counter and resist dominant narratives in CCSL as well as (c) a relational shift in the way that community–university partnerships are envisioned" (p. 48).

Critical scholarship clearly sets the stage for transformative work for students and community partners alike through its invocation of social change. However, there is still not clear guidance about how students can or should be prepared to do transformative work. There certainly exists an abundance of principles for community engagement (e.g., Howard, 2001; Jacoby, 1996), and Donahue and Plaxton-Moore (2018) encourage students to cultivate certain dispositions to approach the experience. But these resources do not provide instructors with much guidance on how to weave these ideas into their teaching and course design. Many questions remain, such as the following: What familiarity will students have with power dynamics, particularly the nuanced dynamics between organizations/communities and HEIs? Are students situated to build authentic relationships? Do they have experience building relationships across difference? Undoubtedly, we can assume that in most situations, students will be coming into circumstances with a wide variety of skills, dispositions, backgrounds, and experiences. Critical engaged scholarship gives us the frameworks to support powerful models of transformation, but preparing students to engage in these frameworks must happen first, meeting students where they are when they come in and helping them move from foundational work through the evolution of thought required so they can process and incorporate newer, even more critical thinking.

Since we submitted this manuscript in 2020, this field has exploded exponentially, and the confines of this volume cannot do justice to addressing the leading edge of equity-centering anti-racism practices and scholarship that are starting to arise out of the critical engaged scholarship of Mitchell and others who have written, as we reference throughout this book, that much of academia (and thus the structure of CE) is steeped in white supremacy (Mitchell, Donahue, & Young-Law, 2012). See more on the topic of building a critical classroom in Chapter 8. We also direct readers to the sources in the appendix as a starting point for other high-level work, knowing that by the time this volume is on shelves, there will be even newer publications that focus on the highest evolution of doing equitable scholarship and practice, and we encourage readers to seek them out.

Community Engagement as Career Preparation

There is robust literature about community engagement as preparation for other parts of students' lives: careers, graduate school, or simply being in the "real world" (e.g., Bowen, 2007; Eyler et al., 2001). CE can be used as a way to try out a career, get to know a particular job or industry, or gain the experience needed to apply for a job later on.

As such, training for CE in the context of career preparation often focuses on particular skills students need to complete a task in their project, rather than focusing on the qualities, attitudes, and approaches that students need to be successful regardless of setting. For instance, training may focus on obtaining particular language skills when working with non-native English speakers (Long & Macián, 2008), understanding the developmental characteristics of a demographic group (e.g., Schmitt-McQuitty et al., 2011), or developing particular skills for the volunteer task (e.g., Duggleby et al., 2018). An example of this type that we have seen at our campus is an introductory computer science course that teaches basic software coding in which the students work with nonprofits on projects such as website updates and building online fundraising platforms. While students need these technical skills for success in their work, they additionally need training to interact with real people in real situations outside of the classroom and laboratory (Capretz & Ahmed, 2018).

When we frame CE as career preparation, there is also the risk of students seeing the community as a lab or place to experiment, rather than understanding that they are interacting with real people and situations that can have potentially negative outcomes. Student mistakes can have lasting effects. Instead, we suggest that career preparation may be one outcome of CE but should not be considered the main focus for students.

Negative Effects of Poorly Prepared Community Engagement

There is also a growing body of work documenting the deleterious impacts of poor-quality CE and the need to orient students toward building good partnerships with community organizations. For many CEPs, Eby's 1998 paper, "Why Service-Learning Is Bad," outlines several issues that we are still grappling with today: that service learning is ineffective in communities, frames communities as deficient and lesser than, ignores systemic transformation, and can create harmful relationships. Eby gets at the heart of the issue by stating, "There is also danger of using individuals and communities in inappropriate ways as laboratories or as subjects for experiment and practice. Community members become objects rather than participants or passive recipients rather than actors. The fact that service-learning mixes objectives has potential for prostituting service by making it serve objectives which contribute to the students or the college or university rather than to the community" (p. 3). Illich (1968) eloquently spoke of the harm volunteers caused over half a century ago:

> To hell with good intentions. . . . Next to money and guns, the third largest North American export is the U.S. idealist, who turns up in every theater of the world: the teacher, the volunteer, the missionary, the community organizer, the economic developer, and the vacationing do-gooders. Ideally, these people define their role as service. Actually, they frequently wind up alleviating the damage done by money and weapons, or "seducing" the "underdeveloped" to the benefits of the world of affluence and achievement. . . . The damage which volunteers do willy-nilly is too high a price for the belated insight that they should not have been volunteers in the first place.

These are powerful words coming from scholars and community leaders that cannot go unheeded by instructors. Too often, the mere fact that volunteers are giving their time for a cause is seen as inherently good, regardless of their actual effects. That in itself speaks to the power differentials that exist between volunteers and those they "serve": volunteers are seen as inherently "good," while those they serve may be viewed as lesser, troubled, or problematic. Additionally, the outcome for those being served is seen as inherently good, regardless of what occurs in reality.

This approach often falls flat, and some CE preparation programs have arisen in direct response to reports of negative impacts that ongoing CE efforts can have (e.g., the UW–Madison's program) or because the cultural divides are so vast that some cross-cultural training is necessary (e.g., Matthew et al., 2018). For instance, Floyd (2013) evaluated a midwife training program in Haiti, which ultimately led to more robust training resources within that organization. Haitian staff and midwives in the program emphasized the need for volunteers to truly understand the context of the situation and the people they were working with. Of the volunteers, one midwife said, "People need to be reminded and encouraged to be respectful and culturally sensitive. They can't come here with the attitude that they are going to change things in one week. This needs to be emphasized to them. Discard that attitude; come here with humility and eagerness to help in whatever way" (p. 563).

In another example, the Seattle Public Library developed more robust volunteer training programs after noticing challenges in the current program: "While volunteering as a Homework Help tutor, Sunny noticed the varying levels of comfort other tutors had with cultures outside their own. Some examples of problematic tutor behavior included declaring that a student's name is too difficult for them to pronounce, failing to support more boisterous students, making assumptions about the culture and homelife of a student, and being unable to relate to diverse life experiences" (Andrews et al., 2018, p. 20). In these examples, volunteer training programs arose out of a history of challenges with volunteers. Unfortunately, these examples are the exception rather than the rule, and student preparation has remained outside the realm of mainstream CE.

The creation of this book was informed by research conducted within our own community through Stoecker and Tryon's (2009) study exploring community perceptions of community-based learning, as well as a 2016 follow-up study we discuss in later chapters and the University of Wisconsin's Civic Action Plan, which identified proper preparation of UW affiliates for culturally informed and mutually beneficial engagement with communities as a top priority. (UW's plan can be viewed at https://scholarshare.tem ple.edu/handle/20.500.12613/8178). Although every institution is unique, we know, through our networks and the literature in the field, that this issue is widespread.

CBOs Preparing Students

In the examples from these sources, you may notice the onus of volunteer training has been continually placed back onto the community organization. Many CBOs have volunteer coordinators who interface with volunteers and prepare them for specific community contexts. Undoubtedly, they are best suited to conduct such training that is tailored to their individual missions and situations that typically arise in their work, and they will have to perform some of it regardless of the circumstances. We do not, however, advocate that we place the task of preparing students solely at the feet of community partners. First, community partners have limited time with students already. A typical CE program asks that students spend twenty to thirty hours working with community partners over a semester, roughly fifteen weeks (and likely even fewer, accounting for settling into and closing out the semester). If partners have to use even more of that limited time to train students, they are getting even less benefit (Tryon et al., 2008). Additionally, it is disrespectful to the community partners and organizations that are coeducating students to send students who are unfamiliar with community context, lack self-awareness, are unaware of systemic oppression and its intersections with that specific community, or are culturally arrogant and inflexible. Last, community partners are typically not compensated or are not well compensated for their time as co-educators, which again places the responsibility of student preparation on university educators.

Although community partners and staff should be seen as collaborators in the goal of preparing students, and certainly should know the intricacies and needs of their communities, instructors have an essential role to play in reinforcing the expectations of community partners and ensuring robust standards of community conduct. By front-loading preparation in the classroom, students are ready to be useful in community settings and CBO staff can focus on specific training for their particular contexts. In this work, we are trying to shift the way CE happens to lessen the burden on our community partners and take greater responsibility for the work our students do.

One solution that HEIs can consider is to involve or hire community partners to prepare students, either as consultants or as university staff. Depending on the staffing level at partner organizations, they may not have capacity to act in this role, so this solution may not be able to support all students in need of education and training. This may be a good fit for smaller programs, classes, or institutions. At a larger scale, we argue that a campus-wide program available to all CE students and overseen by their instructors is a good way to increase the scope of this preparation. The following chapters, and links to video content, will help instructors get started on that journey.

Concluding Thoughts

In summary, there is little information available about specific CE preparation curriculums. CE has been touted as a way to prepare students for other things, such as future careers or graduate school. The little preparation that has been studied has focused on building student skills in certain situations, rather than broadly preparing students. Community partners are well positioned to prepare students for CE but may not have the capacity and time to do so. Additionally, asking our partners to train our students is placing yet another burden on our partners. Instead, we believe that as CEPs, we need to accept responsibility for educating our students prior to their time in communities. This can further the work of critical and anticolonial engaged scholarship and builds on social justice education. This not only supports students in their work but strengthens relationships with partners and allows communities and universities to work together for the greatest positive impact.

Part II

Essential Concepts of Community Engagement Preparation

3

Motivations for
Community Engagement

In this chapter, we explore the various motivations and assumptions underlying students' understanding of community engagement and the implications such ideas can have on communities. We then go on to describe strategies to help students unpack their motivations and understand how to more effectively and critically conceptualize their engagement experience. This chapter fits well into our Level One: Introduction to Community Engagement online module on Canvas (as well as the TU ScholarShare online resource page: https://scholarshare.temple.edu/handle/20.500.12613/8178).

What drives researchers to work with communities? What motivates students to enroll in community-engaged courses? From where do these motivations stem? What assumptions are inherent within those motivations, and how do those assumptions impact engagement? These questions are essential for any of us—researcher, student, instructor, or CEP—to consider as we approach CE. As stewards of community engagement, it is critical to reflect on our own assumptions and motivations before entering a community and in order to meaningfully engage students in this learning. In the words of Teju Cole (2012) in his writing about the "White Savior Industrial Complex" (discussed more later), "if we are going to interfere in the lives of others, a little due diligence is a minimum requirement."

Some common motivations for CE are an inherent by-product of the colonial institution of higher education (Santiago-Ortiz, 2019). Before outlining the primary motivations influencing students, we look at some history on CE in higher education that can be helpful to share with students to help them understand the context and role of the HEI. The last section includes practical approaches, strategies, and activities to help students explore, process, and reframe their motivations for engaging with the community.

Some History of Community Engagement in Higher Education

The history of community engagement in American higher education has a number of theoretical and practical roots, some of which were covered in the previous chapter. However, like most things in American higher education, CE has been influenced by racism, colonization, indoctrination, and other harmful ideologies that require some investigation (Dostilio, 2017; Santiago-Ortiz, 2019). We believe it is essential for facilitators of CE experiences to investigate some of the history pertaining to their respective context in order to more clearly conceptualize the implications this history might have on their engagement. This could be the history of the community or the community partner organization they are working with, the university's relationship with the community, or a relevant social issue impacting the project (e.g., redlining or urban renewal). Through a historical lens, students can gain a more nuanced and informed understanding of community and the way they are contributing to or influenced by its history.

A well-known reading, frequently assigned to students to get them thinking critically about CE, demonstrates the way these ideologies and approaches were seen as harmful as early as 1968. In the same speech quoted in the previous chapter, "To Hell with Good Intentions," presented to attendees at the Conference of InterAmerican Student Projects, Catholic priest and philosopher Ivan Illich laments the paternalism and imperialism he saw as inherent within volunteering, specifically internationally. In speaking with a group of students preparing for a mission-style service trip to Mexico, Illich explicitly points out the power differentials, assumptions, and imposition of Western ideals at that time, especially in the global sector.

The speech continues to be an impactful read for students and professionals alike, as many of the same problems and mindsets criticized in it persist to this day. When assigning the reading to students, be sure to provide sufficient class time for processing through and articulating critiques of volunteering. Illich's speech is suffused with critical insights into systems of power, assimilation, and positionality and is worthy of deep analysis and reflection:

> I am here to suggest that you voluntarily renounce exercising the power which being an American gives you. I am here to entreat you

to freely, consciously and humbly give up the legal right you have to impose your benevolence on Mexico. I am here to challenge you to recognize your inability, your powerlessness and your incapacity to do the "good" which you intended to do. (Illich, 1968)

Within this excerpt of Illich's speech, we can identify another important, albeit marginalized, piece of the history of CE—the actual impact that service has had on communities. As noted in Chapter 1, the focus on community perceptions of working with the university is still fairly new in the literature. Studies have shown great student outcomes associated with CE and have noted CBL as a high-impact practice (Kuh, 2008). However, the actual experiences and expectations of community partners have not been as widely explored. Stoecker and Tryon (2009) revealed common concerns and critiques from community partners regarding the ways universities work with communities. Some examples include the following:

- Partners feeling overburdened by professors essentially pawning students off on their sites in search of service hours
- Students being inadequately prepared to work with diverse populations
- Students not adhering to the expectations and commitments of the community partner

All these concerns can fuel community disinterest or worry in partnering with HEIs.

As mentioned prior, the history of our institutions also has implications for how communities understand the relevance and risks of partnering with HEIs. The founding of many institutions of higher learning, including the history of the lands upon which they are built, offers one lens for understanding partnership. We can use our own university as an example of how history contextualizes institutional community engagement. As authors, we are located at a large, land-grant university in the Midwest. Indigenous communities can trace their occupation of this land back twelve thousand years. Our campus has more Indigenous burial mounds than any other HEI in the United States, some dating back over 1,300 years (University of Wisconsin–Madison, n.d.-b). Previously there were many more of these mounds on our campus and in the surrounding area, but campus and city expansion, as well as poorly managed archeological excavations, have drastically reduced this number.

As a land-grant institution, our university has benefited greatly from being able to build on this land, expropriated from Indigenous peoples (Lee, 2020). A *High Country News* investigation found that our institution made over $300,000 profit selling off some of these lands in the late 1800s. We share this history of our institution to highlight the complex ways and multiple lenses through which universities relate to different communities. Our university continues to grapple with this history. In recent years, our institution has formed a partnership called Native Nations to improve relations between the university and our tribal nations. Many CEPs may also be familiar with the rise of land acknowledgment statements (which we describe later) as another example of efforts to acknowledge and address the histories of harm perpetuated by our institutions.

These sorts of histories impact CE in a number of ways. Histories of harm or exploitation can leave some community partners hesitant to partner with university affiliates. When left unacknowledged, they can erode communities' trust in university researchers and students (detailed in Chapter 5). And repairing such harms can require a great deal of time and resources. In order to avoid repeating the same patterns, CEPs have a responsibility to unpack and situate themselves within such histories and guide their students in understanding why they matter.

Why Motivations Matter

> Nothing about us, without us, is for us.
> —James Charlton, disability rights activist

Recognizing the diversity of students' experiences with CE is an essential starting point to adequately prepare them. The beauty and the challenge of CE is that students come from such different backgrounds, and it is these different backgrounds that often inform students' motivations for and expectations of the engagement experience. For example, consider two first-year students, one whose primary experience with CE was a church mission trip to help build a school in Zimbabwe while the other was a youth activist organizing against oil pipelines on their Native lands. These two students are bound to have drastically different orientations to engagement that can inform how they approach it in the course. When students (or instructors) are motivated by ideas that they are "saving" a community or that they are the experts, they do a disservice to the community they are working with. Holding tight to one motivation or expectation limits our ability to remain attuned to the expressed needs of each community.

CEPs play a crucial role in identifying and unpacking student motivations, as well as understanding their entry points to CE, in order to best orient them toward engagement more strongly rooted in equity, reciprocity, and collaboration. As we have outlined, thoughtful, intentionally collaborative approaches still fail to be the default within higher education. Indeed, we focus on student motivations in this early chapter because we view this as the first step toward helping students understand the work they will be doing with communities. While students may come into CE with ambitious ideas or perceived innovations, instructors must delicately guide students to more fully understand the layers and complexities of a given issue or community, without losing students' youthful idealism and energy. Allowing students to articulate their goals and anticipated outcomes from the experience can provide the facilitator with the opportunity to contextualize and situate engagement within relevant histories, systems, and trajectories of change.

Challenging a student's motivations necessitates a thoughtful approach to the design of the CE experience. When students begin to recognize inconsistencies in their own values or beliefs, cognitive dissonance can result (e.g., Campbell & Oswald, 2018). As much as CBL is helpful in strengthening students' learning around the course topic, it can also change how students make sense of the world and their place in it (Mitchell & Rost-Banik, 2019; Shor et al., 2017). Any seasoned instructor of CBL courses is sure to have at least a handful of anecdotes from students about the impact a class had on their professional and personal development. Just this past semester, I (Cory) received this email from an instructor after facilitating a preparation workshop for her class:

> I also had a senior neuroscientist in the class who's headed off to med school who said that [the training] was a bit of a life-changer. That he knew so many people who complete "service" to get into med school, and that he's had the same attitude, and that these modules, coupled with our work with [the course engagement project] this semester, prompted him to dramatically rethink how he works with patients, attend to empathy and humility, put others' needs first, and consider his influence on the world.

However, not every student receives that sort of mindset shift, and without proper context and preparation, CE can risk perpetuating stereotypes (Peterson, 2009) and other such harms (Dunn-Kenney, 2010). One example noted in the later "Voyeurism and Dissonance" section depicts what can happen when a student explicitly disagrees with the mission or goal of a certain partnership.

Common Student Motivations

Motivations can be deeply informed by context and identity, whether knowingly or unknowingly. For example, at the University of Wisconsin–Madison, many white students from rural communities who come to Madison see it as a big city full of diversity and view CE as a pathway to understanding or exploring diverse communities. Though unintended, this interest can quickly bleed into voyeurism if not reflected on. Students of color, on the other hand, may come from or identify with the very communities that are the focus of a given course and, as such, are put in a unique and often challenging position. Consider the title of the article by Mitchell and Donahue (2009), "I Do More Service in This Class than I Ever Do at My Site," which captured the burden often placed on students of color in CE settings when they are asked to talk about race or perceived as if they can speak on behalf of an entire community. Paying attention to the reflections of students of color in CBL courses can help instructors understand how to support individualized student learning.

An effective way to combat harmful approaches to CE is to explicitly name them and support students in understanding how they may result in harm. In doing so, we can provide more appropriate ways to frame the experience. For us, this has often meant incorporating this idea into orientations to CE or other workshops. We have also seen instructors take these ideas and weave them seamlessly into their classes in ways that deepen student learning. In the following pages, we outline some commonplace but harmful approaches to CE and consider the assumptions and harms associated with them.

The Savior Complex

The savior complex exists across various disciplines from film studies to psychology. Within film, it is often referred to as the white savior complex (or trope), referring to a specific category of movies wherein (generally) a white, female protagonist (often a teacher) is cast as a savior of sorts to a group of seemingly disadvantaged youth of color, as portrayed in films like *Freedom Writers* (2007) or *Dangerous Minds* (1995) (Hughey, 2010). Author Teju Cole, in a piece critiquing the "White Savior Industrial Complex," explains it succinctly: "The White Savior Industrial Complex is not about justice. It is about having a big emotional experience that validates privilege" (Cole, 2012). Across these two examples, we can see these dynamics playing out in both domestic and international contexts.

In a TED Talk given by Ernesto Sirolli, an author and professional with a background in international development, he tells a gripping story detailing an international CE project gone wrong and illuminates the flawed thinking behind the savior complex. The title of Sirolli's talk points to what might be considered a leading principle of engagement: "Want to Help

Someone? Shut Up and Listen!" (Sirolli, 2012).* Note that the first three and a half minutes are the most useful. We have used this video in a number of settings, and the audience response is always strong. He is a humorous, humble, and entertaining speaker who comes across well to students. Although Sirolli does not explicitly name the savior complex, when asked for responses to the video, audiences almost always point it out on their own, also naming other important ideas such as centering community-identified needs and considering the role of identity and/or colonial mindset.

Pity and Charity

As more and more disciplines consider ways to integrate CE into their scholarship, programs, or degree requirements, many conversations that have been going on for years remain unresolved. Pity and charity, offshoots of the savior mentality, are examples of this long-standing, troubling practice. Those who utilize this lens often see communities as made up of downtrodden individuals in need of money, knowledge, and kindness, which can be provided unidirectionally from student to community member (Kahne & Westheimer, 1996; Marullo & Edwards, 2000; Stoecker & Tryon, 2008), rather than as individuals capable of cultivating their own destiny or justice. The focus on charity also tends to favor sporadic or one-time engagement rather than explicitly addressing larger systemic issues or sustainable solutions.

Indeed, when done poorly, CE has been critiqued for its potential to perpetuate hierarchies (e.g., McBride et al., 2006) and reinforce stereotypes (Jacoby & Dean, 2010). The current shift away from "service" language (see discussion in Chapter 1) speaks to the power differentials and the assumption that service is a disempowering approach that maintains oppressive systems without actually moving toward sustainable change.

In recent years, the field has taken a more explicit turn toward social justice and critical engagement, as exhibited through the rise in such literature (e.g., Mitchell, 2008; Vincent et al., 2021). In an early piece about a critical approach to service-learning, Forbes et al. (1999) describe its goals as such:

> We want . . . to empower students to see themselves as agents capable of acting together with others to build coalitions, foster public awareness, and create social change. Our goal is to avoid the trap of

---

* Sirolli, E. (2012, August). *Want to help someone? Shut up and listen!* [Video]. TED. https://www.ted.com/talks/ernesto_sirolli_want_to_help_someone_shut_up_and _listen?lnguage=en

the cultural safari, instead discussing and demonstrating the tools the students will require to pursue the objectives they set forth within the engaged parameters of their own diverse lives and concerns. At the very least, this should short-circuit the stance of charitable pity that traditional volunteerism often produces. (p. 167)

This critical turn is discussed in more detail in Chapter 8, exploring the practice of cultivating a critical classroom.

Voyeurism and Dissonance

Another harmful trend within CE has been a tendency toward voyeurism, wherein communities are cast as "other" and observed/researched in ways that objectify and ostracize them (Butin, 2012; Philipsen, 2003). Like the savior complex or charity, voyeurism disempowers the community and maintains a distinct town/gown separation through its treatment of community partners as a sort of lab site (Eby, 1998). These attitudes can suggest to students that they are not impacted by the issue at hand or do not need to be interested in relationships as part of the learning process. Rather, the mindset enforces the aforementioned "cultural safari" approach, where students feel like tourists venturing into an exotic, faraway land (Forbes et al., 1999, p. 167). Thus, instructors must play a role helping students reflect on the commitments they are subscribing to within the project, rather than merely hoping that students will have an emotional experience that shifts their attitude.

Here, we provide a brief story from *The Unheard Voices* told by a community partner about one instructor's seemingly well-intentioned attempt to challenge a student to get outside their comfort zone that resulted in intense harm to the community:

> It was an instance where we did direct service with [college students] so [our group] had [people] coming in who were struggling with coming-out issues and who were dealing with violence in their dorms, and the LGBT center was the one place that they could feel safe and not have to deal with any homophobia. Then we had the service-learning student come in and talk about how the reason she was there was because she was uncomfortable with these issues because of her faith, and it really made a lot of people uncomfortable. (Stoecker & Tryon, 2009, p. 122)

Of course, such an egregiously harmful mismatch by an instructor might be rare, but it highlights how traditional forms of CE have valued student learning in ways that can ultimately harm vulnerable communities. It is also worth noting that in this example, it is really the instructor who is advocating for voyeuristic engagement here. As we repeat frequently in this book, instructors must be critically self-aware of the motivations, philosophies, and frameworks that inform their approach to teaching to avoid the risk of developing and maintaining harmful approaches to engagement among their students.

Exploitation

This harmful approach can be seen quite clearly when we listen to community partners and learn of the myriad ways they feel taken advantage of by university entities. A number of studies have pointed to trends among CBL courses that place undue burden on communities (Stoecker & Tryon, 2009) and reward researchers and students over community (Eby, 1998; Harmon, 2010; Metz & Youniss, 2003). Exploitation can present in many ways. As an extreme example, consider the Tuskegee experiment, a historically famous study that is probably somewhat familiar to most students but is worth repeating often to underscore the distrust groups may feel toward researchers. The decades-long study, begun in 1932, centered around African American men being treated for syphilis. Fifteen years into the study, penicillin had become the preferred syphilis treatment; however, the U.S. Public Health Services researchers desired to observe the long-term effects of the disease and convinced the participants' local health providers not to provide it. This self-serving and unethical decision ultimately resulted in a proliferation of the disease to participants' families and over one hundred indirect or direct deaths before the study was finally ended after public outcry in 1972 (Centers for Disease Control and Prevention, 2021). This study is just one of many examples of exploitative research that explicitly harmed marginalized communities and only exacerbated their distrust and skepticism of research as a whole.

Exploitation does not always look this extreme. Sometimes it is the attitude the student brings to the experience. A partner in *The Unheard Voices* study said they felt students were treating their population as a commodity; in this instance, "they just want to meet a homeless person." It can also look like a researcher taking the majority of the credit for their "community-based" research and failing to adequately recognize community partners. Today, many CEPs are developing systems to pay community partners out of recognition of the value that partners bring to the experience (e.g., Black et al., 2013; Gelmon et al., 2013), as well as their role in educating the students. As we mention elsewhere in this book, community partners often discuss the burden placed upon them when instructors send students to volunteer at a community partner site without proper support—often stretching already understaffed or overworked organizations—out of a false perception of benefiting the community. Adequately recognizing the contributions of partners and honoring their labor is an essential element of building mutually respectful relationships.

Personal Gain or Obligations

We all know one. The student who engages in a great deal of academic and extracurricular activities—sometimes out of enjoyment, but often stemming from a desire to have as many experiences as possible to boast about or highlight on their social media or résumé (Chesbrough, 2009). It seems worth acknowledging that this approach to engagement, where communities are treated like spots on a bingo card, is sometimes encouraged by academia and the tendency toward hypercompetitiveness and overwork (Leana, 2020).

On the flip side of this syndrome are the students who are required to take a CBL course or engage in service, perhaps for a degree requirement. That is not to say that service requirements are necessarily harmful (though some scholars do have critiques of such obligations; see Chan et al., 2019), but community partners can usually flag these students by their attitude: "Students participated in service-learning primarily to fulfill a class requirement without necessarily caring about the work itself" (Stoecker & Tryon, 2009, p. 52). Similar to the personal gain motivation, both would benefit from a reframing of the course expectation. Instructors should consider how they are supporting students in reflecting on the implications of their engagement and the importance of their commitment. Instructors can also be thoughtful in how they designate time and assignments in the course so that CE does not feel like an extra chore, but rather the primary focus. For example, explain that you are cutting back on a few readings or assignments and are substituting the hours spent in the CE project, which will help ease perceptions of overload.

What to do about the occasional student who, even participating in a well-designed, required project, enters the community behaving as though they were dragged into it kicking and screaming? It is possible for a skilled instructor to help the student shift their views through guided reflection. It is an opportunity as well as a challenge. But unless students are able to understand what effects their attitude could have on partners and temper it, the better part of valor might be to arrange a noncontact assignment for that student to prevent hurt feelings in the community.

Moving Forward

Once students have unpacked the assumptions behind various motivations for community engagement, it becomes easier to discuss what it means to engage more equitably and appropriately. Spending time as a classroom community discussing how to collectively approach engagement is essential. Similar to courses that develop community agreements at the onset of the course (which we encourage and discuss in Chapter 8), such expectations should be collectively shaped by all participants in the course, including both students and community partners. The instructor plays a key role in reflecting and reframing these expectations with students, ensuring they are understood by all and are inclusive of the community.

In the following pages we describe some of the motivations driving community interest in working with students. We also close with some strategies we have utilized for orienting students toward more meaningful approaches.

Common Community Motivations

In the study of community partners for *The Unheard Voices* (Stoecker & Tryon, 2009), chapter contibutors Shannon Bell and Rebecca Carlson, revealed four key motives that informed community partners' interest in working with students:

- Altruism
- Potential long-term impacts of forging relationships with students, including cultivating future employees or sustained volunteers
- Organizational capacity building
- Access to university resources

These motivations serve as a reminder that community partners have their own expectations, hopes, and interests informing their participation in student partnerships. Community partners are invested in and play a huge role in students' learning through CE and naturally expect to engage in reciprocal relationships that meaningfully benefit all stakeholders (Basinger & Bartholomew, 2006). Just as instructors commonly spend course time discussing classroom expectations, dedicating course time to seeing how "the other side" is looking at CE helps establish expectations for how students engage with the community.

Better Approaches to Framing Community Engagement

As useful as it is to demonstrate to students the harms that can be associated with CE and to check their motivations, it is then essential to provide them with alternative framings and examples of successful partnerships. For seasoned CEPs, sharing an example of a past project that went well and discussing the associated outcomes and lessons is useful. For students with no CE experience, understanding how partnerships are formed and sustained is incredibly important. New instructors might consider reaching out to others in their department or connecting with an institutional outreach and engagement office to find good examples (we also share some success stories in Chapter 9). In the following we outline some orientations and framings that can develop students' more nuanced and informed understandings of CE.

Principles of Community Engagement

Community engagement can look drastically different depending on the partnership, the academic discipline, or a myriad of other factors. There is no one-size-fits-all approach. The expectations of first-year students are going to look far different than a senior-level capstone project. Often when we consult with faculty, we are asked for a checklist of best practices or a simple framework of what to do and how to structure the course and prepare students. Although we hope this book provides a shared sense of direction, there will never be an all-inclusive list of how to engage with others—that is not how the real world works, and it can be a disservice to students and community partners to assume that always doing x will always lead to y.

Fortunately, a fairly rich body of literature exists to provide shared approaches to CE that are more strongly rooted in respect and equity, often in the form of "principles" (e.g., Organizing Committee for Assessing Meaningful Community Engagement in Health & Health Care Programs & Policies, 2022; Schlake, 2015; and listed in Appendix B, as well as at https:// scholarshare.temple.edu/handle/20.500.12613/8178). In our practice of CE, we have found great value in using principles to provide a shared understanding of partnership among university affiliates. Rather than specific steps to take, these principles often ask the students, staff, and faculty using them to consider *how* they are approaching the community and what values or commitments might guide the project. As it relates to preparation for CE, dissecting these principles and engaging students in reflection around these existing approaches can open up opportunities for students to discuss values, beliefs, and motivations. In the latter pages of this chapter, we share an activity we have used both virtually and in person to spark students' thinking on this topic. But these discussions are just starting points. Adequate preparation for CE requires the development of the skills and understanding we discuss throughout this book for students to effectively engage with the community and support healthy partnerships.

	INFORM	CONSULT	INVOLVE	COLLABORATE	EMPOWER
PUBLIC PARTICIPATION GOAL	To provide the public with balanced and objective information to assist them in understanding the problem, alternatives, opportunities and/or solutions.	To obtain public feedback on analysis, alternatives and/or decisions.	To work directly with the public throughout the process to ensure that public concerns and aspirations are consistently understood and considered.	To partner with the public in each aspect of the decision including the development of alternatives and the identification of the preferred solution.	To place final decision making in the hands of the public.
PROMISE TO THE PUBLIC	We will keep you informed.	We will keep you informed, listen to and acknowledge concerns and aspirations, and provide feedback on how public input influenced the decision.	We will work with you to ensure that your concerns and aspirations are directly reflected in the alternatives developed and provide feedback on how public input influenced the decision.	We will look to you for advice and innovation in formulating solutions and incorporate your advice and recommendations into the decisions to the maximum extent possible.	We will implement what you decide.

INCREASING IMPACT ON THE DECISION

© IAP2 International Federation 2018. All rights reserved. 20181112_v1

Figure 3.1. Spectrum of Public Participation
(Credit: International Association for Public Participation. [2018]. *IAP2 spectrum of public participation*. https://cdn.ymaws.com/www.iap2.org/resource/resmgr/pillars/Spectrum_8.5x11_Print.pdf)

Levels of Partnerships

A possible starting place to think about the structure of partnerships might be the Spectrum of Public Participation, pictured in Figure 3.1, as developed by the International Association for Public Participation (2018). This model demonstrates how community involvement and decision-making power shifts depending on the approach to the project. On the "inform" end of the spectrum, communities have little power and are generally the passive receivers of information or outcomes. Within the context of higher education CE, this might look like science outreach initiatives that expose elementary students to scientists and researchers. And while such efforts are valuable, through this book we hope to push instructors toward models of engagement aligned more with the "empower" end of the spectrum, where communities have final say in how they interact with the university and what gets implemented in their community.

Focusing on Relationships

The speed of modern life has accelerated rapidly in recent decades. The Western (and academic) culture of overwork has incentivized quantity over quality, encouraging more and more publications, multiple appointments and committees, more emails to respond to faster, and countless opportunities to take on more. Students conditioned to such a rapid pace and productivity-centered model may struggle with the much slower and delicate speed associated with relationships. For overwhelmed, checklist-minded students, relationships may feel like an unnecessary burden, less important than the product being developed or the change being sought.

However, we maintain that the cultivation of relationships is central to any form of CE and as such should be treated with the same rigor that students apply to their studies. This means reflecting critically on the intricacies of how relationships are developed and maintained, such as standards of communication, methods of collaboration, and navigating conflict. Just as important are the development of skills and dispositions such as empathy, authenticity, and self-awareness. Students should be encouraged to view the classroom and reflection as opportunities to process and discuss relationships and how they are impacting the partnership, as well as their own learning. What new perspectives are they being exposed to? What tensions or challenges are present? Whose voices are being centered?

Also worth noting here is that when students are brought into a CE experience, they become pseudo-stewards of the relationship the instructor or CEP (as well as the institution itself) may have with a community partner. For example, if a student is behaving inappropriately on-site and the behavior is not addressed, that behavior will come back to reflect poorly on the holder of the partnership, as well as the institution, possibly limiting future partnerships for others on campus. Ensuring that students are aware of the history of partnerships and the instructor's regard for the community can have positive effects on the level of commitment students demonstrate to the community.

Finally, the importance of relationships within CE has been echoed by numerous scholars, but especially Tania Mitchell (2008), who centers the development of authentic relationships within her model of critical service learning. This approach to CE reinforces the importance of working with the community and others to pursue social change. A focus on relationships can expose students to the complex and expansive networks and active citizens that exist within communities and provide them the opportunity to learn from and with others.

Practical Approaches and Activities for Addressing Student Motivations

While teaching students awareness of harmful or problematic approaches to CE that have commonly colored the practice and about the frameworks and orientations to CE that aim to better center the community, we also want to provide some practical activities and tools to open spaces for these conversations. Following are descriptions of land acknowledgments, CE principles, community partner class appearances, and an activity to define meaningful service.

Land Acknowledgment

Land acknowledgments are becoming a more common practice at a number of institutions of higher education (Keefe, 2019; Wark, 2021). Ours can be found in Appendix B.1.

I (Cory) was pleasantly surprised to see nearly all of the students in an introduction to CE workshop raise their hands when I asked if they had heard our university's land acknowledgment read before. However, when I asked deeper questions, such as students' understanding of the history of Indigenous communities on our campus (which is home to multiple Indigenous burial mounds), almost all students indicated that they were unaware of that history. Land acknowledgments offer an entry point to the deep reflection that should be expected from CE experiences. Often when land acknowledgments are read on campuses, they are read quickly, a breath is taken, and everyone moves on. Within the classroom, instructors can consider ways to connect the history of the land to the communities students may be working with, tracing those historical threads and considering their implications. The following is a slide I created to follow my reading of the land acknowledgment during a recent workshop for an arts-based CBL course (Figure 3.2). It is a simple slide, containing a few pictures of Indigenous burial mounds, including one on our campus and another within our state. Also pictured are before and after photos of children who had been placed in Indigenous boarding schools. During this part of the workshop, we discuss the ways art is connected to culture, community, and land. This example is a way to demonstrate how land acknowledgments can be made more relevant to the course, rather than feeling like an unrelated, performative opening statement to the presentation.

Indeed, as quickly as they arose across campuses, so too did the critique and the feeling that land acknowledgments were mere performances that rather worked to reify colonialism (Tuck & Yang, 2012; Wark, 2021). Through our suggestion of providing space for students to truly grapple with land acknowledgments, we strive to move beyond the performative. We may not be in a position to return the land, but ideally we can help students consider their relationship with the land, the Indigenous stewards of it, and how

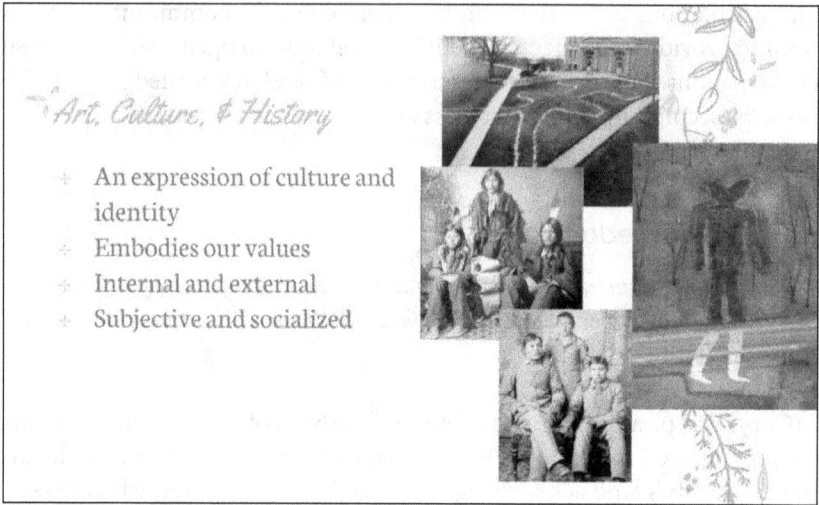

Figure 3.2. Making Land Acknowledgments Relevant
(Credit: Cory Sprinkel.)

that relationship informs how we relate to others and how we each engage in work that impacts our planet in one way or another. Additionally, land acknowledgments can also be strengthened by tying them to calls for action. Instructors might consider opportunities to donate their own dollars to local Indigenous communities or elevate ongoing Indigenous organizing efforts, such as protests against oil pipelines on Native lands and waters.

Crafting and Analyzing Community Engagement Principles

As discussed previously, a plethora of CE principles exist within and outside the academy. Many of these principles contain similarities. As community-engaged teaching and scholarship has become more common, numerous fields and disciplines have also developed their own discipline-specific principles, especially in the health fields. An activity we have frequently facilitated involves comparing and contrasting a thoughtful selection of various engagement principles, some originating from academic literature and some arising from nonprofits and specific community-university partnerships, and reflecting on which amalgamation best fits the program's specific CE work. We provide some principles here (Table 3.1), from both academic and community perspectives, that instructors could use to stoke course discussion and allow students to articulate their values and guiding mindsets regarding community engagement.

TABLE 3.1   COMPARING COMMUNITY ENGAGEMENT PRINCIPLES

Academic and institutional principles	Community-created principles
Bernal, H., Shellman, J., & Reid, K. (2004). Essential concepts in developing community–university partnerships. CareLink: The Partners in Caring Model. *Public Health Nursing, 21*(1), 32–40.	Vu. (2020, February 2). *Guidelines for higher education programs that require students to do special projects with nonprofits.* Nonprofit AF. https://non profitaf.com/2020/02/guidelines-for-higher -education-programs-that-require-students -to-do-special-projects-with-nonprofits/
Bowman, N. R., Francis, C. D., & Tyndall, M. (2015). Culturally responsive Indigenous evaluation. In S. Hood, R. Hopson, & H. Frierson (Eds.), *Continuing the journey to reposition culture and cultural context in evaluation theory and practice* (pp. 335–360). Information Age Publishing.	Cruz, E., & Bakken, L. (2020). *Community guidelines for engaging with researchers and evaluators.* UW Institute for Clinical and Translational Research. https://ictr.wisc .edu/documents/community-guidelines -for-engaging-with-researchers-and -evaluators/
Howard, J. (2001). Principles of good practice for service-learning pedagogy. *Michigan Journal of Community Service Learning, 30*(1), 16–19.	Knowledge Works Foundation. (2005). *10 principles of authentic community engagement.* Strive Together. https://www .strivetogether.org/wp-content/uploads /2017/03/10_principles_community _engagement_2.pdf

Here are some questions you might consider posing to engage students in intentional reflection relating to their expectations for CE:

- Which set(s) of principles/ideas seems most applicable to you? Why?
- Which ideas surprised you or challenged your thinking about how to engage with the community?
- What, if anything, is missing from these principles?
- What values guide how you intend to engage with the community? How, if at all, are they connected to the principles we have reviewed?

An activity like this can also be leveraged to inform other aspects of the course, such as the co-creation of course norms (sometimes called "ground rules"; we think "norms" is a less authoritarian term). The co-creation of norms and the development of shared understanding around good community-engaged practice contribute to a pedagogical approach that empowers students to take responsibility for their own learning and role in the educational environment (Bury & Masuzawa, 2018; Dewey, 1938). More on establishing course norms can be found in Chapter 8.

Inviting in Community Partners

A crucial component of doing good CE is the recognition of the community partner as a co-educator in the process (Vincent et al., 2021). Indeed, the ability to support the development of students is often a primary motivation for community organizations to partner with universities and colleges (Stoecker & Tryon, 2009). And, of course, community partners are ultimately most impacted by the partnership and left to deal with any ramifications, as we discussed earlier.

Inviting the community partner into the classroom can play a helpful role in emphasizing their authority—that community partners have something to offer students' classroom learning and that they are indeed an equitable partner in the CE process. Students' understanding of the community partner as a co-educator and expert on their community, rather than a recipient of services, can enhance students' understanding of the commitment they are making by engaging with an organization (Hidayat et al., 2009). For some courses, this may even mean that community partners can give feedback to the instructor that may shape students' grades. Beyond grades, community partners can also offer valuable and practical insight into the workings of a given organization or effort, giving students an opportunity to hear about individuals' experiences in the field and perhaps opening new career pathways and considerations for students.

Additionally, partners are best poised to contextualize the organization for the students and describe the work and community. Coming into the classroom or other educational setting can be beneficial for the community partner too because it saves them time—allowing them to meet all the students at once, rather than little waves of students stopping by the organization continuously throughout the early weeks in a term. And, of course, the additional opportunity for students and the instructor to see and interact with the community partner supports relationship building. However, attention must be paid to ensuring that the community partner is not taking on the sole burden of orienting the students (see more in Chapters 1 and 2) but rather is inviting the students in to share some of their perspective if they have the time (even better if you can compensate partners). An additional benefit for the partner is that they can "interview" the students and choose ones they feel are the best fit for the project. With the rise in virtual classroom experiences, there is also now the possibility of Zooming in the community partner or taking a virtual tour of a partner site before students leave campus.

Defining Meaningful Service

This is an activity that has floated around the world of CE for quite a few years now. The activity, *Which Service Is the Most Meaningful?* (Koth &

Hamilton, 2003), has been revised and updated by its multiple adapters, but its widespread use is a testament to its ability to cultivate rich discussion among students. This is simple and very adaptable. In essence, it is a ranked choice activity that asks students to articulate what they understand as meaningful community engagement. This exercise includes a few of the choices we use that students often list in their discussions:

Prompt: In this exercise you will rank a list of community engagement activities from least meaningful (8) to most meaningful (1) according to your own philosophy of community engagement. As you go through the exercise, try to notice any patterns or values that emerge for you. Why are you ranking things the way you are?

1. Providing dinner once a week at a homeless shelter
2. Joining the armed forces
3. Conducting research with a community organization focused on health disparities
4. Voting
5. Writing a letter to a congressional leader about campaign finance reform
6. Developing a micro-lending project for low-income teens
7. Giving blood
8. Helping a nonprofit redesign their website for a course

The idea of this activity is not to discourage student participation in any of the listed activities—all are completely valid. The main idea of the activity is to showcase the various ways we understand CE and begin sparking conversation about what constitutes meaningful service.

Asset Mapping and Asset-Based Approaches

Too often, CE efforts are framed through community deficits. Researchers and outsiders are often quick to point out all that is problematic in a community, glossing over the perspectives of those most impacted and overlooking the positives that are present (Ladson-Billings, 2007). This tendency limits the successes of projects and curtails a community's ability to build their own capacity and sustain projects in the absence of university resources. Many of the traditional approaches to service explored in this chapter feed into this lens, often seeking to fit a square peg (i.e., a hyperspecific research project) into a round hole (i.e., one community's unique context). So, when a university partner ultimately wraps up the project, the community is left to either struggle to maintain some new thing they may not yet fully understand or rebuild from their previous efforts, which may have been neglected in favor of university interests.

Asset-based community development (ABCD) asks us to begin by focusing on the assets in the community (Kretzmann & McKnight, 1993). In practice with students and to develop our understanding of a community, we might engage in asset mapping—identifying sources of strength, gathering, and knowledge within a community. Examples could be the church, where folks are already gathering and providing resources or services to different groups; the local newspaper, where community members are sharing their perspectives and advocating for solutions; or a fledgling mentorship program being initiated at the local school. Organizing around a community's assets ensures we are seeking to build the capacity of communities to develop their own solutions that fit their context and interests. Focusing on relationships that increase the students' understanding of the community and relevant histories, groups, and efforts is essential to attuning to community assets. More on ABCD can be found in a contribution from John Zeigler in Chapter 5.

Concluding Thoughts

Community engagement can be truly transformative for students, as well as for the communities and facilitators involved in these experiences. However, care and intentionality must be taken by all stakeholders to ensure the experience is actually meaningful. Student motivations play a significant role in how the partnership and learning take shape. As the rest of this book seeks to reinforce, developing robust partnerships with communities and insightful learning experiences for students is more of an art form than an exact science. Addressing students' motivations is just a starting point for much deeper and critical learning. However, it is a step that should not be missed, considering the impact such insight can have on framing the overall partnership and course.

4

Building Student Self-Awareness— Identity and Socialization

Building upon the previous chapter, student preparation for community engagement requires supporting the development of students' self-awareness. While addressing student motivations is a critical starting point, it cannot end there. This chapter details strategies and tools for preparing students with the skills they need before entering the community in CE, and it maps well onto the Level Two: Contextualizing Community online module.

How we approach CE as an institution and as individuals is heavily informed by our own identities, cultures, socialization, and more. The idea of saviorism, discussed at length in the previous chapter, is deeply connected to those same ideas. As such, supporting students in reflecting on and articulating aspects of their identity plays an important role in preparing students for more critical, and ideally humble, approaches to CE.

Developing students' understanding of their own identities has been a growing interest in higher education over the past few years, as evidenced through the rise in diversity, equity and inclusion (DEI) trainings aimed at students and the literature on student development that informs the field of student affairs (e.g., Patton et al., 2016). Typically, attention to these topics and this aspect of student development is outsourced to institutional offices like multicultural centers, dean of students offices, and other student affairs professionals (Patton et al., 2016). However, acknowledging these topics and dynamics within CE settings (and generally most course settings) can be incredibly beneficial. And while we believe faculty should be informed on these topics in order to best integrate them into CBL courses, we also recommend faculty consider ways to collaborate with institutional DEI resources, including cultural centers and social justice educators (Benenson et al., 2017). These resources can be helpful to faculty who may feel the need to do some deeper reflection on their own identities and their impact on their teaching. As Mitchell et al. (2012) found in their study of CBL courses, these courses have historically perpetuated whiteness through the structure of the class, often centering the learning of white students at the expense and burden of students of color. The savior complex, discussed earlier, is also informed by dimensions of race, class, and other social identities. For the benefit of community partners and all those involved in CE, instructors must strive to develop a basic understanding of their students' identities as well as their own and should consider how those may influence classroom and community dynamics.

Overview

This chapter provides an overview of essential topics related to self-awareness and shares some facilitation strategies that allow students to reflect and build upon their understanding of themselves and their identities and how those relate to their work with communities. These include ideas such as socialization, power and privilege, and bias, which instructors should consider integrating into the course. We conclude with a selection of example activities and suggestions on how to engage students with these topics.

We acknowledge that topics such as race and identity can be challenging to explore in classroom settings, especially in our increasingly politicized world (see Chapter 8 for specific strategies to integrate these ideas into your teaching holistically to create a critical classroom), but failing to discuss these topics does an enormous disservice to both students and communities, and partners will not keep working with students forever if things do not change soon. There are abundant resources available to instructors to better prepare them for creating safe and meaningful spaces for students to engage in complex and vulnerable discussion. We highlight some of these strategies and resources in this chapter, with the caveat that this is not an exhaustive list. At our own institution, we have noticed an uptick in professional development resources aimed at supporting instructor development in this area, such as deliberative dialogue trainings, teaching workshops, and supportive colleagues in institutional DEI offices. A list of resources we have utilized or suggested can be found in the Appendices.

To kick-start our exploration of self-awareness, we use a video (Morgridge Center for Public Service, 2021a)* created by our center's communication staff highlighting the voices of community partners and community-engaged faculty and staff on the topic of self-awareness. This is one video out of a series we put together to showcase to students the community's perspectives on a number of CE topics. Like any other reading or resource, it prompts reflection and provides an entry point to discussion. We welcome you to use it by following the QR code in the footnote, but please also consider resources within your community that present a similar message.

Aspects of Student Self-Awareness

Socialization and Culture

A key aspect of learning to exist in the world involves recognizing the ways our lived experiences shape the way we understand the world. Socialization, as we mentioned in the overview chapter, is defined broadly in social psychology as the process in which individuals develop their own behavior, in accordance with messages and expectations of what is deemed acceptable by the group's standards (Child, 1954). Throughout our lives, we encounter a number of different institutions, such as our schooling, families, or religion, that influence how we understand the world and others. Harro (2013) suggests that the norms and expectations one holds about the world occur in a cyclical nature, as depicted in Harro's Cycle of Socialization. It is not until we recognize the patterns and norms shaping us that we are able to actively disrupt such patterns or assumptions that no longer serve us or that uphold oppression.

As of the early 2020s, we are in a historical social moment where it seems that more Americans are beginning to consider their own socialization, especially as it pertains to race, and how that socialization in turn developed oppressive and unjust institutions. The rise in sales of books like Ibram X. Kendi's *How to Be an Antiracist* or Ijeoma Oluo's *So You Want to Talk about Race* are examples of this discourse becoming more mainstream (although it is worth noting that in parts of our polarized country, how to *not* talk about race could also be considered mainstream discourse). As white authors, we recall the learning that was sparked within us through considering

---

* Morgridge Center for Public Service. (2021a, February 23). *Self-awareness in community engagement* [Video]. YouTube. https://www.youtube.com/watch?v=iX3o78 PnEQM&t=10s&ab_channel=MorgridgeCenterforPublicService

Harro's Cycle of Socialization and the messages we had received from different institutions and people in our lives. Engaging students in deep reflection on the cycle, or at least the idea of socialization, offers an opportunity for them to consider how different communities or institutions enable certain norms and how they too may have unknowingly absorbed certain messages or assumptions.

Briefly, Harro's Cycle of Socialization posits that each of us is born into a world with certain mechanics and norms in place. Over time and through a variety of socialization mechanisms (e.g., parents, schools, media, churches), we come to understand the world in a particular way (for instance, in regards to race, gender roles, religion, and so forth, in addition to many other facets of daily life). In doing so, we consciously and unconsciously absorb or have reinforced certain messages about others and ourselves. As we progress through life and learn more about the world, we may seek to further reinforce the messages and worldviews we have been socialized into—maintaining the status quo and repeating the cycle—or we may strive to reconceptualize our worldview and disrupt the cycle that advances certain ideas while devaluing others. As an example, consider the student who overhears her uncle express a racist remark at the family dinner table and in that moment has to decide if she will say something about it or chuckle awkwardly with the rest of the family. It is in this crossroads of perpetuating or disrupting the cycle of oppressive norms that students will often find themselves when out in the community. Critical to CE (and engagement with the world in general) is the process of unlearning and relearning that needs to occur as students learn to be in active relationship with others. In practice, we have used the Cycle of Socialization as a prompt for reflection, encouraging students to think about how they first learned about different communities or what messages they might have received through the various institutions they have engaged with, as well as to consider instances in which they did question or disrupt the messages they were receiving and what that process felt like.

Another useful graphic and theory to develop students' understanding of socialization and culture is the cultural iceberg (Hall, 1976). The main idea demonstrated through Hall's original depiction of the iceberg is that culture is frequently conceived of as those things that are observable (one's clothing, celebrations, foods, etc.), whereas the much more complex and weighted ideas about culture lie deep beneath the surface—such as one's beliefs (e.g., "there is only one true God") and values (e.g., reciprocity with nature). In the following (Figure 4.1) we include an adapted version of the cultural iceberg developed by Language and Culture Worldwide (2021). We have also employed the iceberg as a stepping stone into conversations about cultural humility, which we discuss in depth in Chapter 7.

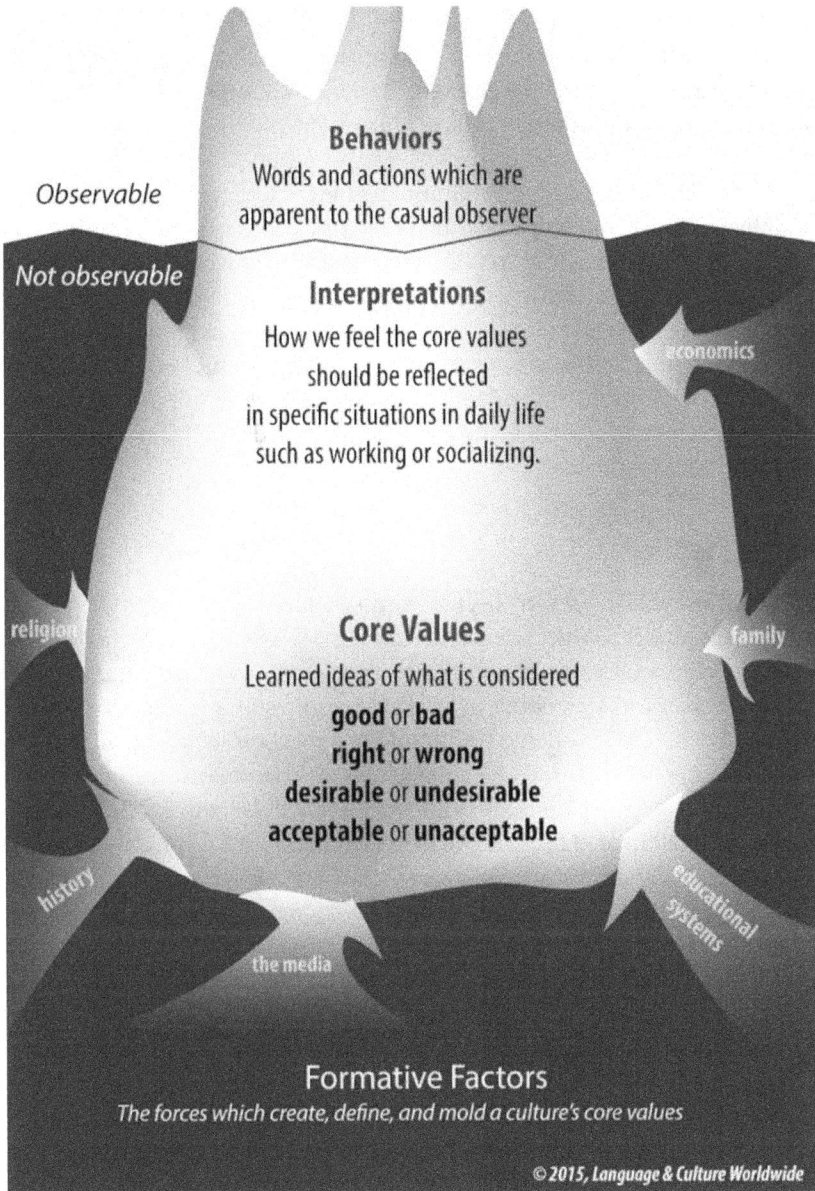

Figure 4.1. Cultural Iceberg
(Credit: Language and Culture Worldwide. [2021, January 11]. *Iceberg or beacon? How the cultural iceberg guides us toward greater inclusion.* https://languageandculture.com/iceberg-or-beacon-how-the-cultural-iceberg-guide-us-toward-greater-inclusion/)

We are drawn to this depiction of the iceberg for its inclusion of formative factors, such as history, media, and other social forces, that impact how one's culture is perceived and enacted, as well as how others may understand it. For example, how different groups are presented in the media can impact how individuals understand themselves and others. The iceberg model is especially compelling because it illuminates the complexity of culture. A point we often reiterate with students is that each of us does not have just one cultural iceberg—we have multiple, intersecting icebergs likely tied to different aspects of our social identities and cultures. Being explicit about the ways our cultures and identities intersect (Crenshaw, 1989) helps emphasize the way culture and identity are not generalizable; rather, students should focus on understanding each individual's story and interests within a community-engaged project, while still being aware of the broader cultural and historical forces that might impact a community.

Social Identity

As noted previously in our discussion of student social identity development, each student's worldview and experiences are shaped by their social identities. Examples include race (i.e., Asian, white, Black), gender identity (i.e., cisgender, trans, nonbinary), and citizenship status (i.e., undocumented, U.S. born, "DACA-mented"), among many others. Social identities are based on physical, social, and mental characteristics; may be claimed by an individual or given to them by others; and may give them privilege or increase the likelihood of oppression. With this in mind, CEPs must recognize and consider the ways students' own intersecting identities and lived experiences inform how they are engaging with and responding to their CE experiences (Green, 2003; Henry, 2005).

One's identity (and positionality, as we discuss later) impacts how one perceives communities and is perceived by communities. Promoting a "race-neutral" approach not only does not benefit anyone involved but is detrimental to communities of color whose unique needs become systemically ignored (Castro Atwater, 2008). As such, it becomes essential for students to have space to do that processing and reflecting on social identity on campus, in a learning-centered environment. Within the classroom or other student setting, this may look like asking students specific questions, such as the following, about disparities pertaining to race or other social identity categories:

- In what ways do you think your identity impacts your understanding of the community?
- How often do you think about x aspect of your identity while in the community?

- What histories or policies have impacted communities with x identity?

Social identity can also be discussed by acknowledging disparities that can exist for different identities. Within our own work with students, we have pointed to racial disparities that exist in our state and city. Wisconsin is unfortunately home to some of the highest disparities impacting communities of color in the United States in areas such as incarceration, unemployment, and infant mortality (COWS, 2019). We also seek to uplift reports, data, and news stories from local organizations and sources, such as a local news story about LGBTQ+ homelessness in Madison (Peek, 2016). Such examples help students see the reality of social identities and the ways certain communities in their own cities experience the world.

Instructors should also be cognizant of how their own identities and perceptions of communities influence their own courses or partnerships. Mueller and Pickett (2015) found that an instructor's identity in terms of race, ethnicity, class, gender identity, sexual orientation, religion, and ability status, among many other aspects, not only has implications for how they approach CE but also how they are received by the community and students. In essence, students are likely making assumptions about the coordinator of a CE experience—their identity, motivations, connections with the community, and so on. As such, CEPs can practice vulnerability by discussing their orientation to and investment in engaged work, as well as how they have grown throughout the experience. More experienced CEPs may already have recognized ways in which CBL courses and projects can become a "site of identity, construction, deconstruction, and reconstruction" for themselves as the instructor, as well as their students (Butin, 2003, p. 1684).

Bias and Microaggressions

One of the most frequent forms of harm we typically hear about when talking with community partners is the combination of unconscious and conscious forms of bias perpetuated by university partners and students onto communities. This has looked like many things—a nutritional science student overheard making race-based assumptions about clients' eating habits, a tutor telling a student that they should want to be more than a mechanic when they grow up, or a researcher discrediting community voice because they believe the community to be uninformed, among many other examples. Bias is frequent and not always obvious, especially if it relates to areas in which we might experience privilege (McIntosh, 1988).

One specific form of bias to consider discussing with students involves microaggressions, which are defined as "brief, commonplace daily verbal, behavioral and environmental slights and indignities, whether intentional or unintentional, directed at minoritized groups" (Sue et al., 2008). In the CE context, examples of microaggressions might include reinforcing an offensive stereotype held about certain communities (e.g., rural communities are less educated) or othering someone based on an aspect of their identity (e.g., asking to touch a Black woman's hair).

Helping students reflect upon and analyze their biases is a critical, albeit challenging, component of engaged work. CE has been critiqued for its potential to reinforce stereotypes (Endres & Gould, 2009) when experiences lack proper space for reflection; additionally, some students seem to deliberately avoid confronting their own biases (Dunn-Kenney, 2010). That is an admittedly tricky space to navigate when working with students and is a reason we encourage multiple forms of reflection, especially written, so CEPs might have the opportunity to push students' thinking further. Here are some questions we have utilized to push students to think more critically:

- What perspectives have influenced your thinking on this?
- What generalizations or assumptions are underlying your perspective?
- What systems, histories, or institutions might be relevant to consider here?
- How might bias, intentional or not, impact relationships?

A great example of this can be found in the University of Connecticut Husky Sport case study Chapter 8.

While it is important for students to understand how to minimize the likelihood of committing a microaggression, it is also important to acknowledge that such slipups are a reality in a society built upon the oppression and exploitation of various groups. We should support students in understanding how to respond when they inevitably make a mistake or accidentally offend. A great deal of literature, blogs, and social media posts exist discussing steps and strategies for how to properly "apologize" or learn from a mistake. However, in our experience, the key is to not lament over a mistake but to treat it as a learning opportunity (more on this in Chapter 8).

It is worth noting that sometimes students (generally those with privileged identities) are dismissive about the realities of microaggressions, seeing them as a sort of overreaction and part of "woke" culture. However, microaggressions do have real implications for CE, whether it be furthering community distrust of university partners or even projects ending because of repeated harm and failure to address it. They also have real implications for students with marginalized identities and can affect their feelings of belonging on campus (Sue et al., 2009). We have used a video from the You-

Tube account Fusion Comedy (2016)* that compares microaggressions to mosquito bites. This video employs some humor to address what can be a challenging topic. We do want to note that the video does include some explicit language as well as depictions of police violence, so CEPs should consider if it is the proper fit for their project.

Power, Privilege, and Positionality

When engaged with community, whether in efforts to enact social change or to support a discrete project, it is important that students consider the lenses of power, privilege, and oppression that shape our reality, support or restrict change, and impact partnerships. In order to prepare students to engage in "wicked problems," efforts must be made to develop students' ability to recognize power and confront the hidden structures that limit the capacity of people to enact change alone (Brookfield, 2005). Although these conversations may be inconvenient and challenging, they are a necessary component of modern leadership development (Barnes et al., 2018), and students benefit from being exposed to the lenses and language needed to actively operate within these systems.

In our own practice of training and orienting students, we do not often have the time needed to dive into the theories and complex conceptualizations of power. With the scaffolding of earlier ideas such as land acknowledgments, socialization (Harro, 2013), and culture (Hall, 1976) to build on, it is pretty clear that students recognize that power exists and has implications. It is up to instructors to provide students with the tools and frameworks to understand how power is operating within CE so they are able to consistently interrogate it.

As a starting point for these conversations, we typically begin with simple definitions of these concepts. The set of definitions for power, privilege, and oppression are in Chapter 1, paraphrased again below. These definitions ensure a shared understanding as conversations unfold. Our research found that many HEIs provide their own definitions of these common terms as well, in order to cultivate a shared understanding of diversity, equity, and inclusion on their campuses (see, for example, Dartmouth and Northwestern University).

- **Power:** The ability or authority to decide what is best for others, who has access to resources, or what is perceived as normal.

---

* Fusion Comedy. (2016, October 5). *How microaggressions are like mosquito bites: Same difference* [Video]. YouTube. https://www.youtube.com/watch?v=hDd3bzA7450

- **Privilege:** A set of unearned or earned advantages and freedoms, given to a group of people based on group membership.
- **Oppression:** The combination of prejudice and institutional power that creates a system that discriminates against some groups and benefits other groups.

In Table 4.1 we map some examples of social identities onto these dimensions of privileged/oppressed groups. Once the shared understanding of these ideas has been established, instructors should provide students the opportunity to process and discuss the information, considering how power shows up in their daily lives or in the course of a project. In order to maintain the conversations throughout the entirety of a CBL course, instructors might consider including theories of power (i.e., Freire, Bourdieu, Yosso) or ethics more specifically tailored to their discipline or assigning case studies and models that demonstrate the complexities of power and how it may arise in practice. These discussions are also likely to come up in students' reflections, and instructors should be sure to create ample space for processing them.

An additional lens to consider is that of positionality, which brings all these ideas together. Coghlan and Brydon-Miller (2014), within *The SAGE Encyclopedia of Research Action*, have this to say about positionality:

> Positionality refers to the stance or positioning of the researcher in relation to the social and political context of the study—the community, the organization or the participant group. The position adopted by a researcher affects every phase of the research process,

TABLE 4.1 DOMINANT AND TARGETED IDENTITIES		
Social identity	**Privileged (dominant groups)**	**Marginalized (target groups)**
Religious or spiritual affiliation	Christianity	Jewish, agnostic, Muslim, etc.
National origin	United States of America	Mexico, Syria, China, etc.
Race/ethnicity	White or Caucasian	Black, Latinx, Asian, Indigenous, etc.
Class	Upper class	Middle, working, and lower class
Education	Ph.Ds., college students	GED holder
Gender	Male	Female, nonbinary
Gender identity or sex	Cisgender	Trans, intersex
Ability status	Physically, mentally able	Wheelchair users, individuals with mental illness, etc.
Sexual orientation	Heterosexual	Gay, bi, asexual, etc.

from the way the question or problem is initially constructed, designed and conducted to how others are invited to participate, the ways in which knowledge is constructed and acted on and, finally, the ways in which outcomes are disseminated and published. (p. 2)

Positionality is commonly understood within fields like anthropology and sociology, but as Coghlan and Brydon-Miller note, researcher positionality affects every phase of an action research project and, we would argue, every form of CE and CES. Consider again the Ernesto Sirolli story from Chapter 3, where a team of Italian nongovernmental organization staff attempt to teach agriculture to locals in Zambia, only to learn the locals were essentially waiting for the project to fail because the organization's staff never sought their perspective or treated them as partners. Simply having knowledge of agriculture was not enough; in order to actually be successful, the project must be informed by a myriad of contextual and power-laden factors.

Students should be taught to consider their positionality as college students. How does their affiliation with the university influence the project and the community? Who is seen as having knowledge and/or power within the context of the project? How is that power being shared? This interrogation is not just an important scholarly skill but, like a lot of learning that comes from community-engaged pedagogies, also a valuable life skill. In Chapter 5 we expand on this discussion by discussing institutional power.

Systems of Oppression

At heart, we hope for students to understand the following about themselves:

- **Who they are:** What identities do they hold? How does their salience and expression change in different contexts?
- **How their identities impact how they move through the world:** How are they seen by others in various contexts? How have they been socialized to behave? Which of their identities may be more or less salient in different situations?
- **Harm they may inflict on others and how to rectify that harm:** How might their actions (often unintentionally) harm others? How can they build awareness of others in order to cause less harm?
- **Power and positionality:** How do their various identities intersect with power individually and systemically? How does their power change in different situations?
- **Socialization into oppressive systems:** Into which systems have students been socialized? How does this affect their identities? How does this affect how they view the world and themselves?

This requires student understanding of oppressive systems—what they are, how they operate and inform socialization and understanding of the world, and how to focus on systems-level change for more meaningful impact. A thorough consideration of systemic oppression necessitates exploring how oppression "is systematic and has historical antecedents; it is the intentional disadvantaging of groups of people based on their identity while advantaging members of the dominant group (gender, race, class, sexual orientation, language, etc.)" (National Equity Project, 2022). These systems support the flourishing of some people and the oppression of others through specific policies, practices, and norms. Systemic oppression typically results in discrimination often described in "isms"—sexism, racism, classism, and so on. As depicted in Figure 4.2 (National Equity Project, 2022), oppression can occur at an individual level, but through an individual's interactions with others and broader systems and institutions, it can result in the perpetuation of oppressive systems. Thus, individuals who hold discriminatory views have created the laws, policies, and practices of every U.S. institution (e.g., education, health care, criminal justice, housing), codifying oppression into law and policy and creating systemic and structural oppression. For instance, in the United States, Christianity is the privileged religious identity, and systems have been built to support that identity, such as federally celebrating Christian holidays.

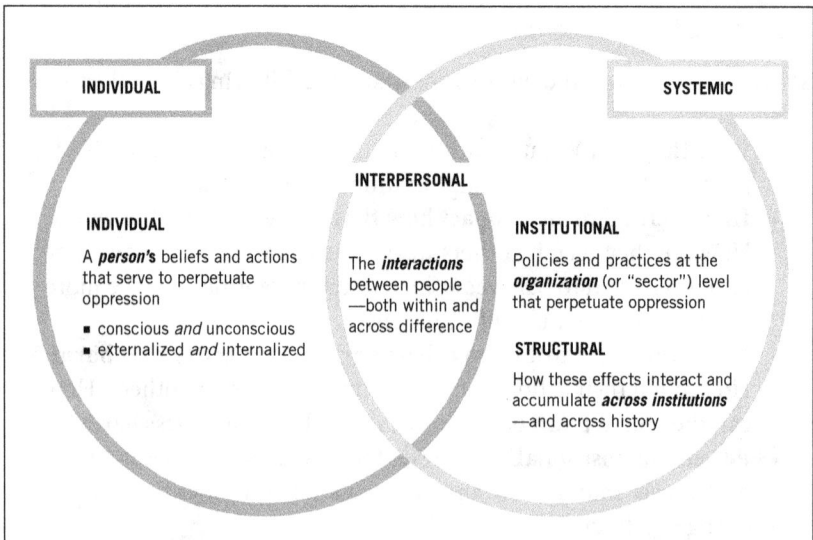

INDIVIDUAL

SYSTEMIC

INTERPERSONAL

INDIVIDUAL

A *person's* beliefs and actions that serve to perpetuate oppression

- conscious *and* unconscious
- externalized *and* internalized

The *interactions* between people —both within and across difference

INSTITUTIONAL

Policies and practices at the *organization* (or "sector") level that perpetuate oppression

STRUCTURAL

How these effects interact and accumulate *across institutions* —and across history

Figure 4.2. Lens of Systemic Oppressions
(Credit: National Equity Project. [2022, May 1]. *Lens of systemic oppression.* https://www.nationalequityproject.org/frameworks/lens-of-systemic-oppression)

One important note when considering systems of oppression is that these systems are often difficult to understand, insidious, and complex. Whereas an individual act of discrimination may be simple to pinpoint, systemic oppression is harder to target and see. It can be helpful to provide examples of systemic oppression and how it affects individual outcomes. Housing discrimination and redlining throughout the twentieth century are useful histories to unpack as an example and have huge implications for the design and makeup of different communities. NPR has a useful and brief YouTube video on this history, titled *Housing Segregation and Redlining in America: A Short History* (2018). We have used this video in presentations with students to demonstrate the impacts of policies on communities and social outcomes. It is also important to note that these systems of oppression can intersect (Crenshaw, 1989), adding more difficulty and complexity for those with disadvantaged identities trying to navigate the world.

In the following we include two examples of useful framings that can support students' understanding of systems of power, privilege, and oppression. There are, of course, many other potential ways to approach these topics, especially depending on your respective discipline or partnership, but for the brevity of this volume, we focus on these two.

Social Determinants of Health

A strong scholarly perspective on systemic oppression and inequality comes from the field of public health. The social determinants of health are defined as "the conditions in which people are born, grow, work, live, and age, and the wider set of forces and systems shaping the conditions of daily life" (World Health Organization, n.d.). Some examples of these conditions include living in an area with limited access to affordable and nutritious food, living in a heavily polluted area, and interacting with discriminatory systems.

These disparate conditions can lead to noticeable differences in the quality of life and life expectancy of different communities. For example, research has found that discrimination can have a physiological impact on the body (e.g., irregular heartbeat, heartburn, anxiety) and can act as a sustained stressor, negatively impacting one's health (Pasco & Smart Richman, 2009). Educators might consider bringing in statistics regarding disparities in their own communities, as we discussed earlier in this chapter with data from our own state. Remaining attuned to the social determinants of health can provide a lens for students to consider how our social systems play a role in influencing the health of communities as well as insight into how our communities can be designed to better support the health of all people.

Much more information exists on this framework that we encourage CEPs to explore if they aim to integrate this lens into their classroom. The Global Health Education and Learning Incubator at Harvard University has an open-access teaching pack available that provides instructors with curriculum and lesson plans that may serve as a starting point (Global Health Education and Learning Incubator at Harvard University, 2018).

The Myth of Meritocracy

One lens that greatly informs how Americans view success and the ability to succeed is through the idea of meritocracy, or pulling oneself up by one's bootstraps. American meritocracy asserts that if individuals work hard enough, they can overcome any barrier and reach (the American vision of) success (i.e., wealth, respectable careers, stable families, etc.) (Kinsley, 1990). In other words, any good outcomes attained in life have been earned due to an individual's own merit—ignoring the reality of privilege and the role of systemic oppression in the United States. This mindset has close ties with the prosperity gospel, a Christian belief that "God grants health and wealth to those with the right kind of faith" (Bowler, 2016); in other words, health and financial success belong to those who earn them.

The logical underlying assumption of the myth of meritocracy is the perpetuation of a mindset that suggests that those who are seen as struggling or unsuccessful are so because they have not worked hard enough. In the context of CE, this might sound like a student working with unhoused individuals who expresses the view that such groups of people are simply drug users and just need to apply for any of the many available jobs, ignoring any real or perceived barriers that impact those in such situations. While students may not explicitly believe in meritocracy, they may have unconscious beliefs that support it. In another example, college students may believe that they got into college solely on their own merit, not considering the other factors that enabled them to gain entry into college, such as the following:

- Living in a middle-class home that had enough food and stable shelter, which allowed them to focus on their K–12 education in a safe, secure, and nourishing environment
- Having a college-educated parent who could help them navigate confusing college entry requirements and apply for student loans
- Citizenship that provides automatic eligibility for many programs

Building student awareness of these systems can expand their thinking around CE, the roots of social disparities, and the challenges they encounter in the community. When students meet others who are less "successful" or are struggling, they can have a fuller appreciation for the impact of systems on individuals, rather than attributing someone's outcomes to a lack of merit.

Interrogating Systems of Oppression

These lenses are complementary to our earlier discussions of socialization. These systems and structures shape our cultural icebergs, inform many decisions about our lives and how we move through the world, and largely define what is considered acceptable or valued. This is why these systems can be so insidious—oppressive structures, from colonization to slavery, discrimination, and more, have influenced most things in our world, even if we are unaware of them. They are the water we are swimming in, as the old parable goes: "There are these two young fish swimming along and they happen to meet an older fish swimming the other way, who nods at them and says 'Morning, boys. How's the water?' And the two young fish swim on for a bit, and then eventually one of them looks over at the other and goes 'What the hell is water?'" (Wallace, 2005). We may not see these structures or know they are there—indeed, privilege is often by nature invisible to the privileged (Mcintosh, 1988)—but they affect most things we do. Understanding of structures and systems and how they relate to particular course content can support student understanding of the root causes of the social issues they are encountering, as we discuss later.

Acknowledging these structures and systems can also help students understand what social change can look like and how social change involves both systems and individuals. This also sets the stage for student learning around how social change occurs, including through political action, social unrest, petitions, businesses and other institutions taking political or social stances, and individual actions.

A helpful recent example of social change may be LGBTQ+ rights. Oppression against LGBTQ+ people existed (and continues to exist) in many forms at the structural level. Homosexuality was listed as a mental disorder in many associations until the 1970s (Burton, 2015), and the World Health Organization removed it from its list of diseases in 1990 (Drescher, 2015). It became legal in all fifty states to engage in same-sex sexual activity in 2003 (George, 2015). Gay marriage was not legal everywhere in the United States until 2015 (Lynch, 2015), denying the benefits of marriage (which is largely a legal contract) to same-sex couples. This forward movement came from a variety of influences, including concentrated political and social campaigns, increased visibility of LGBTQ+ people in the media, and legislation. However, there are also many other ways LGBTQ+ rights have moved forward, including protesting and civil disobedience; the creation of supportive communities, establishments, and publications; and support from businesses in the private sector. While we have seen recent steps forward for LGBTQ+ people, social change can also happen in a regressive way, as we are seeing in 2021 and 2022. Some state legislation has banned trans athletes in sports, required trans people to use bathrooms of the opposite gender, and made it illegal for educators to discuss gender identity with youth (Diaz, 2022). There is no guarantee that progressive social change will last or stay, and this provides a clear example for students of what social change can look like, how change happens on individual and institutional levels, and how community engagement fits into the larger picture.

Supporting Student Development

The activities listed here are examples of exercises we have used ourselves or seen used in similar contexts to promote the level of self-reflection, self-awareness, and critical analysis necessary in CE. However, simply following these activities verbatim does not necessarily mean they will be successful. We encourage educators to consider how they are cultivating a classroom or group environment that ensures students feel able to engage in these activities in honest and vulnerable ways.

Our list deliberately avoids activities some instructors and coordinators might be familiar with, such as privilege walks. For those unfamiliar with this activity, students begin by standing in a horizontal line and then step forward if they have experienced any of the listed privileges, or backward for oppressions, read off by the facilitator. This ultimately results in a scattering of the students such that those who have experienced ample privilege tend to end up drastically distanced from those who have experienced oppression. Activities such as this, although perhaps revelatory for privileged students, can ultimately be harmful to those who have experienced oppression by having their disadvantages used to educate others. We strongly advise against activities that center the learning of privileged students at the burden or expense of marginalized students.

Identity Wheels

This popular activity involves having students reflect on their various social identities (i.e., race, ability status, gender identity, age, etc.) and consider to what extent each identity impacts their daily life. The University of Michigan's Inclusive Teaching at U-M (n.d.) has a version of this activity available to the public that we frequently use to engage students (Figure 4.3). The website also points to studies that emphasize the activity's usefulness in different academic contexts. One of these, as an example, is a study into student retention in STEM courses (Brown et al., 2009). The study found that students' decisions to remain in or leave STEM tracks could be attributed in part to their experience with classroom climate. The website suggests

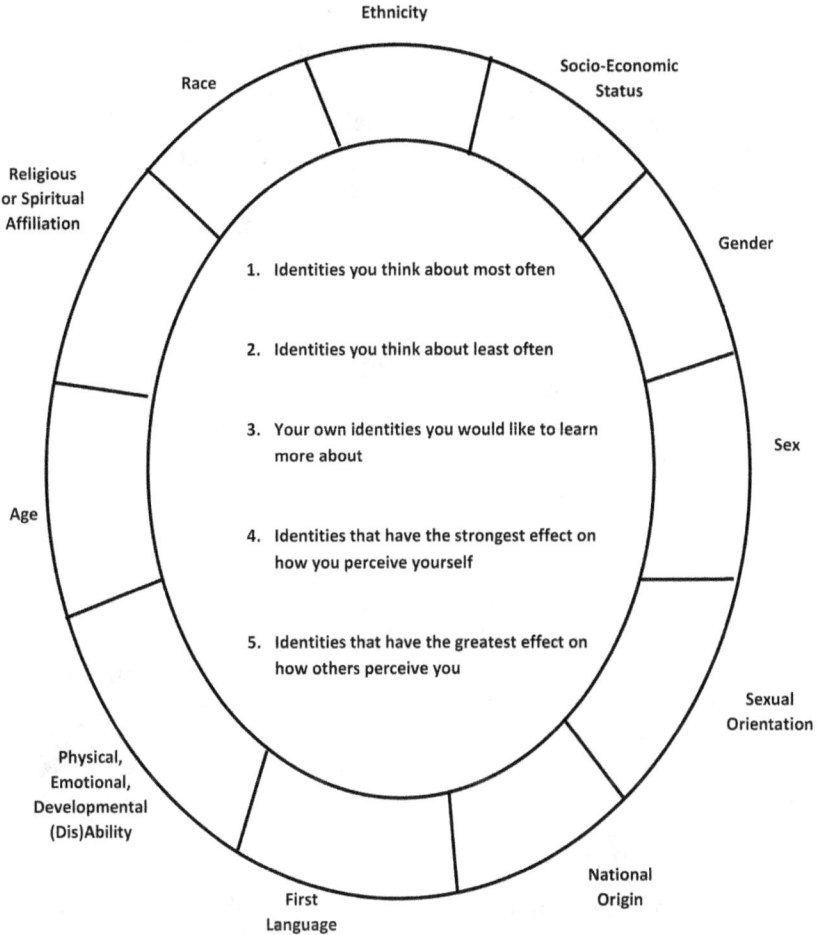

Figure 4.3. Social Identity Wheel
(Credit: Inclusive Teaching at U-M. [n.d.]. *Social identity wheel*. Retrieved April 1, 2022, from https://sites.lsa.umich.edu/inclusive-teaching/sample-activities/social -identity-wheel/)

using the activity as a way of supporting students' relationship development within the classroom. When facilitated with care and intention, this activity has led to deeply fulfilling student engagement.

Some additional considerations for this activity include ensuring you share with students why the activity is relevant to them. You might explain to students that because they are going to be connecting with a community different from those they likely have experienced prior, you want them to consider their own identities and experiences. Without proper framing, students may write off the exercise and fail to engage in meaningful ways. Additionally, we have found from experience that students frequently are uncertain about some of the identity categories, such as the difference between race and ethnicity or gender and sex. If instructors feel comfortable enough to describe the differences, they should feel free to do so, but versions of this activity can be found online that include a list of social categories and their definitions that students may wish to refer to.

Some example reflection questions you might include with this activity include the following:

- What did it feel like to do this activity? Did it feel easy? Challenging?
- Were there aspects of your identity that you felt were not represented on the circle? What are they?
- Why might this activity be useful for community engagement?

We recommend this activity as a stepping stone into deeper discussions about identities and their implications for community engagement. Simply acknowledging identity cannot be where this process ends. Awareness of such cultural differences does not ensure that students have developed a critical understanding of their own or others' identities. Instructors should also consider how they are preparing students to question inequities that might impact different populations and the impact of our social systems on these realities or else risk perpetuating oppressive social structures (Kinefuchi, 2010).

Root Cause Analysis

In order to move toward more impactful and sustainable CE, CEPs can support students in considering the root causes of social issues. A root cause analysis, as used in multiple fields, including health care (Clemmons et al., 2018) and journalism (Francis, 2021), asks students to identify the highest-level cause of a particular problem (Andersen & Fagerhaug, 2006). The converse to root causes is what we might refer to as Band-Aid solutions, or responses that focus more on slowing down the problem and offering short-term solutions. For example, while organizing a clothing drive may offer short-term solutions for families experiencing housing insecurity, more long-term—or at least impactful—solutions might come from increasing the availability of affordable housing, raising wages, or increasing financial support to low-income families.

Within the classroom there are multiple ways you might prompt students toward a root cause analysis. One method that has been applied within a number of disciplines is the five whys technique, which essentially boils down to asking "why" five times in order to develop higher-level insight into the underlying causes of a given issue (Vidyasagar, 2016). In practice, this line of thought might look like this:

- Problem: The community is experiencing housing insecurity.
- Why 1: The community does not have enough money for rent.
- Why 2: The community does not have enough money for rent because they do not have steady employment.
- Why 3: They do not have steady employment because they are unable to work if their mental illness is not treated effectively.
- Why 4: Their mental illness is untreated because the city cut its mental health budget.
- Why 5: The city has denied proposals for better mental health options for low-income people in order to increase the police budget.

When drilling down to the root causes of issues, the results can often be tied to histories or examples of racism, sexism, and other forms of oppression and discrimination, including policy. As such, instructors should be aware of how to address these topics when they do come up. We might not have answers to these realities, but we must at least acknowledge their existence. Again, recognizing that students will run into these very real issues impacting our society requires students to have some understanding of their own identity, as some of the other activities demonstrate.

Development through Reflection

Reflection is truly the foundation of all forms of community-based learning. With roots in experiential learning, reflection is an essential process through which learners make meaning by observing patterns or feelings and relating those to the topic (Kolb, 1984). However, as essential as we may view reflection, it does not fit well into our traditional understanding of education, in which a lecturer stands at the front of the room, dispensing knowledge from a PowerPoint that will be applied to a test. As such, some students may not have much experience with reflection and may struggle to move beyond basic regurgitations of what they did in the community. Being explicit about the purposes and benefits of reflection, along with providing excellent reflection prompts, can be useful to ensure students are sincerely engaging with the process.

Reflection should be woven deeply into all CE activities, and instructors should ensure they are creating ample opportunities for students to process their experience and reflect on their own growth and learning through multiple formats (i.e., verbal, written, artistic representations). Many of the activities listed earlier in this book can be considered examples of reflection when students are provided an opportunity to process and discuss their reactions to different material, as well as the CE experience, with their peers. This demonstrates how reflection can be dynamic and consistent throughout the course.

In addition to in-class reflection activities, it is also important to provide students with the opportunity to process on their own about their experience engaging with the community and the course material. Written reflection assignments can be an excellent way to gauge students' experiences with and expectations of community engagement. Throughout the length of the course, they can also be a useful way to assess students' growth. Choo et al. (2019) found that students perceived stronger outcomes from CBL when instructors more regularly integrated thoughtful reflection and emphasized the impact of the community-engagement component of the experience.

Here we provide a selection of considerations and strategies for reflection; a great number more exist in teaching and learning literature, as well as online. Some reflection methods might include:

- Journaling (written, photo based, vlog)
- Reflective essays
- Discussion boards or groups
- Artistic forms of expression (poems, music, dance, etc.)

Additionally, here are a few tips on reflection we've gleaned from our own experiences, as well as through conversations with instructors.

1. Provide feedback on written reflections.
   If you are having students complete written reflection assignments, ensure that you are not simply providing busywork. Similar to facilitating a discussion, feedback on student writing provides an opportunity to push students' thinking further and for you, as an instructor, to learn their story and experience. Additionally, many students may not have familiarity with reflection, as it is seldom valued in our traditional structures of academia. As such, students should be supported in understanding the purposes of reflection and what it feels like to engage in it meaningfully. Indeed, students who are provided feedback on their reflection in CBL settings have shown a substantial increase in both community service self-efficacy and general self-efficacy (Sanders et al., 2016). In practice, instructors should show appreciation when students demonstrate openness and vulnerability about their experiences and learning. Pay attention to how students' writing grows and their learning deepens. Demonstrating such

care and attention to each student furthers the value students may find in reflection and supports their development of more complex and nuanced thought.

2. **Keep your reflection RICO (relevant, intrinsic, critical, and outcome oriented).**
   When designing reflection questions, we have found success in fostering thoughtful reflection by ensuring our questions are developmentally aware. The four core components we strive to integrate are as follows:
   a. **Relevant:** Ensure the question has some connection to the student and/or the world (e.g., their experience, course goals, or real-world issues).
   b. **Intrinsic:** Ask questions that encourage students to think about themselves and their own values, commitments, and feelings.
   c. **Critical:** Consider how the reflection topic is informed by systems of power, privilege, and oppression (i.e., the societal impacts).
   d. **Outcome oriented:** Especially toward the end of the community-based learning experience, consider how reflection questions encourage students to think about how they will apply the lessons learned from the experience after the completion of the course.

3. **Be attentive to students' barriers or hesitancies.**
   Reflection can be an emotional experience for some students. Whether it be a student who is grappling with their own beliefs or values or a student who, through reflection, might be dredging up some past traumas, reflection is inherently vulnerable. As such, some students may demonstrate resistance to deeper reflection. In their study of reflection among early childhood teachers, Dunn-Kenney (2010) found evidence to suggest that some students may deliberately avoid confronting their own biases out of fear of being challenged. Care again must be taken here to consider how students are experiencing reflection and where and how an instructor may be able to push them to reflect more intentionally. Chapter 8 provides many resources for the development of a supportive critical classroom that can create a productive environment for reflection.

In our center, we are fortunate to work with a number of fantastic interns whom we train to support CBL courses. These CBL interns play an essential role in supporting instructors to engage students in meaningful reflection and educating students on basic community engagement skills. The CBL intern program has been running for ten years, and over the years, these students have played a tremendous role in shaping our preparation trainings into the robust offerings we have today. See Bertha Gonzalez's vignette to hear about how she has approached this experience with humility and insightful advice from her perspective as a former CBL intern and current graduate assistant at our center.

Student Leader Perspective on Community-Based Learning

Bertha A. Gonzalez

A mainstay of support for CBL courses at UW–Madison, the Morgridge Center for Public Service supervises five or more CBL interns, who are the undergraduate students who assist these courses. CBL interns concentrate on helping maintain the reciprocal relationship between students and community partners while supporting instructor capacity. While some faculty prefer having interns facilitate presentations to prepare students for community engagement, others may only need CBL interns to create reflection prompts and provide feedback to students.

Through my role as a CBL intern, I gained a deeper understanding of my identities, how others perceive me, the way I enter spaces, and what this work means for my professional development. As a woman of color, I grew up believing I was *only* disadvantaged. However, I have now realized that there are many aspects of my self that hold privilege, including having access to higher education. Learning about concepts such as cultural humility, implicit bias, microaggressions, and systems of oppression has validated my experiences and given me a vocabulary to voice them. Working as a student intern, I have envisioned ways to continue this work in my professional endeavors. My escalating interest in CBL has led me to focus on community-based research and incorporating this approach into my graduate studies. The following sections outline some of the lessons and insights I have gained into facilitating meaningful community engagement in CBL settings.

Things to Examine during Course Design

It is beneficial for faculty to have a well-grounded understanding of their expectations for student and community partners' experiences, guided by the key aspects of CBL. Reflecting on and reassessing these expectations in collaboration with students and partners throughout the years will allow instructors to revise courses for effective and meaningful experiences. Faculty are then able to incorporate a wide array of learning opportunities for students, ensuring a deeper appreciation for the communities they will be working with. I have both taken and supported CBL courses that have integrated community speakers as part of an introduction to the community. Having community members as part of the curriculum and preparation for CE allows students to develop a deeper connection to prevalent issues affecting the community and to interact with community members. As a student, when community speakers came to class, I felt like I became part of the community and could relate to the issues they faced. For students who do not have experience in working with diverse communities, this may be their first interaction. This is critical in diversifying students' perspectives of communities and recognizing any initial biases.

Reflection

Critical reflection prompts facilitate students' experiences of community engagement and create deeper associations between course content and the real world. Regular reflection makes space for students to process their experiences and encourages students to build their self-awareness. In this process of developing reflection prompts and content, instructors can involve community partners for guidance. As CBL interns, we emphasize the importance of critically reflecting how one's intentions and assumptions inform one's interest in community engagement.

One example of incorporating reflection in class is a psychology CBL course I took in the fall of 2021. The CBL project was to speak with youth in a correctional facility and get their input on the quality of services they receive. With the youth's needs in mind, we provided evidence-based presentations and resources to the correctional facility for implementing change. As groups of students visited the youth throughout the semester, we had class discussions on their experiences and thoughts around what was seen and felt throughout their visits. This made me feel more connected to other students in the class and more excited to visit the correctional facility. Having in-class discussions facilitated the processing of heavy feelings and helped me stay engaged and productive.

Some students and faculty are hesitant to engage in such content. I have found this especially true for STEM classes that historically have had fewer opportunities for self-reflection. Through my experiences, it seemed students were more likely to be engaged and feel connected to course content when there was time built into a course to discuss student experiences with the community partner or ask questions. Since CBL interns are also students, we have found that undergraduates sometimes are more open to asking questions or engaging in reflection with other students than they are with instructors directly.

When students have developed insight into their positionality through looking at identity and power dynamics, they are better equipped to develop cultural and intellectual humility. Having students reflect on their privileges and the ways they hold power allows them to acknowledge spaces where they may need to step back and use their forms of power to amplify the voices of those without. One concept we use as CBL interns when discussing cultural humility is Edward T. Hall's cultural iceberg model (1976). Through preparing students for community engagement, I noticed students resonate with the model as it created a shared language for them to better describe how culture exists in society and how these factors impact identity, communication, and collaboration styles.

Through discussing identities of power and privilege, students may recognize characteristics of themselves that they had not previously considered. When learning about systems of oppression, it can be very discouraging for students to realize the severity of the issue. However, instructors can support students by focusing on resilience in those communities impacted by such systems. Asset mapping is one way, as CBL interns, that we encourage students to focus on the strengths in a community.

Cultural and Intellectual Humility

For students, the aforementioned reflection on identity and culture can solidify the multiple ways of knowing that exist, including from formal education and through first-hand experiences. Cultural humility stems from this recognition and appreciation of the disparate ways we each view, understand, and interact with the world. Practicing cultural humility in the classroom may look like students discussing their own cultural backgrounds or listening to others' stories with the intention of listening to learn. Avoiding correction or comparison shows cultural humility by acknowledging and embracing those differences.

Reflecting on my experience in the psychology CBL course focused on detained youth, it was helpful to learn about and practice intellectual humility. While I learned about different issues with the criminal justice system and methods for treatment of different psychological issues in detention centers, I had to remember that the youth knew more about the system than I did. They knew about the ways the criminal justice system affected their upbringing without ever reading about it. They knew how having family members involved in the criminal justice system impacted their views of the world and their own encounters. Practicing cultural and intellectual humility is critical to students developing strong relationships with people who hold different backgrounds than them. Through practicing and maintaining this level of humility when entering spaces, students are able to effectively understand the community's self-identified needs while developing increased empathy and ability for community connection.

Learning about cultural beliefs, traditions, language, and history allows students to develop an appreciation for different ways of living and communicating so they are better able to interact with community partners, creating the foundation for strong relationships. It is important for instructors to analyze their sources of information when discussing the community's experiences. CBL courses can encourage the use of local news articles, personal anecdotes, and Zoom calls from community members to learn local histories.

Building Meaningful Relationships through Good Communication

Skills that are critical to building and maintaining relationships among students, faculty, and community partners include respecting, actively listening to, and effectively communicating with one another. Students who listen to community members to deepen their understanding, rather than to respond, demonstrate sincere consideration of the community's needs. Self-awareness and openness to feedback are important to maintaining effective partnerships. Through self-reflection and continuous assessment, students are able to consider their own needs and a project's progress. Ensuring students are cognizant of the quality of their work and remaining attuned to the needs of the community keeps a project on track and helps develop a more robust outcome. One example occurred in a CBL course that had students working with elderly individuals who had little access to or experience with technology. Students needed to pivot to in-person meetings or phone calls, rather than video calls, in order to best integrate the voices of the elderly partners.

Summary

Through consistent communication and following through on commitments, trust is built in relationships. Instructors should create and maintain a method of consistent communication throughout a semester to check in and assess whether expectations are being met on both ends. Being open to criticism and feedback is also important when engaging with others and being open to growth, as is cultural humility. As students and instructors, persistence is important when maintaining relationships with community partners, as emails may get lost or schedules may change. Staying in communication throughout a semester through check-ins ensures a smooth collaborative environment.

Concluding Thoughts

We summarize this chapter acknowledging that there are many points of nuance, considerations, and viewpoints missing from our discussion of these ideas. As we emphasize elsewhere in this book, the skill and thoughtfulness needed to best engage students in these discussions require a great deal of self-reflection and learning. This book is intended to spark your interest in integrating these vast, interconnected concepts into your course. The strategies and scholarship you use to do it should be diverse, critical, and practical. Within our context of a research-centered university, we recognize the limited opportunities available to CEPs for conversations around teaching and self-reflection, but making time for these practices is essential to cultivating robust outcomes for all stakeholders. We encourage you to expand your professional network by engaging with units or groups that may already exist on your campus or find national spaces such as the International Association for Research on Service-Learning and Community Engagement, the Engagement Scholarship Consortium, or Campus Compact. These are spaces where community-engaged practices are centered and discussions of challenges, strategies, and opportunities abound. There are important conversations to be had, but you are not alone in your pursuit of them.

5

Institutional Power Dynamics

In the previous chapters, we focused on students' individual self-awareness as it relates to identity, positionality, and cultural understanding. Now we bring in a macro view of the power differentials inherent in campus-community relationships that can impact the student experience and then detail some strategies for neutralizing power imbalances and building better partnerships, as related to student preparation.

Institutional Context

In recent decades, administrators and instructors of both public and private HEIs have felt targeted by lawmakers and members of the public with arguments of being elitist, irrelevant, and undeserving of tax funding (Boulton & Lucas, 2011; Klein, 2015; Mitchell et al., 2016; Oliff et al., 2013; Rizzo, 2004). By the year 2019, according to the UW *Budget in Brief,* our own university received less than 15 percent of its funding from state tax revenues (University of Wisconsin–Madison, n.d.-a), but as a state institution, we are nonetheless subject to a prolific amount of state regulation and scrutiny for everything from COVID-19 safety requirements to distance education (University of Wisconsin–Madison, Office of Academic Planning and Institutional Research, n.d.; Wisconsin Policy Forum, 2011; Wisconsin Public Radio, 2021).

Despite the state's dwindling support, capital from other sources flows into our university coffers at a staggering rate. The Madison campus consistently ranks in the top ten for highest amount of federal government research dollars to public or private HEIs in the United States (National Science Foundation, n.d.). That money helps retain top-notch faculty and researchers to run labs and classes and deliver a high level of instruction and research mentorship to students. Those dollars also directly and indirectly stimulate the local economy by all manner of mechanisms—from campus employee paychecks spent locally to grant-funded supply and expense funds, paying for everything from local contract services to transportation, shovels to test tubes, usually from local manufacturers and service providers. This situation is mirrored in many other cities to varying degrees, depending on university success with fundraising and grant writing. Overall, HEIs are generally considered "power players" in a city.

This begs the question: With all these resources, are students, faculty, and staff contributing in a meaningful way through research and classroom activities to help cultivate better communities? Does all this intellectual capital and energy invested by researchers actually give society the best bang for the buck to solve wicked problems rather than just being knowledge for knowledge's sake? Are peer-reviewed results being utilized in everyday life in different areas? And, whose knowledge is the "best" or the "right" answer (Tchilingirian, 2018)?

There is no doubt the academy develops important knowledge, skills, and inventions that have been meaningful contributions to society throughout the history of higher education. However, we also know that academic knowledge is not the *only* kind of meaningful knowledge. An interesting example comes from Kimberlé Crenshaw, the scholar behind intersectional theory, a legal theory that examines the intersection of multiple forms of oppression. In her work with Black women, who experience layers of oppression through sexist and racist systems, Crenshaw (2015) acknowledged that intersectionality was a lived reality for Black women far before it was a legal theory. She refers to the 1976 court case *DeGraddebreid v. General Motors* that gave birth to the legal theory. This example demonstrates how nonacademics may have knowledge of an issue or topic but not have that knowledge recognized unless it is backed by an institution, such as academia. We discuss this more in Chapter 7 as a dichotomy between intellectual credibility and intellectual humility. Additionally, many so-called scientific advancements may not represent meaningful results. This can be seen in the replication crisis, or the inability of scientists in many disciplines to replicate results published in peer-reviewed journals (Ioannidis, 2005). Others may have deleterious effects on participants and surrounding communities, yet these are not reported on due to the nature of peer review.

Academia supports faculty research and trains students in methods of discovery. In CEP work, it is possible to reassure students that their skills and knowledge have an important place and value in problem solving *with* society while not accepting their academic knowledge as always being the final answer. HEIs pride themselves on being able to sift and winnow in knowledge discovery, but are they doing it in isolation? Looking at HEI marketing materials and press releases, there is often no mention of the role of the community in solving social problems, acting as collaborators, or co-creating knowledge; indeed, academics are frequently heralded as the heroes in the stories. In order to actualize systems and institutions that can be responsive to society, academia needs to critically consider how it engages in knowledge construction beyond the ivory tower and in collaboration with our communities. It is the on-the-ground, in-practice work, often messy and ambiguous, that is utterly essential to developing more robust and impactful solutions. Regardless of whether strong community-university partnerships attract prospective students, these relationships are crucial to the academy's ability to do meaningful research and should play a huge part in an ideal intertwined, interdependent CE relationship. Students gain experience and skills when they interact with the community while also utilizing their academic skills and training to support community objectives.

Universities Have Resources, While Nonprofits Have Relatively Fewer

While HEIs may feel under siege, leading them to operate in a scarcity mindset—constantly readjusting budget priorities to pay ever-increasing fixed expenses—it does bear remembering that compared to most CBOs (and the people who rely on them for services and support), HEIs are perceived as incredibly well resourced (Bradburd & Mann, 1993; Cramer, 2016). Many large universities are typically able to stretch those dollars further by their sheer size. They can negotiate volume prices for everything from toilet paper to student bus passes to frequent computer upgrades with all the latest software at a bulk discount. Students pay fees to fund construction of state-of-the-art fitness and performance centers (highly visible to the community that has no or little access to them) and dining facilities with mind-boggling food choices that they have come to expect as an entitlement of college acceptance. Their libraries have billions of resources available at the click of a finger, as long as the person clicking has online university library privileges. Private schools have endowments that range from struggling to absurdly lavish for their size. Smaller public schools; historically Black colleges and universities (HBCUs) and community colleges are typically less well-endowed, but perceptions of community members can persist no matter the reality.

Individuals and CBOs in the communities in which HEIs are situated, by contrast, do not automatically see the direct benefit of these resources and almost always have fewer resources themselves. They are not privy to the unique perks and access accorded to campus employees and students. Some CBOs are struggling to rub two nickels together to run their programs and pay a skeleton staff or are even run by unpaid volunteers as a labor of love (Besel et al., 2011; Bouek, 2018). This landscape sets up an inherent have/have-not scenario that is not conducive to creating trust with community partners entering into relationships with academia (Lesser & Oscós-Sánchez, 2007; Stoecker, 2005). *The Politics of Resentment* (Cramer, 2016) described an extensive project with rural communities in our state that highlighted widespread perceptions that the urban areas with large research institutions were, to paraphrase, "getting all the state money while we get nothing." The statistics showed that, in fact, per capita, more state tax dollars are spent in rural areas of Wisconsin, but the perceived attitude of feeling ignored and snubbed by intellectuals persists.

Community Perspectives on Academia

This dynamic plays out in even greater amplitude when CE becomes a factor. Stoecker and Tryon's 2009 book, *The Unheard Voices*, retold stories of community partners who agreed to engage in CBL arrangements but felt unequally burdened by a multitude of issues: lack of advance notice, faculty expectations of organizations accommodating more students than they had capacity to supervise, not asking organizations what they needed and instead bringing their own notions of how to address social issues, or instructors directing students to just "go out and find a place to do good deeds." Many partners felt that there was little understanding of the amount of time they spent training and supporting the ongoing "service" of students and little recognition of their *other* work running a nonprofit, typically dealing with funding stresses, staffing turnover, and missions that in some cases address social problems that should be the government's responsibility. The literature review in Karasik's (2020) study of community partners mentions the power differential as playing havoc with many aspects of the relationship, particularly lack of faculty involvement and respect for partners' time and professional expertise (Darby et al., 2016; Williams, 2018). In a community focus group study by Cronley, participants suggested that "the paucity of research on community partner perspectives may be related to a general privileging of the university over the community in service learning partnerships" (Cronley et al., 2015, p. 275).

Similarly, power imbalance concerns have been raised with regard to the "myth of mutual benefit" (Hammersley, 2012, p. 176), where the paternalistic problem of the privileged (e.g., faculty, students) being "here to help" rather than "here to learn" (p. 174) ultimately perpetuates dependency and exploits communities for "free education." Bauer et al. (2015) likewise described the dangers of focusing on what communities are missing (deficit based) rather than on what communities have to offer (asset based).

The trust issue we have discussed frequently throughout this volume speaks to the positionality of institutions as a whole—there is a long history of harm in many communities that is embedded in collective memory and through intergenerational trauma: from the legendary abuses of Tuskegee discussed in Chapter 3 (Heintzelman, 2003; Thomas & Quinn, 1991) to the egregious capitalizing on the genetic material of Henrietta Lacks (Greely & Cho, 2013; Skloot, 2017) as well as others (Harmon, 2010), marginalized communities have these stories in their consciousness about "college people" helicoptering in, extracting data, and leaving without any accountability (Cramer, 2016; Flicker et al., 2007; Goldberg-Freeman et al., 2007; Horowitz et al., 2009).

What Are Some Other Ways Power Imbalances Can Show Up in CE Practice?

These power dynamics are evident in a myriad of ways in the campus-community dyad. Our team has heard many poignant stories from nonprofit staff through the years, including the simple broken contract type, in which the students do not deliver a promised piece of work that the CBO needs. Or it can be a sticky power struggle involving decision-making or funding, or both, or something more subtle.

One example of the first type that we heard from a community partner at an end-of-project debrief involved a CBO that partnered with computer science students during the fall semester to develop a new software program for volunteer registration in January. The undergrads never finished the assignment. When it was apparent that they would fall short, the faculty member told the CBO rep that he would finish it but also failed to deliver. The CBO then had to spend money they did not have for a professional software developer to work overtime on the project over the holidays because their capacity to operate would become greatly inhibited without the online registration system up and running by January 1.

Another story involved a business class's "real world" assignment to develop an accounting program for an underresourced CBO. The students worked diligently all semester in isolation and then finally, at the end of the course, invited the CBO staff into the class for their proud presentation. The CBO later shared with our office that they smiled politely, took the CD-ROM they had been handed with a flourish, and left the class building—by way of the rubbish bin, because the CBO's ten-year-old computers would not be able to run the fancy new program the students created, rendering it useless. The CBO reps did not say anything to the students out of a sense of shame, as well as grace toward the students because they had at least made an effort.

Assumptions were made in both cases that overestimated or took for granted the amount of time, resources, and capital equipment the average CBO has access to. What does that say about HEI behavior when the burden is placed on the partner to behave diplomatically in this unequal dynamic? In the HEI reward system, the priorities are focused on the students gaining experience, so pitfalls in logistics and student skills have not been anticipated and will not be penalized in academic systems and processes.

So What, Now What?

Our campus is finding that due to those individual experiences, and these stories being shared informally in the community, CBOs have become more sophisticated and deliberative in accepting student projects, demanding what they need to have in place beforehand (Tryon et al., 2016). We agree that the burden to tend to the power dynamic should not rest on the community partner. Rather, it is incumbent on the campus—the instructor, the student team, or a professional engagement facilitator—to carry that load, as CBO staff have enough to worry about that is mission critical without making it a dual mission to manage students and their professors. There is also a high amount of turnover in the nonprofit sector, especially when funding is unstable, and a new executive director at an organization may not have the benefit of hindsight from a predecessor's lessons learned, especially if the transition has been abrupt. Because universities are the inventors, if you will, of CE, whatever we can do to smooth the path for busy community partners is not only our ethical responsibility but also creates the foundation for long-term, authentic, and truly reciprocal partnerships. Following are some strategies we hope you find helpful.

Partnering Practices for More Equitable Relationships

Knowing these pitfalls and power differentials, how can we partner in ways that share resources and funding (including grant writing) to ensure equitable allocation to partners while also creating functions for shared power in decision-making, research, and project design? How can the lessons from the prior stories be translated into work to prepare students?

The earlier examples point to a few solutions for both students and HEI practitioners (or CEPs) that begin to mitigate the glaring power differential between campus and community. Many of these issues tie in to developing students' ability to manage interpersonal relationships through an overall lens of learning cultural and intellectual humility, as we discuss in depth in Chapter 7. Here are a few suggestions instructors can attend to and teach about prior to beginning CE:

> In the case involving the volunteer registration platform, the faculty and CBO needed to make a memorandum of understanding (MOU) or "contract" that students, instructors, and community partners sign, stating the scope of the project, the timeline, and what milestones should be met along the path to the deadline, adjusting to the students' skill levels and capacity. Even though written agreements probably would not hold up in court, they have often prevented the disappointment of unfilled expectations. This solution was one of the recommendations from the community in the *Community Standards for Service Learning* (Stoecker & Tryon, n.d.). For more on MOUs and shared decision-making, see Chapter 6.

> Alternatively, the instructor might have decided not to commit to a project of such importance that had any number of ways to fall short. In reality, the partner simply said they would never agree to work with students again on "anything crucial." That could result in students doing very low-value work that neither they nor the CBO will get much out of.

> The students in the business class could have avoided the negative outcome by simply asking up front what format the CBO wanted the product in. It also would make sense to schedule check-in meetings with the partner to discuss how the product was developing and allow feedback on ways to tweak it for the most value to the partner.

Other suggestions in general are as follows:

> Incorporating readings and discussion about the dynamics of institutional power in your local community will help set the stage for students to see their positionality (Preece, 2016). Consider bringing in examples from local newspapers or case studies. Giving your students some readings from the examples of historical harm (e.g., the Tuskegee project) will help them see other perspectives and appreciate what this power dynamic looks like.

> This dynamic is related to the issue of fit, as introduced in *The Unheard Voices* (chapter 3, pp. 38–56, and chapter 4); in other words, how do the pieces line up between institution and partner? Asking to meet in advance at the partner's convenience to gather

ideas is a good method to lessen burdens on both ends. If June or July are less busy months for an organization, instructors can do outreach then, on their summer break, to solicit these "bucket list" ideas for their students to choose from in September. One CBO interviewed in the *Unheard Voices* research suggested keeping a list of "second-level priorities" not critical to mission or strict deadline and "where failure will not disrupt the organization's daily operations." (Stoecker & Tryon, 2009, p. 69).

In addition to your preparation of students for good CBL practice, some issues will require more of a structural solution. The problem of project fit suggested by one CBO staff in Madison led to an innovation at our center:

It doesn't really do me any good to get an email in Sept. from a graphic design class that says "We're going to take on a logo project this fall" but for us it's the busiest time of the year, and they have to have it done by December and I haven't thought about it yet, but then when we get to the point in the spring where we want to work on logo development . . . if I could do the background work and put the project in the "hopper," and if there was a place to bring a list of projects for the whole year (not academic year) that the classes could access, that would work. (Tryon, n.d.)

The partner wished to mitigate the campus issue of CE partnerships being initiated piecemeal instead of through a streamlined, coordinated process—mirroring a priority our center had discussed but had not devoted enough resources to. With her impetus, we created a database for making matches (actually referring to the back end as "the hopper"). A caveat: data maintenance and updating must occur frequently for it to be truly time saving. Other solutions include a request for proposals process from an instructor and phasing work over several semesters so that a larger goal can be reached by a series of student projects.

Overcoming Distrust

We have written about this issue in other work—in the *Sage Sourcebook of Service Learning and Civic Engagement*—on the building of trust that allows for the benefit of the doubt:

Is there transparency in decision-making? Is there follow-through on promises? Are relevant parties included throughout? Without trust, there is little chance of developing a relationship where all parties are given the "benefit of the doubt." Without this factor, if a partner's action produces harm, the other partner may assume that the harm was intentional. (Tryon et al., 2015, p. 194)

One of the co-authors of that chapter, Marian Slaughter, came up with the analogy of thinking about these relationships like a checking account—you deposit money and then can make withdrawals . . . until you are out of funds (or write a check for more than what is in the account and receive a nasty overdraft notice with a hefty fee!). A trust relationship can be viewed the same way: if you show up when you say you will, follow up with good communication, and complete agreed-upon deliverables, you are adding "trust deposits" into your partnership account. Over time, you create a solid relationship as a basis to work from. So when you (inevitably) screw something up, even minor things like forgetting to return an email or getting signals crossed on the date of a site visit, you have that solid trust account to help the partner say, "That's OK, I know they just made an honest mistake." This commonsense trust-building analogy is apt in other personal relationships (see Bringle & Hatcher, 2000; Cutforth, 1999).

Listen

Listening to community partners is crucial to build that trust relationship. Chapter 6 covers ways to help students build listening skills in detail. In early explorations about community organizations in Madison, one CBO director said, "Whenever I hear the word 'research' I want to run the other way screaming! *If*, however, grad students or faculty would come to just listen to what we have going on, that they could help with, then I would be open to continuing that conversation" (personal conversation, 2006). See Kathy Cramer's vignette for her reflections on the importance of this skill.

Listening to the Community

Kathy Cramer

When I try to prepare my students to go out into the community with humility, I tell them about my experience as a public opinion researcher traveling around Wisconsin. From about 2007 to 2012, I was doing fieldwork for a project about attitudes among rural residents toward urban places and people. In the process of inviting myself into conversations in places like gas stations and diners, people occasionally told me stories about their encounters with researchers from my university. Some of these stories were positive tales, but sometimes they expressed resentment. For example, I once visited with a group of fishermen who wondered aloud why people were doing research on the lake they frequented to figure out where bass spawn when all they had to do was ask the locals. These fishermen had a great deal of knowledge about that lake and felt disrespected that the folks from the university had not bothered to ask for their wisdom.

Maybe these fishermen did not actually have accurate insights on where bass spawn. Maybe they misunderstood the nature of the research being conducted on their lake. But my hunch is that they had insights and years of lived experience that might have been useful to the people doing research in their neck of the woods.

The lesson I learned from this that I try to impart to my students is that taking the time to listen to the people you encounter in the community is important. It does at least two things. First, it conveys goodwill and sends a signal that you respect them enough that you want to take the time to hear what they have to say. Second, listening to the people on whose turf you are treading just might teach you something valuable. You will only know if you ask.

Validating Community Knowledge and Incorporating It into CES

What does it actually mean, in practice, to "validate"? You may hear that validation of community knowledge is important, but *how* do you actually do it, since community knowledge looks different from the traditional scholarly knowledge that instructors have been trained to accept as the final authority? The following provides some suggestions.

One way is to invite community partners, when interested and willing, to co-author an article or contribute a chapter to a book. Be aware of sticky power issues that may crop up. A tenure-track faculty member, for example, needs to show solo publications and first authorship in order to make progress toward tenure. What if they feel their community partner co-author in an article deserves lead authorship due to the amount of work the partner did but the faculty's senior mentor pressures them to take first authorship anyway? Even if those conflicts cannot be resolved, other types of "nonacademic" output, such as reports or media interviews, can bring community partner contributions to the forefront. Whenever possible, share the spotlight or back out of it if you can. See Chapter 9 for a discussion of how tenure and promotion guidelines are starting to allow for a more inclusive view of what constitutes an artifact or accepted publication.

An aside—another power dynamic can be the "unbiased" research argument. Tenure or dissertation committee members who are unfamiliar with CBR may critique scholarly work that includes "too much" community input as biased. However, more social scientists are accepting of constructivist paradigms and the social construction of reality, which should support the acceptance of CBR at least in those fields. Bias is also overcome through good data collection and research design that includes calibrating questions with a broad cross section of the affected population to get at the most salient areas for exploration.

Another strategy is to build a relationship with a partner to the point where they might accept an invitation to co-teach a class with you. Sometimes there are administrative hurdles, and usually the academic HR system is unwieldy about providing proper compensation, but by persevering and being creative, these challenges have been overcome. A campus-community teaching team like this became a yearly course at our university and was not only wildly popular but influenced the career trajectory of the community partner by creating a special position for them.

Other ways of incorporating this knowledge that many of our peer centers, especially those with off-campus, place-based CE centers use:

1. Begin a discussion of how lived experience has informed the community's frame of reference and beliefs about addressing issues. It can take the shape of a discussion of different ways of knowing that make community partnerships more equitable and help them have more meaningful impact. Use specific scenarios to begin. If a course is studying a social issue (e.g., homelessness), ask the students who is better equipped to give an "on the ground" picture of the issues of being homeless than those experiencing homelessness? Who can give more relevant information on specific local issues and causes better than CBOs whose lifeblood is working with the people affected?

2. Convene a group of community members and broad representation of CBO staff to find out which current issues seem to be of the highest priority to communities and then solicit faculty and students to contribute to ongoing efforts by communities with energy and academic knowledge. Granted, some individuals and even organizations have narrow lenses and entrenched opinions, but the best way to find out what is going on is to attend as many different group meetings as possible and listen. Time constraints dictated by the academic calendar often preclude this activity. However, a course design could include teams of two or three

students attending different events or meetings in the community on the same issue and comparing notes in class, recording common themes as well as individual nuances, and developing a course curriculum from the combined information.

ABCD

The well-known concept of asset-based community development discussed in Chapter 3 was developed by Northwestern University faculty John McKnight and Jody Kretzman in the 1990s. Now an institute in the Steans Center at DePaul University, it is at "the center of a large and growing movement that considers local assets as the primary building blocks of sustainable community development" (DePaul, Asset-Based Community Development Institute, n.d.).

John Zeigler's vignette shows an example of how ABCD can be used to help students understand and advance goals of social justice in a long-term partnership between DePaul's Egan Office of Urban Education, where he is an ABCD-trained CEP, and the public schools nearby.

The Threat of School Closure and Staying Community Engaged through ABCD

John W. Zeigler Jr.

Background

The West Side community of North Lawndale is home to some of Chicago's poorest residents. The community has been challenged with disinvestment, high unemployment, a declining population, and a high crime rate. School reform and educational equality have been consistent issues for Chicago Public Schools (CPS). A growing body of literature has investigated the impact of communities with weak social capital, frayed social networks, and low levels of religious participation and collective efficacy. Having few social connections beyond the immediate neighborhood was likely to lead to weak essential support for schools. Previous research has also established that a high crime rate in a community contributes to weak essential supports. Sampson (2012) identifies that neighborhoods with high rates of crime and "signs of disorder" are prone to develop a reputation as "bad" and to be avoided. Sampson maintains that racial segregation and poverty are bound up with patterns of disinvestment. Warren et al. (2001, p. 4) wrote that "the main problem for poor communities may not be a relative deficit in social capital, but that their social assets have greater obstacles to overcome, and are constantly under assault." Larsen et al. (2004) argue that though poor communities may have a high degree of bonding social capital, this does not result in collective action. Warren et al. (2001, p. 202) assert that "urban schools can create or enhance a key aspect of social capital-intra-community ties." Schools provide the intracommunity linkages for actors who have access to resources. Schools prove to be a training ground for active parents, particularly women of color, to cultivate a broader understanding of organizing. Active parents are often supported by community-based organizations that are involved in school-base organizing.

DePaul's Role

DePaul's Egan Office of Urban Education and Community Partnership supports place-based students in the Lawndale Community Academy, a K–8 school in the North Lawndale community. The Egan Office ethos is aligned with Egan's spirited work (Satter, 2009) for equality in the North Lawndale community. This case study investigates the role of Egan students who are not only tutors for students in the school but also act as advocates for the parents as the school faces the threat of closure. The study examines the Egan students as they become vital "gappers and connectors" in the community and the process of building trust with residents outside of the school.

In the spring of 2013, approximately twelve thousand children in Chicago Public Schools (CPS) were informed their schools would close. CPS is the nation's third-largest school district, and its administrators closed fifty-three schools and displaced thousands of students, claiming underutilization of school buildings and poor academic performance. Of those students, 94 percent were low-income and 88 percent were African American. One of the most affected communities was North Lawndale, where neighborhood decline began with the riots that followed the 1968 assassination of Martin Luther King Jr. The riots devastated much of the community's infrastructure, and by 1970, an estimated 75 percent of local businesses had left, taking jobs with them. The population plummeted by more than half between 1970 and 2000. This exodus affected public school numbers, and the fear was that with more school closures, the population would continue to decline. On the eve of the announcement, community activist Valerie Leonard accused Rahm Emanuel, then mayor of Chicago, of wanting to make a new Chicago, which meant "no Black folks" (CBS Chicago, 2013). School closures and privatization in North Lawndale came at a time when it had the third-highest crime rate of the seventy-seven community areas in Chicago and 43 percent of people lived below the poverty line (Rush University Medical Center, 2016). Community activist and educator David Stovall (2016, p. 39) reminds us that "the residents and organizations in the area have little time to engage in individual and collective healing from the trauma of long-term disinvestment and community upheaval."

Community Work

Despite these challenges, there have been aggressive efforts in the revitalization of the North Lawndale community. In 2005, a heavily resourced quality-of-life plan, primarily funded by the MacArthur Foundation, gathered community stakeholders together to design and guide potential investment in the community. Work groups of engaged community residents were formed to address critical needs in the community and, in recent efforts, proposed to close and consolidate three elementary schools and establish a PK–8 STEAM education academy in North Lawndale. Plagued by memories of past school closings, other community residents formed a group to organize against the plan. The North Lawndale Parent and Community Coalition (NLPCC) is creating an alternative parent-led proposal that calls for $65 million proposed for the academy to instead be invested into existing schools in ways that genuinely address the root causes of underenrollment.

Egan Partnership: Grad Students Trained as School-Community Organizers

The Egan Office has been a critical partner with the NLPCC in support of their efforts to keep their schools open. The Egan Office promotes the understanding and support of sustainable community schools. Rather than closing schools or turning them over to private, unaccountable managers, priority is made to support and build schools as strong public institutions in the heart of every community. The Egan Office realizes that successful community-based schools serve as anchors in the community and helps stabilize young people and their families. Egan's school community organizers (SCOs) initiative employs graduate students who are taught to understand and engage community from an ABCD lens. The tenets of ABCD are based on the premise that every community possesses unique (gifted and skilled) individuals, organizations, and institutions; no matter how disadvantaged, those gifts need to be recognized and mobilized. The SCOs also understand the importance of building social capital and knowing where the social networks exist within the schools and community.

The students go through an eighteen-hour workshop that introduces them to the core principles and application of ABCD in the context of local communities. This approach is regarded as a positive alternative to traditional needs-based approaches (Kretzmann & McKnight, 1993). The SCOs, through the ABCD training and continual reflection, help other students see their role as working to create opportunity so the people they serve can use their gifts. Some would classify this role as a "gapper" (McKnight et al., 2015). Gappers are considered staff who work in the community as well as the institution, with one foot in each, and are working to put ABCD into practice through their organization. The role of the gapper includes understanding the construction of community partnerships, including one of the Egan Office partner schools in the North Lawndale community slated for closure. The SCO there has built sound partnerships with the school and key community stakeholders. To better understand the issues, the SCO engaged the community in several ways:

- One-on-one interviews with parents and community and faith-based leaders
- Sitting in on community meetings, which includes local school councils
- Door-to-door engagement and community walks
- Dialogue with the youth in the community
- Talking with the elders in the community
- Volunteering at various community events

This process allowed the SCO to realize that nonprofit organizations within a community do not necessarily represent all the community's constituencies. The SCO is determined not to simplify the understanding of the term "community driven" but to complicate the concept in support of the notion that Chicago communities are complex systems of contested space, power dynamics, and struggle.

The SCO co-chairs the NLPCC meetings with the schools' parents, teachers, and residents; understands the importance of the community's history; and knows there are long-standing disconnects with the residents and community-based organizations. The SCO's analysis of their engagement of the school and community helped the Egan Office and DePaul find appropriate ways to help build capacity and develop tangible relationships with stakeholders in the North Lawndale community. The SCO understands that authentic engagement depends upon real relationships that are built over time, engender mutual respect and acknowledgment of equality of voice, and are maintained through meaningful actions and responsiveness.

Research or Project Design

An important way to equalize the power dynamic in community-based research is to negotiate the level of involvement the partner or partners wish to have in the process (see Figure 3.1 in Chapter 3). The only ground rule in this endeavor for scholars interested in CBR is to listen to the affected stakeholders in the community and co-design the research in partnership, asking what level of hands-on involvement they desire and accommodating institutional barriers. We have mentioned the idea of shared decision-making, or shared power, in project work. And the community-based participatory research (CBPR) process (see the following) is meant to involve the community partners in every aspect of the work. But some partners really do just ask for information or other technical expertise, as they may not have time to be closely involved. One project we heard about from a community partner involved a Ph.D. student doing a comprehensive data analysis of membership information and private donations to a CBO to better detect and predict new giving patterns. The CEO of the CBO met three times with the student: once to outline the type of info needed and turn over the raw data to scour, once midsemester to make sure things were on track, and then at the end to accept and review the analysis with grateful satisfaction. The spectrum ranges from this fairly hands-off approach from the community side to a wish to partner fully in the research process.

Assumptions of CEPs have ranged from believing community partners do not have the time or inclination to become co-researchers (Tryon, n.d.) to assuming they have the same amount of time capacity as the students and faculty to be involved (Arieli et al., 2009). The truth, as is often the case, is in the middle. In a number of cases, community mentors and citizens are willing and eager to become co-investigators (Suarez-Balcazar, 2020; Vaughn et al., 2018). A CBR methods class at UW–Madison in 2011 that looked at racial bias in the media included three community mentors who received stipends and took the human subjects training alongside the grad students in the class, completing the research together in mixed teams. When research can be done this way, the findings can be more authentic, as the community researchers may already have a level of trust with many of the constituents in the study and so are not told whatever the constituents think the researchers want to hear to get rid of them (Bales, 1994; Stoecker & Tryon, 2009). This falls under the subset of CBR called community-based participatory research. Dr. Philip Nyden, former faculty director of the Center for Urban Research and Learning (CURL) at Loyola University Chicago (see Chapter 9), wrote in 2003 that "some traditional academics see CBPR as a radical approach because it recognizes that the knowledge of individuals outside of academia can be equally as important in defining, guiding, and completing research" as traditional academic research. He went on to compare the two types with an apt analogy:

By effectively tapping community knowledge, CBPR is particularly effective for gaining insights into persistent social problems and developing solutions. Traditional research can be compared to an old-fashioned marriage, where the husband has more power and resources than the wife. In this case the university uses its power to call the shots in the relationship with the community. In contrast, CBPR resembles a more modern egalitarian marriage. When university and community get together, they recognize that they each have resources and responsibilities in the relationship. Both parties see . . . this marriage of community-knowledge and discipline-based knowledge as critical to understanding pressing problems and doing credible research. (Nyden, 2003)

Funding

In grant writing, having partners included as direct funding recipients, principal investigators (PIs), or co-PIs obviously goes a long way to showing good faith and building solid trust relationships and is highly recommended whenever possible. Some grant funders insist all the money must flow through the HEI, which is unhelpful to furthering even a short-term relationship built on trust, much less a long-term partnership. An argument we heard in the early 2000s from the grantors was that, paraphrased, HEIs "are more stable than CBOs, who might shut their doors in any given year and then the grant money would disappear with no results." In equitable practice, pursuing this type of grant might be best to pass up.

Compensation for community partners even when not part of a grant is highly desirable. Some HEIs have dedicated lines in their CE office budget for honoraria to community partners who come onto campus to give guest lectures in classes, participate in conferences and campus-wide presentations, support curriculum development, or advise in other capabilities. At the least, everyone should be compensated for their time and expertise.

Logistics, Timing, and Other Issues

There are some factors beyond cash that can also help ease the ability of CBOs to participate in CE activities. If constituents of an organization are asked to attend focus group sessions on or off campus and lack transportation, either paying for bus fare, coordinating ride shares, or providing other means of getting people where you need them is helpful. Another factor cited by community members as a barrier to participation is childcare. We have seen CBR and other community projects succeed when faculty or staff coordinate to have on-site childcare, perhaps supervised by an early childhood education department using students who need practicum hours anyway. Something else mentioned by community partners in the *Community*

Standards is the idea of "zero-dollar appointments" for partners who commit to long-term projects. This could mean access to the online resources of the university libraries, parking permits, or even discounted membership at rec centers. These noncash items are still value added and serve to make partners feel their time is more respected, even if it cannot be compensated by dollars.

Infrastructure Changes

An extremely encouraging sign of the evolution of CE toward authentic, equitable partnerships is borne out by the number of institutions making structural changes that level the playing field for community partners, which can also streamline project processes and limit duplication. The discussion of infrastructure in Chapter 9 contains more sources to follow up on regarding schools that have created structures to equalize CES partnerships. Although outside the lens of specifically preparing students in the classroom for culturally humble engagement, this work is related and important to consider in the long term for any HEI interested in equitable partnerships.

Educational Privilege, Writ Large

In this chapter we have been speaking at a macro level about the imbalance inherent between communities and HEIs. At the interpersonal level, institutional power also has implications for how we are perceived by and able to engage with the community, as discussed in Chapter 1. In the bird's-eye view of this tangled, sticky HEI/CBO power dynamic, this is seen and experienced as an academic partner having resources (education, credibility, money, power) and a community partner lacking them. It follows that the conversation about privilege also needs to happen at the institutional level since the institutional disparities directly create the individual differences. HEIs in the United States, as well as Europe, are neoliberal, colonized institutions, virtually all headed by white males until relatively recently (some Catholic schools notwithstanding). It is important to discuss this overarching concern with students in tandem with training regarding individual identity, as discussed in earlier chapters.

Concluding Thoughts

The unbalanced community-university power dynamic is entrenched and endemic and in some ways a fact of life in HEI relationships with community organizations. Community organizations almost universally have less resources at their disposal than HEIs due to the nature of how each entity functions and how HEIs came into being. It is easy to get frustrated and feel helpless because of that intransigence; however, we are seeing many shifts where caring CEPs across the United States are beginning to collaborate on ways to serve their communities more equitably and usefully. The first step is awareness. As you share these concepts with your students, they will become part of their shift in consciousness and will provide students a better understanding of how to flatten power dynamics as much as possible while working for new systems of change. CEPS themselves can also focus on tangible ways to support more equal power dynamics—initial and ongoing attention to trust-based relationships, co-creation of projects and courses, clear and realistic partnership expectations, focusing on useful community outputs, and providing whatever resources community partners need to engage in partnerships, such as compensation and appointments. These power dynamics may be nuanced and entrenched, but a basic understanding of these realities will support students in their CE work.

6

Student Skills for Community Engagement

For students to succeed and grow through CE, and for community partners to achieve useful outcomes, instructors and coordinators must consider how to develop students' professional and interpersonal skills in order for them to engage effectively. As important as it is that students learn the theories and concepts underlying a field of study, students must also learn how to artfully apply those theories through tangible skills and engagement with others in order to be meaningful collaborators.

In this chapter we explore a list of concepts and skills that students should be cognizant of as they prepare to engage in the community. Many of these skills, such as relationship building or listening, may seem outside the scope of the average course learning outcomes. Indeed, we might expect students to navigate and learn some of these skills on their own through the broader context of their college experience. However, we assert that we are all always learning, unlearning, and relearning how to engage with one another—especially after years marked by fluctuating social environments spurred by the pandemic and political polarization—and as such should take seriously the role of the classroom in cultivating relationship skills.

Community-engaged scholarship is not the pursuit of knowledge for knowledge's sake. Rather, it is the pursuit of knowledge for social impact. The social implications of this pedagogy also bring forth the complexities of working with others that students should be encountering and learning from during their time in college in order to best prepare them for real-world settings. Consider how you can provide students classroom space to process through these complexities and reflect on their professional (or even personal) goals.

Additionally, this chapter comes from acknowledging the reality that the real-world application of theory, readings, and ideas is quite complex. CBL instructors bear a heavy load, needing to develop students' understanding of course concepts while also providing some level of professional readiness coaching. Indeed, the rise in literature such as this book stems from the recognition by educators that there is a large gap between students' levels of preparation and what is actually required for students to be useful in a community context (Floyd, 2013). As such, interpersonal and professional skill building must be given as much weight within learning outcomes as understanding of course content.

A Student Development Lens

A central consideration to weigh as you consider how these skills and topics can fit into your classroom is the role of student development. By this, we are referring to "the ways that a student grows, progresses, or increases his or her developmental capabilities as a result of enrollment in an institution of higher education" (Rodgers, 1990, p. 27). There are many aspects to student development, including but not limited to students' identity, moral, and epistemological development. Most models of CBL seek to disrupt classroom and academic hierarchies, encouraging students to be more self-directed in their learning and less reliant on the instructor to dictate meaning (e.g., Freire, 1970). However, this approach to instruction cannot be equally applied to all classes. For example, the way you structure and prepare a first-year student for CBL is going to look drastically different than what you cover with a fourth-year student in a capstone course.

Howe et al. (2014) have developed a useful model, referred to as the three-phased model for service-learning course design, that outlines considerations about the design of CE experiences based on students' level of coursework. The three phases, designed for students to progress through, include exposure, capacity building, and responsibility. The exposure phase focuses on building students' understanding of CBL and introducing them to foundational skills and reflection. Engagement in this phase is primarily through discrete, one-time direct service experiences, where the instructor plays an essential role in the development and coordination of the engagement (e.g., tutoring). The second phase, capacity building, starts to provide students with opportunities to develop more practical, high-level skills. At this phase, students might begin to work in collaborative teams and engage in longer-term, strategic projects with communities. Finally, phase three, responsibility, intended for students with ample exposure to CE, engages students to take on more ownership and accountability for the project. In this phase the program manager or instructor may serve more as a coach, providing feedback and framing to support student learning.

This model allows instructors to consider the level of support or development that students may need in order to engage with the partnership, depending on their level in school. As an example, higher-level students should be well suited for small group work and may be able to develop their own relationships with community partners, such as preparing educational programming for a local nonprofit. However, first-year students are better suited to enter into experiences that are more structured and discrete, recognizing they likely have not yet developed the skills necessary to form their own partnerships and produce the most meaningful outcomes.

We have structured this chapter by considering two dimensions of student skills related to effective community engagement: relationship-building skills and practical CE skills. These dimensions are informed in part by the work of Donahue and Plaxton-Moore (2018), who developed a companion reader to guide students in their preparation for CE. These authors incorporate many of the following concepts under the lens of the responsibilities of community-engaged learners. Viewing the following dimensions of skill building as the responsibility of student learners emphasizes the sincerity and humility needed for students to engage in meaningful partnerships. Toward the end of this chapter, we also share a few strategies for incorporating skill building into student preparation activities.

Before we close out this section on student development, we want to bring special attention to graduate-level programming. We have not parsed out many of the distinctions between graduate and undergraduate students as they pertain to CE. Of course there are many, and preparation for different levels requires different content to meet students where they are. Most of the content in this book is appropriate for undergraduates but can also be helpful at the graduate level, being aware of their advanced ability to assimilate information. Several schools, including Michigan State University and Merrimack College, have programs and/or majors in CE at the graduate level. At UW–Madison, we codeveloped a doctoral minor and master's certificate in CES with the Department of Civil Society and Community Studies to provide support for grad students pursuing CE. This program foregrounds student preparation so students can do CE equitably and impactfully, and it also provides training to the next generation of faculty and CEPs (see vignette by Laura Livingston, Chapter 10).

Relationship-Building Skills

Relationships are the bedrock of strong CE and inform the success of a project. Although the instructor is generally the primary relationship steward within CBL contexts, it is important for students to actively reflect and build upon their relationship skills through the everyday interactions they have "on the ground" with clients or organization staff as well as their peers. Numerous activists, scholars, and community partners have emphasized the long game of social change work and the importance for those engaged in it to recognize the long-term implications of relationships in shaping this work (Doran et al., 2021). In this section we list some key skills that impact students' ability to build relationships with community partners. These same skills frequently appear across CE literature, regardless of discipline. This is not an exhaustive list, but merely a few that lend themselves well to class activities for practice. Other skills and qualities, such as cultivating humility, self-awareness, and patience, are discussed throughout the book.

Active Listening

Listening is such a basic concept that we often overlook how challenging true listening can actually be. No matter what context students are entering into, based on the specific partners or focus of a particular CBL experience, listening is essential to respectful engagement. CE can be an incredibly intimate experience depending on the project. For example, consider the large number of students who go into schools each year to tutor younger children. When working with children, especially in certain settings or environments, university students may be exposed to a variety of painful realities, from poverty to hostile home environments and youth mental health challenges. But even the urban planning student seeking community feedback on a neighborhood redevelopment plan or the medical student explaining a condition to a patient also needs the skill of active listening to ensure their audience feels heard. Truly listening, understanding, and responding to where folks are coming from requires an intentional approach to listening.

Framing listening as a valuable professional skill and providing different models and approaches to listening has been helpful in our work with students. Certain disciplines, such as nursing (e.g., Haley et al., 2017), social work (e.g., Rogers & Welch, 2009), and education (e.g., Vostal et al., 2015), already incorporate development of listening skills into their degree programs and professional training. We urge instructors to consider how to equip all undergraduates, across any course, with a skill set that will better prepare them to engage with others as peers, citizens, and collaborators in all their future endeavors.

When we talk about active listening, we are referring to listening that communicates empathy and builds trust by indicating unconditional regard and affirming the other's experience (Lester, 2002; Orlov, 1992; Rogers, 1951). Weger et al. (2014) conceptualize three core aspects of active listening, including nonverbal engagement (i.e., body language), reflecting back what is heard (i.e., verbal paraphrasing), and "asking questions that encourage speakers to elaborate on his or her experiences" (p. 14). One common model for active listening is referred to as the LARA method: Listen, Affirm, Respond, and Ask Questions (Tinker, 2004). This method is frequently applied in intergroup dialogue settings and applies well to environments where students may be encountering new ideas and realities. Students should be encouraged to listen deeply in order to understand the communities they are working with, as well as their peers in the classroom.

Beyond the act of listening in real time, students may also need to understand what it means to integrate what they have heard. We have all likely been in frustrating situations in which feedback is sought and then ignored, which can be an exceedingly harmful practice in CE. During their CE, students may be part of formal ways of listening, such as conducting focus groups or facilitating community listening sessions. In these spaces, students should also be considerate of which voices are present and which might be absent. Depending on the project, it may also be necessary for students or university partners to be explicit about why certain feedback was or was not integrated into a project. Additional ways in which listening and CE might be conceptualized within different fields include stakeholder engagement (e.g., Concannon et al., 2014) and participatory evaluation (e.g., Cousins & Whitmore, 1998). There are a number of excellent activities that can develop students' listening skills. We list a few that we have utilized here (The GLS Project, 2022):

- **Drawing:** In this exercise, students are in pairs, with one person in each pair receiving a picture. The person without the picture can ask questions about the picture to encourage its description and then attempts to draw it through what they hear. This exercise helps students reflect on asking more open-ended questions, listening thoughtfully, and listening in a way to collaborate on a project. Reflection questions are as follows:
  - How did this exercise feel?
  - How did your drawing compare to the initial drawing?
  - What strategies were helpful? What strategies were unhelpful?
- **Listening:** In pairs, have students take turns speaking about something for a full five minutes. The listener cannot interrupt or say anything at all but must simply listen. At the end of the speaker's time, the listener paraphrases what they heard. This exercise helps students listen without trying to come up with the next thing to say, focus on understanding, and notice their internal urges to interrupt. Reflection questions are as follows:
  - How did this exercise feel?
  - What did you notice when it was your turn to listen?

- What do you notice about yourself when you are listening in conversations?
- How did it feel to be the speaker?
- What can you take away back to everyday conversations?

- **In pairs, have students take different stances on an issue:** You can pick an issue that is more or less comfortable or emotionally charged, from a favorite meal to religious beliefs. In the first part of the activity, ask students to have a five-to-ten-minute debate to try to convince their partner of their beliefs. They can interrupt, talk over each other, or engage in whatever kind of conversation they want. In the second part, ask each student to talk about their side of the conversation for three minutes without interruption. At the end of three minutes, the other person can ask questions. This exercise can help students notice their desire to interrupt, contrast listening to understand versus listening to be right, and develop their curiosity. Reflection questions are as follows:
  - What did you notice about each of those treatments?
  - How did you feel in each part?
  - What do you think was more effective?
  - What was challenging for you?

- **Ask students to write down and reflect on two different situations:** These should be a conversation that went poorly and a conversation that went well. What happened in each? What emotions were present? How did each person speak and behave? What helped the good situation to go well? What inhibited the poor situation from going well? What do you wish you had done differently? This exercise can help students identify specific characteristics of good conversations.

- **Sympathy versus empathy video and reflection:**
  - We have found value in engaging students in a discussion about the difference between sympathy and empathy. Our approach to this discussion is heavily influenced by the work of Brené Brown and her viral TED Talk (from 2011). We specifically use a YouTube video by RSA (2013) that condenses the TED Talk to focus on the topic of empathy.* As of the time of publication, this video can be accessed through the QR code in the footnote.

---

* RSA. (2013, December 10). *Brené Brown on empathy* [Video]. YouTube. https://www.youtube.com/watch?v=1Evwgu369Jw&t=5s&ab_channel=RSA

- **General helpful listening questions:**
  - Tell me more.
  - What does that mean?
  - What does that look like?
  - This is what I'm hearing—is this what you mean?

Communication

Communication, the "mother" of listening, is another essential skill for successful collaboration and has great personal and professional value. Within CE, communication should be consistent, transparent, and clear.

Instructors should be sure to discuss with students the course expectations related to communication, especially in communicating with their community partners. We frequently hear from community partners who receive last-minute emails from students about having to miss a volunteer shift right before their scheduled session time (Stoecker & Tryon, 2009). Instructors are likely familiar with this tendency among students, as well. When stakeholders are impacted by students' poor communication, instructors should emphasize to students the importance of timeliness as well as demonstrate how to communicate professionally, and they should hold students accountable. This means ensuring students know how to compose an email or even how to be efficient and professional in calling an organization or leaving a message. These skills are often taken for granted and may not be obvious to all students, especially those who may have limited experiences operating in more professional environments. Additionally, instructors can explain how students' poor communication negatively impacts community organizations who may be relying on certain staffing numbers or how their absence can impact the clients served by a partnership or CBO.

Another dimension of communication relates to students' ability to respectfully and effectively communicate with diverse audiences. Much has been written about intercultural communication and the importance of making academic knowledge more accessible, especially in regards to science communication throughout the COVID-19 pandemic. But another aspect of intercultural communication that especially impacts the ways students are interacting with the community is the importance of communicating in respectful and patient ways. The story related in Chapter 2 about library volunteers deciding students' names were too hard to pronounce emphasizes the need to promote respect, care, and consideration as related to communicating with others.

Finally, instructors should also consider how to support students in advocating for what they need from the learning experience. For example, if students require accommodations, instructors should find out what may be

TABLE 6.1   DOS AND DON'TS OF RELATIONSHIPS AND
COMMUNICATION WITH COMMUNITY PARTNERS

Dos	Don'ts
Do speak with/call/email your community partner frequently, and in advance, especially as it relates to absences.	*Don't* email your community partner about missing your shift an hour before you are scheduled, unless there is an emergency.
Do listen sincerely and actively when engaging with others.	*Don't* look down at your phone or dominate the conversation with your voice.
Do speak with respect, clarity, and patience.	*Don't* speak in a condescending or academic, jargon-heavy way.
Do make sure your language or messaging is accessible (i.e., printing posters in multiple languages).	*Don't* assume everyone speaks/reads English.
Do be flexible to the shifting needs of community partners, and try to be helpful where you can.	*Don't* consider yourself better than any specific task and complain if the partnership needs to adjust.
Do practice cultural humility by being open to and respectful of different perspectives or beliefs.	*Don't* seek to change people or question the beliefs and practices of different communities.
Do aim to be an active and curious learner, listening to the wisdom and expertise of the community.	*Don't* ignore or belittle contributions or priorities of the community.

needed to ensure students are able to easily work with the community partner and support students in communicating those needs to the partner. It also means incorporating multiple feedback loops into the course so that students have the opportunity to express any concerns or frustrations with their experience. Similarly, these same safeguards can be useful for marginalized students who may experience microaggressions while engaging with the community. Instructors who learn of these incidents should ensure they are openly communicating with the partner to improve the experience for all stakeholders.

Communication needs and skills are bound to differ depending on the scope of a CE project, but in our student trainings, we have boiled it down to some essential ideas (Table 6.1). We also discuss with students the importance of body language and to be considerate of how they "show up" in a community. We encourage them to bring their energy and authenticity while showing respect in order to nurture more meaningful relationships.

Preparing for Discomfort and Accountability

As discussed in Chapter 4, discomfort has often been seen as an unavoidable component of some CBL scenarios. We also know discomfort and dissonance impact students differently depending on their social identities (Taylor & Reynolds, 2019). For white students, dissonance can arise from essential CE conversations around race and privilege in ways that bring about feelings of shame or guilt (Sue, 2016). But for students of color or other marginalized students, these discussions might fuel discomfort as a result of trauma associated with life experiences impacted by systems of oppression, thus risking the perpetuation of negative outcomes such as withdrawal from the experience (King et al., 2011). Because the directive from community partners of our predominantly white institution (PWI) was "train your majority-white students in better cultural understanding and behavior," most of the content in this book is necessarily directed toward that.

In order to best meet the needs of diverse learners, instructors must be cognizant of how they are including support for students and how students' identities may impact their experience in the classroom and community. Much has been written about helping students of color cope with discrimination on campus (Hussain & Jones, 2021; Sue et al., 2009), and instructors can follow up with resources specifically for students of color (such as Taylor & Reynolds, 2019, or Yosso, 2005).

Discomfort within CBL can arise in many different ways. When out in the community, students may exhibit nervousness and uncertainty about how to behave, often coming off as disengaged or inauthentic. In the classroom, this may look like students shutting down or withdrawing from difficult conversations. In their analysis of the role of discomfort in college student development, Taylor and Baker (2020) offer considerations for pedagogical moves that can lead to more positive outcomes. Some of the core components of CBL, such as critical self-reflection or dialogue with peers, can serve as tools to help some students move through dissonance and process their discomfort (Kiely, 2005; Mezirow, 2006). Instructors can also ensure students feel supported by taking active steps to ensure their classroom is inclusive and a safe space for complex and heavy discussions (such as through the development of course norms) and by being cognizant of how discomfort may be connected to students' social identities. More on cultivating these intricate but transformational learning environments can be found in Chapter 8.

An additional element of discomfort, predominantly relevant to students with dominant and/or privileged identities, is considering how to respond to it in the moment, especially when students find they unintentionally caused harm. This happens when, for example, a student commits a microaggression. But discomfort in the moment can also look like students experiencing fear and trepidation out of concern that they will accidentally commit harm. However, in reality, harm will occur from time to time, and it is important that students understand that and consider how to learn from it. We are not asking them to be perfect, but rather to be responsive and accountable to community partners and their peers. Instructors have a role to play in ensuring students are held accountable for microaggressions and missteps as well. But rather than calling out students who make mistakes, we advocate for *calling in* students, to better understand where they are coming from and to inform them about the impact of their words or actions. Some of these ideas are well captured from an online article about how individuals can respond when they learn they unintentionally committed a microaggression (Kothari, n.d.), which we have adapted here:

- **Understand intent versus impact:** Rarely are we ever intending to offend someone, but alas, our intentions do not really matter when another person's feelings have been hurt. So rather than seeking to clarify our intentions, we should own the impact that our words or actions had and seek to remedy them.
- **Throw away your defenses:** Do not make the mistake all about you. Apologies rooted in defensiveness are often easy to see through and come off as disingenuous. To truly sit with and understand how our words may have impacted another requires some vulnerability, but that is needed in order to move forward.
- **Embrace learning:** Being accountable to the impact you have on others also means learning about how to be a better person. When someone is willing enough to inform us of the way our words or actions impacted them, we should be grateful. This can be an opportunity for further learning and can improve how we relate to people later on in our lives.
- **Move forward:** There is no use dwelling on past mistakes, but we can rather focus on learning from them and committing to improving in the future.

The program overview from Edgewood College shown in Virginia Lee's contribution provides an example of a strong integration of aspects of stu-

Edgewood College Bonner Project and Community-Engaged Learning Initiatives

Virginia Lee

Background

This project evolved from faculty ideas on recruiting students to undergraduate community-based research through their interests, utilizing the Bonner Leaders program, a national service-learning leadership program that allows students to provide community service while growing as leaders. Bonner Leaders strive to understand issues in our own community and work with community partners to work for social change. The program fosters an inclusive community of practice and a pathway to institutionalizing asset-based undergraduate research for students at different development stages. Edgewood's Bonner Leaders spend a minimum of two years working on community service initiatives and meet regularly as a group to learn about social justice issues, community leadership, and civic engagement. Students receive a stipend and complete 220 hours of community service and training. After discussions, we focused on our COR 2 (see the following) curriculum as the vehicle for this work, which aligned with the intent of the request for proposals from Bonner and helped prepare students for community-engaged work.

What Is COR?

Edgewood College includes CBL as a central piece of the undergraduate education experience through the COR Program, a three-course sequence designed to introduce students to the school's Dominican tradition to "Study, Reflect, Act." These courses "encourage students to examine connections among learning, beliefs, and action, to participate in building a more just and compassionate world" (COR, Edgewood). An essential component of COR is a set of reflection questions that encourage every Edgewood student to think about their skills and strengths and their role in the world:

- Who am I and who can I become?
- What are the needs and opportunities of the world?
- What is my role in building a more just and compassionate world?

COR's Use in the Bonner Research Cohort

Meetings for this inquiry and research program were designed so faculty members could share good practices with the group and lessons learned. The process of sharing faculty expertise served to illuminate the practices of faculty who had developed successful pedagogies and partnerships. We utilized our second-phase, "COR 2 Enhancement Pathway" as a means of streamlining access to undergraduate research opportunities, particularly for traditionally underrepresented, low-income, and first-generation students and by developing a culture of community of practice and reflective space.

The students and Bonner Leaders meet regularly through a cohort using the Haas Center's Pathways of Public Service tool to help students identify the types of service they lean toward, community asset mapping to steer clear of deficit thinking, and the development of "river stories" to hear and reflect on why they are interested and vested in community service. The Bonner Wiki site has open-access resources for all this work, including the river stories and a good root cause analysis tool. The cohorts are oriented toward the work through capacity building, continuity, and ongoing training/reflection.

Many guides that offer best practices for developing undergraduate research offer structural details of what to consider in terms of program design, typology, and best practices for pedagogical approaches that support asset-based approaches for engaging youth, faculty, and the community as collaborators. There are many considerations: ethics, social impact, agency, and pedagogical and epistemological approaches. Considering the "social justice youth development" model (Pryor & Outley, 2014), two of the considerations are developing critical consciousness and being mindful of acknowledging the contributions of all stakeholders. Examining other program models and pedagogical practices also offers methods for supporting students' sociopolitical development and critical consciousness coupled with their academic development.

The president of Bonner advised me to take a look at some of these guides and models, which led me to the following resources:

- Christens, B. D., & Dolan, T. (2011). Interweaving youth development, community development, and social change through youth organizing. *Youth and Society*, 43(2), 528–548. https://doi.org/10.11 77/0044118X10383647
- Ginwright, S., & James, T. (2002, Winter). From assets to agents of change: Social justice, organizing, and youth development. *New Directions for Youth Development*, 2002(96), 27–46. https://doi.org /10.1002/yd.25
- Healey, M., Jordan, F., Pell, B., & Short, C. (2010). The research-teaching nexus: A case study of students' awareness, experiences and perceptions of research. *Innovations in Education and Teaching International*, 47(2), 235–246. https://doi.org/10.1080/1470329100371 8968
- Jones, J. N. (2017). The development of youth purpose through community service and social action. *American Secondary Education*, 45(3), 50–67.
- Kiyama, J. M., Lee, J. J., & Rhoades, G. (2012). A critical agency network model for building an integrated outreach program. *Journal of Higher Education*, 83(2), 276–303. https://doi.org/10.1353/jhe .2012.0009

- Luedke, C. L., Collom, G. D., McCoy, D. L., Lee-Johnson, J., & Winkle-Wagner, R. (2019). Connecting identity with research: Socializing students of color towards seeing themselves as scholars. *Review of Higher Education, 42*(4), 1527–1547. https://doi.org/10.1353/rhe .2019.0074
- Maclure, R. (2017). Youth reflexivity as participatory research in Senegal: A field study of reciprocal learning and incremental transformations. *Social Inclusion, 5*(3), 251–261. https://doi.org/10.17645/si .v5i3.991

Program Change and Developing a "Students as Colleagues" Model

In student development theory, students of color are often the subjects of the research but not the purveyors of knowledge. Community-engaged learning and practices such as participatory action research provide students with the opportunity to develop skills in collaboration with faculty/staff, with classmates or in a cohort, and with community partners at various developmental stages to effect social change. There are many benefits to these students, including a sense of belonging that contributes to retention, building critical consciousness, sociopolitical development, policy literacy, and cultural competency. This project can serve as a model for intentional, inclusive programming through the development of an undergraduate research program that supports student agency, drawing on the academic expertise of faculty and staff, and addresses real societal issues by collaborating with community partners.

dents' civic, social, and career development into CE. Multiple aspects of the program are specifically designed to support student skill building and access to a community of support and mutual learning.

Practical Community Engagement Skills

In this section, we outline professional and leadership skills that we associate with CE. Compared to relationship-building skills, we consider the following skills to be more associated with project-based work, although positive relationships can certainly improve the way these skills are navigated. This is not an exhaustive list, and we encourage instructors to discuss with their partners what skills students might need in order to be successful.

We have shared links to two videos, created by staff at our center, that elevate community and campus voice to share an assortment of perspectives and words of wisdom for students to consider as they prepare for their CE experience (Morgridge Center for Public Service, 2021b).* These videos do a great deal to highlight the reality of CE and how that experience has gone well, not so well, or could be better. At the same time, these videos demonstrate to students the vast network of individuals and professionals from both within and outside the university who are working to improve the community in one way or another. Your university may not have these sorts of video resources, but we are sure there are other articles, videos, or platforms within your community that you may consider utilizing.

Community Voice and Stakeholder Engagement

We have discussed the importance of communication and how it relates to stakeholder engagement. But we want to go deeper here, encouraging CEPs to consider how students are taught to identify the varying stakeholders potentially existing within a project (e.g., clients, boards of advisors, custodial staff, neighbors, etc.) and what it means to incorporate the voices of groups that might often be silenced or overlooked (e.g., individuals with disabilities or non-English speakers). How can students make space to integrate multiple, diverse voices into their work? How are students considering how to communicate to these audiences? This also involves weighing questions about decision-making and incorporating different perspectives, as well as ensuring communities have all the information necessary in order to participate fully (see Chapter 5 for more on power dynamics).

Professionalism and Appropriateness

"Professionalism" is a word we are using loosely here (knowing that the concept has often been coded to promote racialized and gendered attributes) to capture those behaviors and dispositions associated with students showing commitment to the CE project and care in their interactions and quality of work. "Appropriateness" may be a more precise term, since we are expecting students to behave in ways that are appropriate to each situation (e.g., it would be appropriate for volunteers to wear relaxed clothing when

---

* Morgridge Center for Public Service. (2021b, February 23). *Words of wisdom part 2* [Video]. YouTube. https://www.youtube.com/watch?v=sR_MV7I33_w&t=8s&ab HYPERLINK "https://www.youtube.com/watch?v=sR_MV7I33_w&t=8s&ab_channel =MorgridgeCenterforPublicService"_channel=MorgridgeCenterforPublicService

working with youth, rather than wearing business attire). Appropriateness and professionalism include big things such as students communicating in advance to their community partner about any absences, as well as more basic things like wearing appropriate clothing (i.e., close-toed shoes for outdoor work) and writing coherent and respectful emails. Ample research has shown how important these skills are to community partners in order to ensure a partnership is worth their energy (e.g., Karasik & Hafner, 2021; Stoecker & Tryon, 2009).

Professionalism in CE requires that students be educated about and held to basic standards of conduct in community settings, especially as representatives of the college or university. Many aspects of what we consider "professional conduct" are often taken for granted, but younger undergraduates likely have limited experience writing emails, corresponding with stakeholders, or interacting on a site. For example, if a student is unfamiliar with the context of the CBO or the scope of the work (e.g., clearing brush at an environmental preserve), some clothing errors are bound to happen. Etiquette or expectations around email communications (forwards, cc'ing, follow-ups, etc.) can be overwhelming even for seasoned professionals, and students may not understand how to best employ these functions or tools without some guidance. We recommend tailoring this content to the specifications of the partner organizations (e.g., appropriate behavior, language, clothing) and creating basic communication guidelines that feel relevant for your context (e.g., promptness in responding to communication, how to write an email).

The rise in social media posting and photography/videography over the years has also brought about issues of students violating privacy or even exoticizing community partners. There are certain laws and protections that students should be aware of. When working with children, for example, students should absolutely avoid all photography unless parents have signed permission waivers, as minors are a protected class. It is always best practice for students to ask permission from the community partner or *any* individual before taking photos.

Finally, another common complaint shared among community partners relates to the lack of professionalism exhibited by students who may show up late or act tired or disengaged when they arrive, generally lacking a positive attitude or interest (Blouin & Perry, 2009; Cronley et al., 2015). Instructors should consider how they can limit students' barriers to engaging appropriately. Students may be impacted by improper planning for transportation. Consider allowing time in class for students to schedule their engagement or map out their commute. Some campus CE centers may have funds available to support student transportation as well. If they are truly disinterested in what they are doing, switching to another project might be an option instead of limping along and making all parties dissatisfied.

Flexibility and Adaptability

Life does not always go according to plan. This sentiment feels especially relevant when reflecting back on the initial years of the COVID-19 pandemic that continue to have an impact on everyday life and a profound influence on organizations, projects, and partnerships. Even during the "before times," community partnerships and projects frequently had to alter their initial goals, expectations, or timelines as a result of our ever-changing world. Whether it be a staff member at a partner organization needing to take medical leave, a new policy that reshapes how an organization can offer services, or a global pandemic that changes how we are able to work with one another and brings about a new set of emergencies, change is inevitable, and students should come to understand how to respond to change with flexibility and adaptability.

Instructors can support students' adaptability by staying attuned to the students' CE experience and regularly reflecting on a project's timeline and progress. When a change occurs that derails a project, instructors can help students consider how they can adjust their projects to still be useful to community partners. For example, say something shifts within the community partner organization toward the end of the semester, such as a major staffing change, and the project needs to go in a different direction. Rather than feeling that all their time has been wasted, students can be supportive by summarizing the work they have done thus far into a transition plan as a useful starting point for others who may step into the project later on. This sort of flexibility is especially valuable for students as they begin to experience other professional settings, where such adaptability is often needed among staffing transitions, funding parameters, and changing environments.

Time and Project Management

Instructors can support students in building time management skills by providing time in class for students to schedule their visits to the partner site or map out their transportation route in advance. For students new to urban environments, the need to rely on public transit such as buses or subways may feel daunting. When possible, students can be encouraged to commute to the partner site with their peers. Instructors should also seek out additional transportation resources that might be made available through institutional CE offices or other units. For example, our center offers students free access to rentable e-bikes available in our community and provides free cab rides for students heading to destinations that are farther from campus.

In order to avoid instances where students procrastinate on their project or wait until the last minute to fulfill their required hours, instructors should consider establishing benchmarks throughout the semester so students are actively building toward the end goal. For example, by midsemester, students should have completed the initial phases of a long-term project, and with a month left in the semester, they should have completed over half of their required hours. These benchmarks not only support student success but also ensure that community partners are not overwhelmed by a flurry of end-of-semester procrastinators begging for more hours and will not receive thrown-together project deliverables.

Understanding the elements, needs, and timeline of a project is also central to student and community success. This process of actualizing complex collaborations is frequently referred to as project management, and it is becoming an increasingly valuable skill in all sectors. There are innumerable project management tools and resources available depending on the type of project students are embarking upon. A few basic considerations include the following:

- Goal setting
- Project mapping (timeline, responsibilities, deliverables, etc.)
- Utilizing project management software (Trello, Asana, Excel, etc.)
- Stakeholder group engagement

Understanding Community Context

Campuses are their own mini-communities, as we discussed in Chapter 5. These design factors inform what many of us might refer to as the "campus bubble"—creating a division between the campus and community and making it easy for students to be disconnected from the community. Supporting students in *bursting* the campus bubble requires pulling back the curtain of any community by learning about local interests, leaders, demographics, histories, and more. Such activities allow students to develop their ability to understand, navigate, and collaborate with different communities. Here are a few examples of activities we have used.

Community Partner Mission Analysis
This activity is pretty straightforward but nonetheless valuable. When students and instructors fail to really understand the mission of partner organizations, they are doing a great disservice to those partners. A good understanding of the organization's mission helps students contextualize their role in the partnership and the value of their work. An overall exploration of the scope of the organization can also develop students' understanding of the broader community.

Instructors can exercise ample creativity in designing this activity for their courses. Depending on the resources of your community partner, your students may be able to do a deep investigation into the organization's website, considering the organization's history, past or current projects, or news stories about the work of the organization. In our trainings with students, we present the mission, vision, and history of an organization in our community and have students collectively unpack it, sharing any reactions or observations about the organization. Often community partners even have presentations or resources they want to share with students to best orient them to their work and setting, but instructors can also play a role here as well.

Local News Issues

Students in the campus bubble are seldom attuned to the goings-on beyond the boundaries of the campus. They might have no idea of the vast amount of activity taking place in the cities or towns their universities are situated within, such as local elections, urban development, and local concerns around food insecurity or homelessness. Most colleges have their own student newspapers that focus exclusively on campus events, further limiting students' exposure to issues and happenings beyond campus. This exclusive focus on campus may isolate students from cultural assets; for instance, on our campus, a PWI within a predominantly white city, many students of color were also unaware of local places such as Mexican markets, barber shops or other cultural community spaces that they would likely be interested in frequenting (M. Nellis, personal conversation, 2010).

To support students' understanding of the community, we have facilitated activities wherein students engage in analysis of the local news. We generally do this by selecting articles that have both explicit and implicit connections with the course topic and the CBO. As an example, in our work with an arts-based CBL course, we asked students to engage with an article from a local news outlet regarding a series of temporary murals that were installed on the storefronts of a prominent commercial street during the height of the Black Lives Matter protests during the summer of 2020, in the wake of the murder of George Floyd. When assigning these readings to students, we ask them to pay close attention to the names of folks being interviewed or cited. What organizations are represented? Who are leaders within the community? What work is already being done? What history or context does the article provide? Educators can also make use of alternative forms of news that might cater to different communities. Our city has a number of community Facebook groups, blogs, and mutual aid pages, as well as newspapers and magazines catered to the local LGBTQ+ community and communities of color.

Conceptualizing Social Change

Social change can be an aspect of community engagement that is often brushed aside, perhaps due to the politically charged nature of the phrase or the limited scope of a course. However, social change is a goal of most CBOs and is often an interest and motivation of college students enrolling in CBL programs. Community-engaged scholars have been discussing the importance of a social justice and change orientation toward CE for some time (e.g., Butin, 2007; Grain & Lund, 2016; Mitchell, 2008). In recent years, such a perspective has felt increasingly crucial as our students come to grips with the crises of our time—ranging from climate change, growing inequality, and gun violence to the rise of fascism and white supremacy, to truly name just a few. Also on the rise are concerns regarding students' mental health, certainly tied to these growing crises. Grappling with our current world requires care and humility, as we have hopefully illuminated throughout this book, but it also requires hope. Grain and Lund (2016) assert that a level of "critical hope" (Freire, 1994) is needed, and can be fostered through CBL, to combat the despair that may arise through learning associated with systems of oppression, histories of harm, and modern injustices.

Building on this, we encourage CEPs to consider how they can be intentional around discussing goals related to social justice, as well as in supporting students in understanding their place within "social change ecosystems" (Iyer, 2018). Social change is a process and can be exhausting work. As educators, we have the privilege of cultivating spaces that need not reproduce all the oppressive norms of our society but rather foster the imaginations and communities we hope to see in the world. Helping students realize the long game of social change and contribute to spaces that support vulnerability and connection can go a long way in nurturing that hope. There are ample ways to approach this topic that we cannot fit within the scope of this book. But within this vein, we want to emphasize a few concepts, in the form of quotes, that might provide jumping-off points for further reflection:

- **Solidarity:** "You don't fight racism with racism, the best way to fight racism is with solidarity."—Bobby Seale, cofounder of the Black Panther Party
- **Liberation:** "The revolutionary sees his task as liberation not only of the oppressed but also of the oppressor. Happiness can never truly exist in a state of tension."—Steve Biko, anti-apartheid activist
- **Justice:** "There may be times when we are powerless to prevent injustice, but there must never be a time when we fail to protest." —Elie Wiesel, Holocaust survivor

Notes on Virtual Engagement

Virtual forms of CE existed long before the COVID-19 pandemic made it a shared necessity. While the abrupt shutdown of HEIs in March of 2020 allowed all of us to learn how to engage with others in new ways through long-distance and virtual platforms, emphasizing some shared expectations around respectful virtual engagement with the community is still useful practice. Here we offer a few simple tips and considerations to keep in mind when preparing students for virtual engagement:

- Barring connectivity issues, students should aim to always have their cameras on when engaging with the community in order to foster stronger connections and communicate with their body, as well as their voice.
- Students should minimize distractions by avoiding multitasking and doing their best to set up in a quiet environment.
- Especially when working with youth, students should ensure their backdrops are free of inappropriate posters or paraphernalia.*
- Students and instructors should become familiar with some of the accessibility features available on video conferencing platforms, such as captions, in case such tools are needed to best engage all members of the community.
- Patience should be emphasized, especially when students may be working with populations that are less tech savvy.

The COVID-19 pandemic continues to shift into a different mode as we write this book, but regardless, the realm of hybrid and virtual engagement is not going anywhere. Although in-person forms of engagement are the gold standard, we cannot disregard the vast opportunities and new forms of engagement that virtual platforms allow for, and virtual technologies even make engagement feasible when it was not before, such as in rural under-resourced areas or abroad. It is reassuring to know that Krasny et al. (2021) found that students are still able to receive positive outcomes from online engagement methods when they are done with care. On the part of the instructor, embracing these virtual opportunities means discussing with partners how to best utilize technology within projects, whether that be having

---

* Note: It came to our attention shortly after the COVID-19 shutdown that after-school tutoring one on one does not always translate to online virtual tutoring, even if it is a convenient substitute for in-person interaction. Most college students in CBL courses are above reproach, but when there is no in-class adult supervision, an environment of older students working with younger peers in a chat room situation is a place where "funky stuff" can and does happen—whether initiated by the college student or the younger peer—if boundaries are not observed. Besides using student trainings to provide a grounding in what boundaries look like in an online tutoring relationship (asking or being asked for personal information, making inappropriate comments, etc.), the strategy we used to ensure safety and avoid liability issues was to include classroom teachers or CBL instructors as participants in the Zoom meeting so they can "Zoom" around between sessions and check in on the content of the conversation and the chat bar.

meetings online or collaboratively developing internet-based resources such as video content or websites.

One useful resource we found when researching for this book comes from the realm of data science. Racin and Gordon (2018) explored the experience of CBOs engaged in community-academic research partnerships, focusing on digital contexts. Their study acknowledged the role of differing technological resources and knowledge in perpetuating power imbalances within partnerships. They noted that "developing partnerships that improve the technological know-how and infrastructure of [CBOs] may go a long way toward bridging the digital divide between the academic community and the communities with whom they partner" (p. 11). They also provide example MOUs and deliberate reflection questions CEPs can consider when planning partnerships.

Strategies for Student Skill Building

Thoughtful Assignments, Projects, and Activities

Given the heavy task instructors have in preparing students for CE while also assigning discipline-specific materials, it might feel challenging not to overload students with content. However, we believe that thoughtful, transparent, and intentional structuring can help students develop while also preparing them to deliver results that are of value to the community.

As discussed earlier in this chapter, Howe et al. (2014) propose a model for CBL course design that considers students' academic level and provides suggested course design elements. We see that model as a great starting point and emphasize the importance of providing students with thoughtful and relevant course projects. The model has implications for the planning and organization of both curricular and cocurricular CE experiences. The following are some useful considerations:

- **Assignments build off of each other:** How can students work on aspects of their project throughout the semester? This practice reduces the risk of procrastination and serves both the student and the community partner well.
- **Be transparent:** Ensure students understand your reasoning for the assignment. What do you want them to get out of it? How does the assignment fit the learning objectives of the course?
- **Reflect with a purpose:** As discussed in other chapters, reflection is central to community engagement, but so is ensuring that students understand why they are reflecting and how to reflect sincerely.

Students without much experience reflecting are likely to struggle to understand what they should be articulating or why they need to reflect. Instructors can be transparent about their understanding of the role of reflection within learning and can model and share their own strategies for meaningful reflection.

Feedback Loops

Just as we encourage CEPs or instructors to ensure that community partners have ample opportunity to share feedback on the progress of a given partnership or project, students should be extended the same courtesy. This provides benefits to all stakeholders—students, faculty, and community partners—by ensuring open communication throughout the process and providing insight that can allow for adjustments that improve the course experience, as well the outcomes for communities.

In our own practice, we have created an anonymous Google form that remains on the course web page for our graduate-level course on CES that students can provide feedback on at any point. We set up the form to send notifications when new responses are submitted so we do not have to worry about frequently checking it. Other instructors may also use more formal feedback opportunities, such as a midsemester check-in survey. Students' reflections also can provide insight into the experience, especially if instructors build in reflection prompts that ask about the learning process or course experience.

Additionally, for projects that utilize group work, we also suggest providing students with opportunities to provide feedback on group dynamics throughout the group experience and not just at the end of a project. When issues within groups do arise, this provides CEPs with valuable, albeit delicate, opportunities to engage students in problem-solving and other professional skills. Providing students the opportunity to authentically communicate with peers and share their needs or concerns is incredibly valuable and ideally improves the outcomes for all stakeholders.

Goal Setting

Setting intentions and goals pertaining to one's educational experiences has been shown to be an effective tool for adult learners (Petty & Thomas, 2014). In the context of CBL, goal setting can also strengthen students' sense of commitment to the partnership by allowing them to critically reflect on their aspirations for the experience. Having students reflect on the professional skills they want to build or the perspectives they want to learn provides the instructor with useful information that allows them to better support student growth and development throughout the experience. Depending on the scope of the collaboration, community partners may also be interested in learning students' interests and goals in order to best support them or leverage student interests to train them for certain tasks or needs.

Leverage Campus Resources

The beauty of the college environment is the opportunity to exist among a network of educators and knowledge hubs. From career services offices to culinary staff or human resources (HR) professionals, we (and other large institutions) have access to many, many colleagues to engage with us in a shared mission of educating students. We encourage instructors to cultivate a diverse network of connections across their institution and to make use of that network, when applicable, through the classroom. For example, what resources might career services have available to get students thinking about project management? Are there diversity, equity, and inclusion professionals on campus who can support students in reflecting on their social identities? When dealing with intergroup conflict, does HR have any resources to share? If you are working on a project related to food systems, what insight do your campus kitchens have related to sourcing local foods?

Not only does this provide students the opportunity to learn about new or possible career pathways, but it also exposes them to a vast network of individuals on campus who might play a role in their education and are likely also members of the local community. Engaging students with an array of different professionals and audiences can expose them to the vast, increasingly complex, and also increasingly interconnected world that we live in.

Concluding Thoughts

Higher education often does a good job of developing students' understanding of different disciplines and exposing them to new knowledge, theories, and models—what we might call the hard skills. An area that does not get as much attention, at least within course-based settings, relates to the soft skills that students need in order to work effectively with others and be engaged leaders and citizens. CE is an excellent laboratory for students to develop and actively build upon such skills. Instructors should be thoughtful in how they are supporting students in navigating the intricacies of collaboration and the realities of modern work. Reflecting on the ideas within this chapter may also serve as an opportunity for students to consider the type of professionals they want to be and how they can grow as collaborators and leaders. We have been building toward what we consider perhaps the most important soft skill needed in good-quality CE—that of humility. This concept is so important that we have devoted the next chapter to this topic, hoping to give CEPs and instructors some tools to help foster the characteristic in themselves and their students prior to engagement. Read on!

7

Cultural and Intellectual Humility

Cultural and intellectual humility are crucial skills in working across differ-ence, which is perhaps the single most important goal for engaging in com-munities. In this chapter, we discuss what humility is, why this concept might be at odds with university missions and how to overcome that challenge, and how to cultivate humility in your students.

Many universities have outreach and engagement as part of their stat-ed mission and/or purpose. For instance, UW–Madison includes it as part of the Wisconsin Experience (Wisconsin Experience, n.d.-b):

> Purposeful action—Badgers strive to find greater meaning every day through purposeful action. We work for the common good—for some-thing that's bigger than ourselves. We apply knowledge and skills to solve problems; we engage in public service, partner with others, and contribute to the community; and we lead for positive change.

This goes hand in hand with the Wisconsin Idea, which theoretically guides work at UW and states that the work of UW–Madison should benefit the broader community and that education should influence people's lives be-yond the classroom (University of Wisconsin–Madison, n.d.-b). UW–Mad-ison is not alone in its service mission. While other universities may not have such clearly defined service expectations for their students and faculty, they all have missions and guidelines for students. Often these missions include "public service" or the importance of the campus in creating a positive community impact. For instance, Stanford's is as follows:

> Supporting our community of faculty, students and staff who underlie Stanford's beneficial impact in the world. (Stanford University, n.d.)

Here is one from a private school, Drexel:

> Drexel University fulfills its founder's vision of preparing each new generation of students for productive professional and civic lives while also focusing the University's collective expertise on solving society's greatest problems. Drexel is an academically comprehensive and globally engaged urban research university, dedicated to advancing knowledge and society and to providing every student with a valuable, rigorous, experiential, technology-infused education, enriched by the nation's premier cooperative education program.

Faith-based colleges and universities have the concept of service fairly well "baked in" to their mission and values, in keeping with the Christian doctrines they were founded on (Daniels & Gustafson, 2011). For example, Loyola University Maryland's mission states the following:

> Loyola University Maryland is a Jesuit, Catholic university committed to the educational and spiritual traditions of the Society of Jesus and to the ideals of liberal education and the development of the whole person. Accordingly, the University will inspire students to learn, lead, and serve in a diverse and changing world.

There are several themes that tie together these statements about student experiences. First, they focus on one-directional outreach and service, with knowledge and skills flowing from the university ("experts") to surrounding communities for the benefit of those communities. Second, there is an underlying assumption that this outreach is beneficial—that students are inherently bringing something useful to the world around them. Last, there is an assumption of student competence as both a goal to strive for and a goal that will be reached during students' university education. In other words, students can and will become proficient in their areas of expertise.

Given these premises, it is no wonder that students often experience challenges when they go into the community. The messages they receive from the university can be interpreted as follows: Students should be confident in what they are learning and what they have to offer, and it is their duty to go into the world to do good, where they will be welcomed as proficient helpers and experts by community partners who do not have the knowledge, expertise, and proficiency that students have. While student experiences in community settings are often not as described by the marketing brochures, students are indeed often welcomed into community settings. They bring enthusiasm, energy, new ideas, and new knowledge. However, universities may be inadvertently creating challenging situations or unintended harm by focusing on unidirectional relationships and student competence. Instead, we believe that for students to have positive and useful experiences in community settings, they need to understand and exhibit cultural and intellectual humility, in addition to the intellectual confidence they may need to succeed in the classroom.

Cultural Humility

Merriam-Webster's dictionary definition of the word "humble" as an adjective is as follows (Merriam-Webster, n.d.a):

> 1: **not proud or haughty**: not arrogant or assertive. 2: reflecting, expressing, or offered in a spirit of deference or submission (a humble apology). 3a: ranking low in a hierarchy or scale: insignificant, unpretentious. 3b: not costly or luxurious.

By encouraging cultural humility in CE, we are not implying that students are low ranking or insignificant or that anything is wrong with any student's home culture; rather, we are emphasizing that students enter the community without pride, haughtiness, or arrogance. The second meaning is illuminating because it shows that one can offer help or service, but "in a spirit of deference." Students often enter communities with great enthusiasm and some useful skills; when they also enter with cultural humility, their offerings can be put to use in ways that are most beneficial for students and community partners alike.

In our experience, community partners want students who are humble—open to learning, nonjudgmental, curious, and eager to learn. Humble students know they are going into communities to learn as well as to support the work partners are doing. We can further define the types of humility necessary by focusing on cultural humility, the openness to other cultures, and intellectual humility, the openness to other ways of knowing and types of knowledge. In this chapter, we explore these terms, connect them to missions of HEIs, and describe some strategies for successfully guiding students to humility.

Cultural humility assumes that we can never be up to date on culture in any context. We can never fully know the depth and nuances of culture in contexts we are not part of or are unfamiliar with. Rather than striving to be competent in our knowledge of another's culture, we can instead strive for humility. We can try to be curious, open, and nonjudgmental (Tervalon & Murray-Garcia, 1998). Tervalon and Murray-Garcia in their scholarship on cultural humility within the field of nursing, add: "Cultural humility incorporates a lifelong commitment to self-evaluation and self-critique, to redressing power imbalances in the [partnership], and to developing mutually beneficial and nonpaternalistic clinical advocacy partnerships with communities" (p. 117).

One of the best explanations of culture we have heard is this: Culture is the *way* we do things around here—and *why*. This encompasses both the outward markers of culture (food, dress, speech, customs, practices, behaviors) and also the driving forces behind those outward markers, which can include beliefs, value systems, attitudes, systems and structures, biases, and conceptualizations of important structures such as the self, time, family, community, government, and more (Clifford, 1988). Culture describes not only those things we are aware of but also those structures that unconsciously guide behavior and life (such as implicit bias). The image of the cultural iceberg (Chapter 4) may be helpful for students.

Cultural humility can also be described as the "ability to maintain an interpersonal stance that is other-oriented (or open to the other) in relation to aspects of cultural identity that are most important to the [person]" (Hook et al., 2013, p. 2). In other words, cultural humility is the ability to understand and respect another person's culture without judgment. In terms of CE, this means that students can both have awareness of their own culture and interact with those from other cultures with respect, responsiveness, and care.

Here is an example of what that might look like from our university. As we have said earlier, UW–Madison is a PWI and admits many students from rural backgrounds (Ansari, 2019; Palasz, 2016; University of Wisconsin–Madison, 2020). A typical student could be white, cisgender, female, straight, and raised in a middle-class, two-parent home in a small town (fewer than two thousand people) with an economy based in agriculture and manufacturing. This student might be working with a middle school student at a community center who is Black, transgender, queer, and raised in a single-parent, low-income household in the state's second-largest city, where the biggest employers are in higher education, health care, and biological sciences. These two individuals not only have different demographic characteristics but may have different outward presentations of culture as well as different attitudes, beliefs, and value systems. Cultural humility gives the UW student the ability to have awareness of her own culture and how that influences how she moves through the world. It also gives her the ability to interact across cultural differences without judgment; she does not believe that her cultural ways of doing and being are better, just different, which is part of living in a diverse, democratic society.

Difference between Humility and Competence

Notice that we are focusing on cultural humility rather than cultural competence. Cultural competence, a common thread of "cultural sensitivity" trainings, implies that one will reach a time when one is competent in another's culture, or potentially in all cultures, and that this is an attainable goal (Tervalon & Garcia-Murray, 1998). This is, in fact, an impossible and irrelevant goal. Suggesting that one can reach a completed level of learning about an individual or an aspect of their culture completely disregards the complexity and sincerity of both cultural communities, as well as the diverse individuals within them. On the other hand, humility acknowledges this and instead strives for openness, curiosity, and respect. Humility also implies that competence is not attainable; we cannot have the knowledge to be culturally appropriate in all situations. By striving for cultural humility, we are instead clarifying that we do not need to strive for universal competence. We will be in cultural settings and situations different from those we are used to. When we are experiencing a culture different from our own, we can instead be curious, open to new experiences, and without judgment, rather than thinking we can know the intimate nuances and traditions of any culture. In some ways, this also takes the pressure off students. They do not need to become "experts" in other cultures. We do want to note that we are careful in our word choice. We recognize that in years to come, we may well learn about other terms that will be more appropriate than "humility," and we encourage you to update language as appropriate.

What Does This Mean in Practice?

Nonjudgment

Our instinct when faced with the unfamiliar is often to make assumptions and judgments, as we discussed in Chapters 3 and 4. Cultural humility asks that we instead remain free of judgments and try not to assign value to different ways of behavior. Instead, we can simply notice, even appreciate, differences.

Example: A university student is working at an after-school youth center. When he works with Indigenous youth, he notices that they are rarely on time to their meeting, often lingering with the other students or the center staff. When he asks one of the youth about it, the student says that his community interacts with time differently. Rather than wanting to adhere to a strict schedule, the youth tries to let things happen when the time is ready for them. So rather than rushing through a conversation with a staff member, he takes the time to finish the conversation and then is ready to meet with the university student.

A culturally humble student understands that the youth has a different understanding of the meaning of time and how to interact with it. Even though it is different from his own understanding of time, he does not judge the youth taking his time in conversation as being wrong but rather looks for ways he, as a partner, can be more accommodating, such as building in a bit of extra time following their scheduled session to allow for starting later.

Curiosity

Cultural humility recognizes that competence is not the goal; rather, the goal is that we remain curious and excited to learn about different cultures and ways of doing things. This curiosity is based in a desire to connect with others, rather than a voyeuristic sense of gawking at an exotic other. A curious student is eager to learn with and from those in the community.

Example: A university student is volunteering with high school youth in a science club. Several youth identify as nonbinary, and one youth is transgender. The university student has not knowingly interacted with nonbinary or transgender people before. She is learning about pronouns, names, and more inclusive ways of meeting and interacting with people. As she is learning, she makes mistakes, misgendering a youth.

A culturally competent model would ask that the student be an expert on gender and gender terminology. A cultural humility model would ask that the student stays curious as she learns more about gender, trusting that those educating her are experts on their experiences rather than feeling like she has to be an expert. When she makes mistakes in the learning process, she apologizes and makes amends. She approaches gender with curiosity but also respect for others' willingness to share, rather than feeling like she has to know everything right away. She is eager to learn more and open to listening to the youth she is working with. She also uses that curiosity to seek out new sources of information on her own to deepen her own education on this topic.

Openness

In models of cultural humility, openness means that we are open to different kinds of knowledge and cultural ways (Hook et al., 2013). We do not assume that our way is the right way; instead, we assume there are many ways of doing things for many purposes. We are open to learning more along the way and having our methods or ideas challenged.

Example: A university student is working with an organization that supports refugee resettlement. The refugees have different religious traditions than the university student is used to, with religious practices occurring several times a day and practices that affect their eating habits. The student brings snacks to share during his time with the group, and the people he is working with do not eat them because it is against their religious beliefs to do so.

In a culturally competent model, the student would be expected to be an expert on the culture of the people he is working with. In a culturally humble model, the student would be encouraged to ask about any food preferences and dietary restrictions before bringing in a snack. If he does not do so (there may not be time or opportunity) and does bring in a snack that others cannot eat, he is open to learning about different foodways and practices. Rather than feeling ashamed of his mistake or irritated that his food is rejected, he is interested in learning more and sees the interaction as a learning opportunity and a chance to deepen his connection to the people he is working with. Rather than judging the people he is working with for being different, he is open to learning more about these differences.

Cultural humility asks that we are open to difference, stay curious about this difference, and remain nonjudgmental about difference. We understand that culture runs deep and that no culture is "right" or "wrong." When we interact across difference and culture, we can do so with grace, connection, and care.

Cultivating Cultural Humility

How can we support students in developing cultural humility? Here are some strategies that have worked well for us, as well as other strategies grounded in the literature.

Self-Learning, Self-Awareness, and Reflection

Like so many things, cultural humility begins with the self. When students can understand themselves, they will have an easier time understanding others. Students can begin by exploring their own culture. What does it look like? Where does it come from? What are deeper cultural beliefs, attitudes, and values? How do these influence their lives? How are they seen by others? One exercise that can be helpful is the social identity wheel, as we discussed in Chapter 4. This can be modified to include more personal characteristics, such as values, personality characteristics, and so on.

Another helpful exercise is to use specific reflection questions in discussion or writing assignments. Some examples include the following:

- How would you describe your culture?
- How does your culture influence your behavior? Your spiritual beliefs? Your values?

- Describe an experience of meeting someone from another culture or being in another cultural space that helped you better understand your own culture.
- What parts of your culture are you proud of? Are there any parts of your culture you would like to change?
- What is something you learned in your culture that you later unlearned? How have your values changed over time?
- What is a part of yourself you would like to know more about?

Mindfulness and Nonjudgment

A recurring theme in developing cultural humility is awareness and nonjudgment (Gottlieb, 2021; Hughes et al., 2020). Mindfulness, a valuable skill that can support the practices necessary for cultural humility, is defined as being actively in the present and noticing what is going on inside one's mind and in outside circumstances without judgment (Mindfulness, n.d.). Mindfulness encourages one to both notice what is going on in the present and accept it. It can be associated with religious practices, such as Buddhism and Hinduism, as well as with health practices, such as mindfulness-based stress reduction. However, mindfulness can also be presented as a powerful secular tool with benefits such as self-compassion, stress reduction, resilience, and increased compassion for others (Mindfulness, n.d.).

In the context of cultural humility, mindfulness can be a tool to increase attention to the present *without judgment*. This can help students better notice what is happening around and within them and reduce judgment for themselves and others. Then they can be more thoughtful in their responses rather than immediately reacting, especially when their immediate reactions are based in judgment or bias.

There are many forms of meditation that are helpful for increasing mindfulness, as well as many meditation resources available online (Mindfulness, n.d.). A basic meditation practice asks practitioners to sit quietly and focus on their breathing; they may also focus on a particular word or phrase, if that is helpful. During this time, thoughts may be flowing through their head. Ask that they notice them and release them, returning again to focus on the breath or phrase. The point of the exercise is not to banish all thoughts but rather to notice them without judgment and practice returning to the present moment and the breath. A simple way to incorporate this in your course is to start a class, activity, or reflection session with a grounding or mindful moment, asking students to connect with their breath and quiet their minds.

There are also other kinds of meditation. A body scan meditation asks practitioners to scan their body one part at a time, noticing how they are feeling and what is going on in each part. A walking meditation asks practitioners to walk slowly, concentrating on each step and how it feels. You can also support meditations around really examining an object, such as a raisin, asking practitioners to imagine they have never encountered one before and to explore it without judgment.

In practicing mindfulness, your goals for students can include the following:

- A habit of nonjudgment in challenging situations
- Taking a moment to reflect and then respond rather than immediately reacting
- Increased awareness of the self
- Increased compassion for the self and others
- Increased comfort with silence and pauses in conversation
- Curiosity around strong emotions and situations rather than judgment

Some reflection questions that may be useful include the following:

- How does mindfulness meditation make you feel?
- What is challenging about this?
- What came up for you?
- What did you notice?
- How can you use this skill in everyday life?
- How can you use this skill in challenging conversations?

Relationship Development

A prepared student is focused on relationship development, as we stress in other chapters. This is a key part of cultural humility. A student who is culturally humble is focused on prioritizing relationships over other outcomes—academic goals, finishing a project, time constraints, or preconceived ideas of community work. If this is made explicitly clear as a goal for students, they can be better placed for success. The focus on relationships should also be visible in student assessments. For instance, rather than focusing solely on a project outcome, a more complete assessment may also consider community partner evaluations, time spent on the project, and student reflections on the work.

Luckily, much has been written about relationship development in community engagement (Pompa, 2002; Stoecker & Tryon, 2009), and see Chapters 6 and 9 in this book. Focusing on students' understanding and development of their relationship skills will enhance their cultural humility.

Self-Development

If you have followed the progression of this chapter, your students should be comfortable with active listening and should have a better understanding of themselves, some skills to interact with curiosity and without judgment, and a focus on relationships. There are additional skills and attributes that can support the development of cultural humility in students (Trainings and other activities and strategies to develop cultural humility, n.d.):

- **Patience:** Work in communities takes time. Getting to know others takes time. This is often at odds with academic traditions and culture, which tend to value and reward speed and efficiency. Model the importance of patience for your students and be realistic with their expectations to help them cultivate their own patience.
- **Assume complexity:** Culture is complex and multifaceted. Even what may seem like straightforward behaviors or customs can have deeper and more complex meanings.
- **Flexibility:** We are writing this while entering the third year of the COVID-19 pandemic. While hopefully you are reading it in a packed coffeehouse, without a mask in sight, this pandemic has taught us that flexibility is mandatory, not optional. As CEPs, we have already learned this, but it has become a whole new ballgame. Stress that flexibility and change are necessary and will be part of your students' work in communities.
- **Humor:** A sense of humor, appropriately used, can go a long way! This helps alleviate tension in situations, build trust, and forge connections.
- **Comfort with the unknown:** Cultural humility is about acknowledging that no one has all the answers and knowledge—and that is OK! In academic training, students are often asked to learn how to be and see themselves as experts, which can be antithetical to cultural humility training. Encourage students to be comfortable in situations where they are not the experts.
- **Ambiguity/uncertainty tolerance:** When working in communities, there will likely be more uncertain and ambiguous situations than in traditional academic work. This can be uncomfortable for students, who may be used to educational models that are more straightforward, simple, and clear. Ambiguity tolerance is a huge learning goal for community-engaged work generally and cultural humility training in particular.
- **Empathy:** Last, empathy, or the ability to acknowledge, allow space for, and build connections to another person's feelings and experiences, is a primary goal of cultural humility (Brown, 2019). This differs significantly from sympathy, or feeling sorry for another's feelings or situation. In CE, a student's initial response to a challenging situation might be sympathy. This response is disconnect-

ing, as sympathy distances us from the situation at hand. Sympathy says, "I feel pity for you," which inherently means that I am in a better situation. Empathy says, "I am trying to understand this from your perspective." Empathy helps level the power dynamics and create space for connection, while sympathy indicates power over and can be disconnecting. Please note that empathy is not saying that I explicitly understand exactly what you are going through but rather that I am trying to understand what you are feeling and what it would be like to be in your shoes.

As we stress throughout this book, cultural humility is a crucial piece of successful CE. Both our communities and our students would be better served if we focused more on humility and less on competence. Cultural humility creates opportunities for connection, collaboration, and impact. It is not a hard concept to grasp, but it requires practice to develop, instead of falling back on previously conceived notions of one's role in any situation. Read the sidebar interview with a student named Daniel Rodriguez for his experience with learning to be humble.

Re: Self-Awareness, Humility, and Empathy: Interview with Student from UC San Diego

Daniel Rodriguez, a former leader in the Border Immersion Program at the Mulvaney Center of the University of California San Diego, spent three years taking students to the border and hearing stories from families about deportation and family separation. In a phone call, Daniel described how his own experience as an undergrad in the program had helped him in "learning how to be humble" as well as grateful. As he related, "Even though I am of Latino descent, I have the privilege of being a U.S. citizen, and all of us would be traveling back across the border at night, while these people cannot." He continued, "You can have orientations and small groups about being introduced to someone else's reality, but you can't be totally prepared." In those orientations, he told students to be aware of that and to do their best at listening instead of talking, and he asked them, in their listening to the stories, to try to recognize and see themselves in someone else's reality—and thus "see themselves as a stakeholder" (phone interview, March 14, 2022).

Intellectual Humility

Cultural humility has been discussed in CE literature for a number of years (Floyd, 2013). Intellectual humility is newer to the discussion and guides one's interpersonal behavior. The Templeton Foundation gives the following information about intellectual humility:

> Intellectual humility is a mindset that guides our intellectual conduct. In particular, it involves recognizing and owning our intellectual limitations in the service of pursuing deeper knowledge, truth, and understanding. Such a mindset appears to be valuable in many domains of life—from education to interreligious dialogue to public discourse. It promises to help us avoid headstrong decisions and erroneous opinions, and allows us to engage more constructively with our fellow citizens. (John Templeton Foundation, n.d.)

Intellectual humility recognizes that each person has their own limited knowledge, yet every person comes with their own valuable knowledge. This dovetails well with a core component of CE: that all of us have unique and worthwhile wisdom and expertise (Strand et al., 2003).

Let us look again at our example of the university student volunteering with youth at a community center. The university student is more advanced in her academic education than the youth. This could lead to the student coming into the space feeling intellectually superior. Indeed, she has learned a lot at her university and is studying hard for a goal. An intellectually humble approach means that she would stay curious and open to learning from and with the youth while also being unconcerned with intellectual domination or the need to make intellectual comparisons. The student would be eager to learn from the youth she is working with; she may think about questions regarding what they know and what their life experience has been. How might their knowledge contradict and add to what the student knows? Intellectual humility can support the development of a trust relationship and help reduce the power differential between the youth and the student, helping communities become more receptive to the academic knowledge students are eager to share.

The Importance of Intellectual Humility in Community-Engaged Work

Although intellectual humility might be a newer topic in the CE world, practitioners will clearly see its value and often integrate it in their practice, even without specifically naming it. We have discussed the problems with traditional unidirectional academic CE, and intellectual humility helps us name some of these challenges. These models are predicated on the belief that university work is inherently valuable, is always wanted by communities, and has the answers and knowledge that communities lack. Older ways of thinking about CE are continuing to be challenged and updated, through scholars such as in Mitchell's (2008) critical service-learning model and Stoecker's (2016) liberating service-learning model. Mitchell's model prioritizes social change in the broader community, centering community voice and systemic change. Stoecker's model prioritizes community outcomes and recommends focusing first on community priorities and building CE experiences from there, knowing students will still learn, and more authentically, from this perspective.

However, the harm that has been done is evident in many community-university relationships. Kathy Cramer outlines some of these in her book *The Politics of Resentment: Rural Consciousness in Wisconsin and the Rise of Scott Walker* (2016). Cramer describes how rural Wisconsinites feel that the university is not there for them. Their children are not really wanted as students, it is too expensive for those in rural areas to attend, and the university is, overall, felt to be disconnected from the rest of the state. What is more, she notes that academics see themselves as intellectually superior to "ignorant" people in rural areas:

> These perceptions of distance [between UW–Madison and rural places] are very much about resources and economics, but they are about so much more: respect, acknowledgment, and understanding. All of these things together—not just resources—constitute people's perceptions of their relationship to power. . . . Through the conversations, I heard about interactions with the rare UW—Madison employees who traveled out to do work in rural parts of the state. The issue people raised with me in these conversations was not that UW—Madison ignored their communities but that it ignored the knowledge and norms of the people living in their communities. (p. 123)

One of her participants described his interaction with university researchers in a lake where he fishes:

> I went looking along and they, had, there were bass spawning and there was a little peg in the ground with a little red flag with a number on it. I seen these all over the lake. Well, they were there one day when I was fishing and I said, "what's with the red flags?" and [they] said, "Oh we're trying to determine if bass spawn in the same place

every year." And I said, "well if you'd have asked anybody who lives up here they could've tell ya 'yes' and just save yourselves a whole bunch of trouble." They don't want anything to do with ya. They think they're smarter than ya. Got that book learning. People go to college, they come out dumber than they went in. They got the books there, those books, it's not like the experience. (p. 126)

Cramer's work clearly outlines the importance of intellectual humility in community engagement. Perceptions of academics as elitist, aloof, and ignorant of local knowledge exist in many spaces outside the academy. People believe that university folks look down on nonacademics. Even when CEPs and students work in humble ways in community, these perceptions may precede their work. If the university has been doing CE for any length of time, community members may have already had negative interactions with university constituents. Considering that our brains are wired to pay attention to negative interactions and that negative interactions outweigh positive interactions (Gottman, 2008), this history could mean that those doing CE are often starting their community relationships with a deficit, rather than with a fresh slate.

Is there merit behind these beliefs? There is some evidence that some academics do think of nonacademics as ignorant (e.g., Besley & Tanner, 2011; Cook et al., 2004). A 2016 study (Simis et al., 2016) examined the attitudes of scientists toward the public and found that over 50 percent of respondents, who were tenured and tenure-track professors at a university, conceptualized the public as nonscientific, and some specifically felt negatively toward the public. One participant shared that the public are "well-meaning people who think that they are informed, but are not really all that informed on matters of science and philosophy" (p. 407). Respondents had a range of negative feelings about the public. Some professors thought the public cared only about subjects related to them and that people are inherently narrow minded. One participant stated that the public is "a broad spectrum of individuals with diverse interests, expertise and experience, generally rather unaware, indifferent or sometimes recalcitrant to the importance of science in society" (p. 407). Participants often had strong emotions when conceptualizing the public, including arrogance, frustration, and hostility. One respondent stated simply, "Most people are idiots" (p. 407).

Scientists who felt most antagonistic toward the public were also more likely to adhere to the information deficit model, which states that any lack of support for science or uptake of scientific recommendations is due to a lack of knowledge of science (Simis et al., 2016). According to this model, simply providing information to people will cause them to change their minds. The deficit model does not have strong support (e.g., Brossard & Nisbet,

2007), as there are many other factors affecting one's attitudes and beliefs. However, one can see how an intellectually humble approach is necessary for quality community-engaged work—and that it may be at odds with both traditional academic approaches and the views and beliefs of some academics. Intellectual humility allows academics to enter community spaces with a mindset that says the following:

- I am open to learning.
- I may be wrong about what I think I know.
- It is OK to change my views based on new information.
- It is OK to be uncertain about things.
- Everyone has something to teach me.

People who are high in intellectual humility are open, curious, tolerant of ambiguity, not dogmatic, nonjudgmental, and tolerant of people changing their viewpoints (Leary et al., 2017).

So, if intellectual humility is as important as cultural humility, how can we cultivate it in our students?

Cultivating Intellectual Humility

Understand the Difference between Shame and Guilt

Understanding the difference between shame and guilt is a hugely powerful place to start. The work of social work professor Brené Brown is fantastic for understanding shame, guilt, and how to differentiate between the two. In her words, "Shame is a focus on the self; guilt is a focus on the behavior" (Brown, 2019). Feelings of shame tell you that *you* are bad and that you as a person are wrong. Guilt, on the other hand, separates the worthiness of the person from the behavior. Feelings of guilt indicate to you that you *did something* bad. When you do something bad, you can be held accountable for it, try to rectify your mistakes, and work to improve next time. When you are the bad thing, there is no such path forward. Shame leads to disconnection from others, the opposite of the feeling of belonging.

On the other hand, when we refuse to shame, we can see the inherent worthiness of each person and that no action could make them less worthy as a person. As famous lawyer and human rights advocate Bryan Stevenson said, "Each of us is more than the worst thing we've ever done" (Stevenson, 2014, p. 17). Therefore, every person has inherent value and is worthy of belonging. This mindset can help us move through disagreements, mistakes, and misunderstandings with care, connection, and belonging. If your students understand this, they can feel more comfortable with humility and the process of making mistakes and accountability. Making a mistake will not mean disconnection and a lack of belonging but is instead expected throughout the learning process.

Create Comfort with Being Wrong and Failure

Students often come to the university for the sake of learning and becoming experts in their own right. The work of professors is an example; peer-reviewed publications prefer to publish positive findings and results, not experiments and studies that failed or did not find anything of significance (although failure is an established part of the scientific method and learning). In fact, many universities ask that their students feel confident in what they are learning. For instance, at our institution, students are asked to be intellectually confident:

> Intellectual confidence—Badgers fearlessly sift and winnow until we achieve intellectual confidence. At our core, we're learners and teachers. We develop competence, depth, and expertise in a field of study; we integrate ideas and synthesize knowledge across multiple contexts; and we exercise critical thinking and effective communication. (Wisconsin Experience, n.d.-a)

This can be interpreted as needing to have the right information and be the expert in an intellectual situation. While there is value in intellectual confidence, it must also be paired with intellectual humility—and feeling comfortable being wrong and making mistakes. This is where learning and growth occur. If we can communicate to our students that they can have both intellectual confidence and humility, they will be better prepared for success in the community. Indeed, there is nothing wrong with being wrong, except insisting that you are not. Being wrong gives you the opportunity to learn and grow. As you know better, you do better! Encouraging students to be comfortable with failing may be a new endeavor for them, but it will be a big step toward intellectual humility.

Focus on a Growth Mindset

This foundation can be enhanced by encouraging students to focus on keeping a growth mindset. A growth mindset believes that skills and abilities can be improved through effort, rather than being set in stone (Dweck, 2006). A student who has a growth mindset believes they can improve their own skills and will be more resilient through mistakes, failures, and setbacks. A mistake, problem, or setback is not a tragedy but rather an opportunity to grow and improve. This mindset can support students through challenging situations and help them even if they struggle.

Remember That We Are All Ignorant

There can be immense pressure to feel like we have to be the expert in every situation, particularly in university settings that take pride in their knowledge production. In reality, we are all ignorant on different topics and in many situations. Normalizing the fact that we cannot be experts in every situation is really helpful for students and can take some pressure off them, as well.

Seek Out Multiple Experts and Cultivate Respect for Other Views

Who are you bringing into your classroom? Are you bringing in guests and readings with different views and different areas of expertise? Encouraging your students to listen to and seek out people with different expertise—and different kinds of expertise—can be really helpful. This can encourage students to keep an open mind, feel comfortable with some ambiguity, and respect different forms of knowledge. Even when students are listening to those with whom they disagree, maintaining intellectual humility can support them in engaging respectfully across difference.

It may also be helpful to discuss how things look different depending on where you are coming from. Our brains process information differently, have implicit biases, and view the world through the lenses of our experiences (Resnick, 2019). We also often have flawed understandings of our own expertise, which is illustrated in the Dunning-Kruger effect: people of low ability in a skill often overestimate their ability, believing themselves to be of high ability (Kruger & Dunning, 1999). On the other hand, people with high ability often underestimate their ability.

Concluding Thoughts

Cultural and intellectual humility are key pieces of successful student preparation and CE. Students may be going to many different contexts, interacting across identities, and collaborating across difference. Humility, characterized by being nonjudgmental, curious, and open, can set students up for positive community interactions. Students can be supported in developing cultural humility by focusing on learning about themselves, developing listening skills, practicing mindfulness, and continuing their own self-development. Intellectual humility can be cultivated by learning how to be wrong, focusing on a growth mindset, remembering that everyone lacks knowledge in some areas, and seeking out multiple experts. Being gentle with yourself and others, while not always the quality fostered foremost in universities, makes this content easier to digest and practice.

Part III

Additional Skills, Contexts, and Considerations

8

Building a Critical Classroom

In this chapter, we outline the need for creating a critical classroom, what that looks like in practice, CEP strategies for developing that classroom, and how to troubleshoot potential challenges. A critical classroom foregrounds justice, supports student growth and development, and creates space for liberatory frameworks.

What Is a Critical Classroom?

Critical pedagogy is instruction that "rejects oppression, combats injustice, gives voice to marginalized people, fights the maintaining of the status quo; [it] is achieved through a reflective search for wholeness" (Milner, 2003, p. 199). A classroom that is ready to do CE is a solid community. Students feel like they belong, are supported, and are cared about. They care for each other. They know they are cared for by their instructor. Students feel like they can be as vulnerable and authentic as they would like to be. They feel like they can make mistakes and be held accountable for their mistakes. They value and respect each other above all things. They know they are learning from the community and have a deep responsibility to be useful in community settings. They know to invite participation and teaching and learning from others, but they do not demand or rely on it. People feel safe to share from their lived experiences. They are eager to question assumptions. They embrace difference and find community in multitudes, not hegemony. We list the characteristics of a critical classroom here.

Interrogation

A critical classroom supports the interrogation of assumptions, common practices, and preexisting beliefs of the entire learning community. What actions, patterns, and norms are named and unnamed? What is the status quo? The word "critical" is based on "critique." What facets of the course topic, the university, and one's experiences are students critiquing? Milner (2007) provides an excellent list of questions to support interrogation in the classroom. Some examples include the following:

- What is my racial and cultural heritage? How do I know?
- In what ways do my racial and cultural backgrounds influence how I experience the world, what I emphasize in my research, and how I evaluate and interpret others and their experiences? How do I know?
- How do I negotiate and balance my racial and cultural selves in society and in my research? How do I know?
- What do I believe about race and culture in society and education, and how do I attend to my own convictions and beliefs about race and culture in my research? Why? How do I know?
- What is the historical landscape of my racial and cultural identity and heritage? How do I know?
- What are and have been the contextual nuances and realities that help shape my racial and cultural ways of knowing, both past and present? How do I know?
- What racialized and cultural experiences have shaped my research decisions, practices, approaches, epistemologies, and agendas? (p. 395)

Interrogation also comes with acknowledgment. This includes acknowledging the history of your campus, including its community engagement, the experience for students with marginalized identities, and the relationship of the university and the community they are working with. What is this history? How is it reverberating into the present? Are there amends that need to be made? Who is accountable? What accountability does the classroom need to take?

A critical classroom also interrogates traditional conceptualizations of CE that focus on individual action along with the individualization of oppression. In other words, CE has often focused on individual actions, rather than interrogating structural causes and systems that cause inequity and societal problems. Critical classrooms locate individuals within systems to build a more comprehensive picture and understanding of people and issues. They also support students in focusing on structural solutions to structural issues, rather than focusing on individual-level solutions and placing the blame for issues at the feet of those affected.

For example, students in a critical classroom working with individuals who are unhoused will examine their preexisting beliefs about homelessness, learn about structural issues and solutions around homelessness, better understand the intersection of other issues and homelessness (such as mental health, the economy, and transportation), learn from the lived experiences of those who are unhoused, and focus on meaningful solutions to create equitable housing. They may also consider the role their university has played in creating unaffordable housing markets, as well as discuss the experiences of unhoused students on campus and the circumstances that lead to homelessness in the student body. A critical classroom will think about both how their individual actions can support justice and how they can support greater justice and accountability in the broader systems that impact housing.

Dr. Ruth Kassel's essay from Siena College's Center for Academic Community Engagement describes how students in the community development certificate program build toward more critical understandings of the community that better center the experiences and perspectives of communities.

Ethnographic Sensibilities in Community-Engaged Learning

Dr. Ruth Kassel

"Why don't they just go to the City Rescue Mission?" said James, a service leader taking Higher Ed and Community Development, a class that students in the community development certificate program take during their sophomore year. In this class, students practice elements of the ethnographic process to prepare to engage communities and reflect on privilege and personal motivations for community service. James, for example, was talking about individuals facing homelessness who often loiter at a local bus stop. His question might prompt us to think that James is a student with high privilege, but the reality is more complex. He identifies as Black from an inner-city background and has been surrounded by chronic homelessness in his daily reality. This quote, like many others that I hear from my students, becomes the locus of learning in this class, a starting point for the teaching of ethnographic sensibilities—what I refer to as moments of "justing." Often, when we use "just" or words like it, we ignore moments of cognitive dissonance, avoid personal reflection, and silence marginalized voices and authentic connections with people who identify differently from us.

We are often asked how we know students are prepared to participate in community work. We create survey instruments, develop orientations and workshops introducing students to concepts, and send them out into the world. In my opinion, these steps often fall short and, when done poorly, reinforce stereotypes of poverty and reaffirm positions of privilege. How can we do better? What follows is a short summary of three lessons in "justing" that I use to help my students think ethnographically about communities and the issues they face, which, in turn, can create a more thoughtful and culturally humble service leader.

Lesson 1: "Justing" Flattens the Community Issue and Community Members

I asked James to rephrase his question as, "I wonder why they don't go to the City Rescue Mission?" When James moved from a "just" to an "I wonder" statement, he made room for unanticipated narratives and motivations of the people he was interested in studying. He took time, through field observations, to notice new things about the City Rescue Mission and the people who often loitered just outside. He took some time to chat with people at the bus stop and found that they were happy to share their stories. He learned that the Rescue Mission is highly evangelical and that there is often violence in the shelter. He also discovered, through interviews with nonprofit leaders, that the community sees the organization as a barrier to development. The Rescue Mission continues to expand its number of beds (and thereby state funding for the institution) without offering wraparound services that would give individuals facing homelessness something to do during the day. For that reason, they spend their time at bus stops and in front of businesses in the surrounding neighborhoods. In the end, he learned that behaviors and identities are complex and that the tendency to simplify community issues related to poverty can be detrimental to development. In class, I use experiential activities as a launching point for identifying and processing the dissonance that is often articulated as "why don't they just . . ." Some semesters this is done through a pre-semester travel component to rural Appalachia or participation in a local service day. When getting off campus is not possible, we use culture-clash simulations like BaFa' BaFa' (a face-to-face learning simulation. It is intended to improve participants' cultural competency by demonstrating culture's impact on behavior). This starting point helps students start to recognize what a moment of dissonance feels like and how to engage in new modes of inquiry.

Lesson 2: "Justing" Creates Opportunities to Challenge Identity and Privilege

Even while "justing" often simplifies a complex issue, it can also challenge aspects of the researcher's own identity. Ethnography is highly reflexive and does not shy away from recognizing the impact of researcher identity on the community and the research products. The presence of loiterers and panhandlers on corners often elicits strong reactions that urge us to examine the elements of our identity that block us from fully engaging marginalized communities. James, for example, examined how his family needed social service systems growing up and reflected on how that shaped his approach to community development and his reaction to those who refuse services when they are available. Most students in this class are also in community engagement programs and clubs. As they start to look at the communities they serve in new ways, the class provides a forum for them to challenge words like "normal," "natural," and "objective." We process these moments as a way to understand how we bring our own identities into research—from the way we formulate questions to the ways we describe injustice and even the things that we notice in the first place. To cultivate insight, the class uses double-entry journals where students use the left page to write field notes and the right side to process their reactions and thoughts. This often leads to authentic (and sometimes difficult) class conversations on how identities such as race and gender put people in the same room but for very different reasons.

Lesson 3: "Justing" Creates a False Division between the Researcher and the Community

Finally, "justing" creates distance between the researcher and the community and can be a tool to make moral assumptions about the actions of an individual or community. Ethnographers, in contrast to more traditional styles of research, are expected to live within the community and study it from the inside out. While authentic and long-term fieldwork is not an expectation in the Higher Ed and Community Development class, we do practice deep listening and seek out an "emic" perspective, in which the community in question controls the narrative. During class we use modified Quaker discussions and process our discomfort with this type of listening. We process what it means to be with a community as a member as well as a researcher and discuss how to suspend judgment in order to get to thick and contextualized analyses. We read excerpts from ethnographies over the course of the semester and discuss the ethics of researchers bringing subjects to court dates, and we process provocative pieces like "Letter from a Crackhouse," a critical ethnography that describes the culture of a New York City crack house as a way to humanize individuals facing addiction and advocate for just policies. We have honest conversations about what it takes to suspend judgment and understand human realities from the margins as they are and not how we want them to be. I find that not all students are successful in this third lesson but all of them start to understand why this emic perspective is important.

Once my students learn to recognize moments of dissonance and take an "I wonder" stance, check their privilege and understand how they bring elements of their identity to the research, and see things for what they are rather than what they want them to be, they bring these skills to new situations. After the semester ends, many students in this class start to bring an ethnographic approach to their service sites; they teach classmates these new ways of approaching community, and others bring this approach to their capstones. Some have even started experimenting with autoethnography as they engage in student teaching, nursing practicums, and social work field hours. Ethnography has become a language that connects us because when we engage in ethnographic thinking, we are transformed and see the world in new ways.

Multicultural Identity

Historically, multicultural classrooms have often been described as classrooms where everyone can blend together, similar to the melting pot idea of the United States, where people of many different identities can combine into a more homogenous identity (e.g., Dantley, 2002). Our goal with the multicultural classroom is rather that students have the opportunity to bring whatever part of their identity they are comfortable with to the classroom, with attention paid to the space created for minoritized identities in particular, since they have historically not been welcome in educational spaces (e.g., Peters-Davis & Shultz, 2015; Sleeter & Carmona, 2017).

Creating a multicultural classroom also means there is awareness of oppression and identity and how these topics affect the classroom and those in the classroom. Students are not expected to speak for their identities, as too often occurs when instructors try to include students with minoritized experiences in conversations. Students have the chance to participate and share their own experiences, thoughts, and ideas, which are grounded in their identities, as they feel comfortable, and they know that this sharing will be met with respect, care, and empathy.

Interdependence

Hardiman et al. (1997) argue that "social justice involves social actors who have a sense of their own agency as well as a sense of social responsibility toward and with others and the society as a whole" (p. 3). In the critical classroom, students feel accountable not only to their instructor but also to their fellow learners and their community partners. Have you ever been in a classroom where there was such a deep sense of community that it felt magical? I (Haley) remember teaching a first-year communications course as a young graduate student. Over the course of the semester, I watched as a group of intimidated, uncertain first-year students came together as a community unit. They felt free to discuss, argue, laugh, and learn in a comfortable, enjoyable, boundary-pushing space. The success of one student was the success of every student, and everyone worked to make sure their fellow classmates did well. Developing such a strong sense of community and collective care is a goal of social justice work and should be a goal of our work as CEPs.

We have experienced the same magical phenomenon in a graduate-level course on CES. Students felt this was the first place or one of only a few places on campus where they truly felt they belonged. Belonging is one of the most important human needs (Brown, 2007). Students who feel as though they belong will feel more comfortable taking risks, making mistakes, failing, and persisting anyway. Venkatesh et al. (2021, p. 1162) described useful outcomes and implementation tools for building community in the classroom, including the following:

- Developing shared communication tools
- Identity-based check-ins
- Diverse modes for student participation
- Opportunities to share feedback anonymously

One of the most challenging things about CE for students is the unpredictability of community interactions (e.g., Cahuas & Levkoe, 2017; Soukup, 1999; Witmer et al., 2009). Projects change, people drop in and drop out of community work, priorities shift, and the outcome rarely looks like what was initially pursued. For students without this educational experience, this can feel stressful and unsafe. Creating an interdependent community focusing on belonging, accountability, and growth gives students what they need to weather the uncertainty. There can be a focus on getting it right, rather than knowing everything and perfection. As Bettez (2011) notes, "We can define community as continually shifting groups of people that dialogue with, actively listen to, and support each other, through reciprocal responsibility and accountability, regarding a common interest or concern. Community in this sense is both a process and a goal" (p. 10).

This relates directly to the concept of liberation—that the liberation of every person matters to everyone else and that our liberation is bound with everyone else's, as Lilla Watson has articulated (Aboriginal activists group, Queensland, 1970s). This sense of interdependence can support students in developing a nuanced, advanced understanding of what CE is and why we do it so students can engage respectfully, ensuring "that the educational institution is not merely using the community as a social laboratory with human guinea pigs whom students can go out and look at, prod, and snicker at as they 'learn' about social problems in the classroom" (Marullo & Edwards, 2000, p. 908).

Development of Critical Consciousness

Fittingly, a critical classroom supports critical consciousness in students, and as Kim et al. (2013) point out, "there is no clear consensus on how to practice critical pedagogy, three central components must be facilitated in the college classroom: dialogue, critique, and praxis" (p. 157). Critical consciousness is a deep understanding of the world and moving against oppression (Freire, 1970).

A part of this is developing an understanding of the world and viewing it in its entirety. A helpful analogy is put forth by social justice educator Tim Wise (2008). He describes understanding the present-day context as a new CEO might do when coming into a company. The CEO would ask for a full accounting of the organization: assets, income streams, production, and debts. It would be unthinkable if the new CEO said:

> It was great to know we have all these assets and some really amazing income coming in, but the next time I ask you to come in and show me that, don't bring me the debt material, all that stuff about what we owe, because, see, I wasn't here when you all ran that up. That was that other guy. That was your last CEO. The debts of those older leaders, those are on them. Have them pay them. I am going to make use of the assets, oh yes. I am going to make use of the income, oh yes. But I am not going to pay the debts because they are not mine. (p. 17)

An honest reckoning of a business or of society means understanding what is going well and what is unjust and knowing they are the responsibility of all of us.

Classrooms and programs that engage in CE are particularly well suited to supporting these components, particularly praxis—the combination of theory and action (Lather, 1986). There are several excellent examples of the critical classroom that can be helpful to draw on (e.g., Kajner et al., 2013; Leeman et al., 2011; Mitchell & Rost-Banik, 2020). Marullo and Edwards (2000) describe the change to a transformational classroom as one that supports self-motivated, interdisciplinary student learning; faculty who are responsive to community needs and have egalitarian relationships with community partners; and an institution that values engagement. In other words, in a critical classroom, students are able to see the world through a variety of lenses, stay awake to the suffering and oppression of the world, and work toward their own liberation and the liberation of others. The tools of interrogation, reflection, interdependence, and multiculturalism will support this development.

How Does Oppression Show Up in the Classroom?

One point in creating a critical classroom is to create a space where everyone is allowed and encouraged to grow, thrive, and change. This means acknowledging what education is, including where it has fallen short. Beginning from this starting place acknowledges reality for what it is, rather than disregarding how oppression has shaped the very educational institutions students are in. While many CEPs agree that a main purpose of education is liberation, the history of education is full of oppression, including many structures and systems that exist today. While it is not the purpose of this text to describe oppression in education, touching on how this may show up in your classroom can give you practices for moving toward liberation.

White Supremacy

White supremacy is insidious, with deep roots in the educational system. Educational opportunities have been routinely denied to people of color, and curriculums have been designed to promote and normalize whiteness and white ideals, such as the policy of removing Indigenous children from their homes to send them to U.S. boarding schools (e.g., Jacobs, 2009). A huge amount of data supports the claim of unequal treatment of children, youth, and young adults of color in the education system from preschool through higher education (e.g., DeCuir & Dixson, 2004; Leonardo, 2013). This discrepancy in treatment can be ascribed to both individual racism (such as teacher biases, often unconscious, that result in disproportionate punishment of BIPOC students) and systemic racism (such as the drastically different resources available in schools depending on income level and how the schools are funded).

To better understand white supremacy and racism, critical race theory employs the following six central tenets:

> (a) racism is endemic to American culture; (b) rejection of dominant narratives, processes, or systems that claim race neutrality, colorblindness, and meritocracy; (c) racism has deeply rooted origins that attribute White people with dominant status and non-White people with subordinate status; (d) the voices and lived experiences of people of color are legitimate and used to generate oppositional discourses; (e) recognition of interest convergence, which describes the conditions by which racial justice will be accommodated in a white power structure; and (f) racism's eradication is tied to eliminating all forms of oppression. (Haynes, 2017, p. 88)

Jones and Okun (2001) outline how white supremacy infiltrates spaces, including educational spaces. They describe characteristics of white supremacy culture, including perfectionism, a sense of urgency, defensiveness, quantity over quality, worship of the written word, only one right way, paternalism, either/or thinking, power hoarding, fear of open conflict, individualism, I'm the only one, progress is bigger, objectivity, and a right to comfort. With this history informing the present day, white supremacy is a huge part of educational spaces. Building a critical classroom creates a container for discussions of race and white supremacy so students can understand how they are affected by white supremacy culture. In the following, we outline some examples of how white supremacy might show up in the CE classroom.

White supremacy culture privileges individualism and self-reliance. When students are working in community settings, they most likely will rely on others as they are doing their own work and will focus on the outcomes of the group rather than their own individual outcomes. This is quite different from many other educational settings and could cause student anxiety, confrontations with community partners, and frustration with community work. Challenging the standard of individualism can help students disentangle white supremacy values from their work and support meaningful processes over outcomes.

Systemic racism means that different schools are funded very unequally, which has a huge impact on student outcomes. Students in a CBL course may be working with youth at an underfunded school. This lack of resources greatly affects students' achievement at that school. When university students work with these youth, having that background information can support them in understanding where students are coming from and knowing that potential underperformance is related to lack of resources rather than deficiencies in the youth themselves. University students can act with greater compassion, empathy, and kindness.

Paternalism is another characteristic that can show up in community-engaged classrooms at multiple levels. Instructors may feel paternalistic toward students, and students may want to treat community members in a paternalistic way. Creating a learning community where everyone is invited in as equals can combat paternalism.

Injustice in the Classroom

Oppression and injustice, of course, are not limited to race. Just as we described in Chapter 6, it is not only essential that students understand oppression around identities, but it is equally important that educators understand which identities have been oppressed or privileged. How is your class comfortable and supportive for all students? What learning do you have to do? Consider some of the following topics in your discussion with students:

- Race
- Gender
- Ethnicity
- Sexual orientation
- Disability status
- Immigration status
- Income level
- Family education level
- Language proficiency/comfort
- Cultural background
- Religion

This is not, of course, an exhaustive list. However, it is crucial to be thoughtful about how oppression has made its way into your classroom at both individual and systemic levels. Consider a recent misstep by our university—scheduling the first day of classes to coincide with Rosh Hashanah yet closing the university during Christmas. Keeping the goals of anti-racism and anti-oppression at the forefront of your classroom will support the creation of a nourishing environment. In the next section, we discuss strategies for doing that.

Instructional Strategies for Creating a Critical Classroom

Meeting Students Where They Are

This may be one of the most challenging parts of working with students in CE contexts. First, it is almost inevitable that there will be cultural differences between you as an educator and your students, even as simple as the age gap between you. After all, do you and your students have the same taste in music or use the same slang? Students come into college with a wide variety of backgrounds, identities, and experiences. They may be more or less familiar with CE and social justice. They may be deeply oriented toward the charity model of service. They may hold many marginalized or privileged identities. They may have no experience interacting with those who are different from them. While some CE courses address these challenges through pre-course screening regarding familiarity with critical CE and social justice, that is neither feasible nor advisable for many courses and programs. Instead, we must meet students where they are and try to minimize the (usually unintentional) harm that students can cause each other and their community partners while creating an environment where students can grow.

Some strategies for doing that successfully follow here.

Clarify the Approach to CE Early and Often

One of the most helpful things instructors can do is clarify what CE is, what the semester or program will look like, and what this approach entails. Critical CE with a focus on student preparation might be totally new to students or very different from how they have approached this work in the past. Defining CE and expectations will guide students to more updated understandings and away from charity mentalities. This will also help them connect the dots between the preparatory work they are doing and the CE they will be doing. Social justice and CE cannot be disentangled, as they are two pieces of a larger whole, and CE is meaningless without the larger goal of social change. If this is delineated at the beginning of the CE experience, students can better understand what is expected of them, why this preparatory work is important, and how it relates to the CE work they do. Those students coming in with a deep well of experience in charity or savior models will have a chance to rethink their approach and consider why other approaches are more appropriate. This will also clarify for students what CE is:

- Collaborative among all involved
- An opportunity for all to learn from each other

- Co-created by university and community constituents
- Rooted in social justice
- Involving real people and situations that necessitate respect and appropriate seriousness

It will also reveal what CE is not:

- A chance for academics to help community members
- A unidirectional approach in which "benefits" only go to community members
- Focused solely on what the university needs
- A chance for students to practice on people in the real world

Front-Load Self-Reflective Work

Early in the semester, students can be expected to do work around understanding themselves, their identities, and how they move through the world. This can often be achieved through individual reflection assignments and other activities (see the activities in Appendix A). This will not only help you understand who is in your class and their experiences, but it will give students a chance to understand how their own identities will impact their time in class and in the community. One of the most important goals of preparation work is to increase self-awareness in students. Providing ample reflection opportunities with guided questions is crucial. Even for students who are just beginning their learning journeys around social justice, self-reflection can support them in going inward—examining themselves and their knowledge, biases, assumptions, and preconceived ideas. This can also foster a tradition of self-reflection that will support students in thinking critically before speaking, noticing their own feelings and reactions, and developing a habit of contemplation when they feel challenged. Some potential reflection questions that could help understand where students are coming from include the following:

- Why did you take this course?
- What experience (if any) do you have with community engagement?
- What does community engagement mean to you?
- What do you hope to learn in this course?

Share Useful Resources to Help Students Engage in the Classroom

Providing seminal works to students early in the semester can be helpful. This ensures that students can have a common ground, as well as topic definitions. While this may be review for some students, it can help bring everyone toward a common understanding. Some other resources to consider include *The Unheard Voices*, Tania Mitchell's work, Ivan Illich's essay, Ernesto Sirolli's TED Talk, and adrienne maree brown's work. Also see other recommended readings in Appendix B.

Additionally, a handout that describes the language and terms to use in the course may be helpful. This can include differentiating between outdated terms that students may see in texts but that are inappropriate for use in class discussion (e.g., negro), preferred terms for racial and ethnic groups (e.g., Black/African American, Latinx, people of color), and definitions of different groups and terms. For students who are newer to discussions of identity, this resource can help them feel more comfortable in their language use while reducing avoidable mistakes.

Recognize That Everyone Is Learning, but Accountability Is Crucial

Block (2008) argues, "Commitment and accountability are forever paired, for they do not exist without each other. Accountability is the willingness to care for the well-being of the whole; commitment is the willingness to make a promise with no expectation in return" (p. 71). In critical classrooms, each person is positioned as the educator and the learner. We are asked to have patience for each other, care for each other, and recognize that this comes with deep accountability. It is expected that students will make mistakes, fail, and inevitably harm others, regardless of how hard you work to avoid this outcome. It is also expected that students will listen and understand when they harm someone, not question the harm that has occurred, and will make amends for the harm. This may occur through an apology, a private discussion, or a larger classroom discussion. Learning is not an excuse to harm others.

Classroom Commitments

Instructors can share resources about accountability and create an environment where accountability is the norm. For instance, creating classroom common commitments or guidelines that are co-created and agreed upon by all students can support accountability practices. As an example, the American Association of University Women (n.d.) recommends these guidelines:

1. Listen actively—respect others when they are talking. [This may also be framed as "listen to understand, not to respond."]

2. Speak from your own experience instead of generalizing ("I" instead of "they," "we," and "you").
3. Do not be afraid to respectfully challenge one another by asking questions, but refrain from personal attacks—focus on ideas.
4. Participate to the fullest of your ability—community growth depends on the inclusion of every individual voice.
5. Instead of invalidating somebody else's story with your own spin on her or his experience, share your own story and experience.
6. The goal is not to agree—it is to gain a deeper understanding.
7. Be conscious of body language and nonverbal responses: They can be as disrespectful as words.

Creating common commitments or classroom guidelines at the beginning of the semester and revising as needed can support a productive critical classroom. It also gives students both expectations and support as they grow and learn. These guidelines can also create a blueprint for what to do when harm occurs. For instance, they might include something like the following:

- Apologize if you have harmed someone.
- Speak privately to the person (with the support of the instructor as needed) to learn how you can make amends for the harm you have caused.

Invite Rather Than Demand Sharing

While you can encourage students to share from their experiences, do not lean on students to educate each other involuntarily. Students with marginalized identities are often tasked with educating those with majority identities inside and outside the university. This labor is often asked for without consent, uncompensated, and unvalued. It is more than likely that these students have already been asked to speak for all members of their identity group(s), singled out for a part of their identity publicly, or publicly asked to educate others on topics that are sensitive, painful, and uncomfortable. These students have been othered and viewed with curiosity and exhibitionism, rather than compassion, caring, and the goal of being in community.

For example, I (Haley) have been in spaces where the only Black man has been asked to speak about what police violence is like for Black men. In largely male spaces, I have been asked to share what women think about an issue. I have seen instructors ask BIPOC students to teach others about microaggressions and social identity. Calling students out based on their identities is othering, pejorative, and hurtful. This is a separate issue from creating space for everyone to share. Certainly, some students are eager to speak about their experiences and educate others. However, this can only be done ethically with consent and the desire to share one's story. Without those elements, these exchanges may be extractive, hurtful, and potentially traumatizing.

Indeed, some argue that the academy generally enjoys extracting and fetishizing pain narratives:

> Damage-centered researchers may operate, even benevolently, within a theory of change in which harm must be recorded or proven in order to convince an outside adjudicator that reparations are deserved. These reparations presumably take the form of additional resources, settlements, affirmative actions, and other material, political, and sovereign adjustments. Eve has described this theory of change as both colonial and flawed, because it relies upon Western notions of power as scarce and concentrated, and because it requires disenfranchised communities to position themselves as both singularly defective and powerless to make change (2010). Finally, Eve has observed that "won" reparations rarely become reality, and that in many cases, communities are left with a narrative that tells them that they are broken. . . . Academe's demonstrated fascination with telling and retelling narratives of pain is troubling, both for its voyeurism and for its consumptive implacability. (Tuck & Yang, 2014, p. 227)

In short, the experiences of our students are their own experiences and theirs to share or not. If and when students would like to share, instructors can create environments in which it is safe to do so. It is important to note that while students can refuse to respond to these requests, the power dynamics between students and instructors mean students may feel uncomfortable refusing. Instructors control grades, assignments, and, in some cases, access to professional connections and opportunities. Students may fear jeopardizing their future or their relationship with the instructor if they do not positively respond to requests. One way we have worked through this issue is by hiring student staff to support facilitation of these conversations in classrooms. These students enjoy participating in challenging conversations and are paid for their support in providing education. They can gently redirect instructors and help create supportive environments for students.

Calling In versus Calling Out

Inevitably, things will go wrong. Students will make mistakes, say the wrong thing, and make poor choices, such as committing a microaggression in class. They may also feel afraid to accidentally commit harm. None of this is cause for panic. Hopefully, by creating classroom commitments, guidelines, humility, community, and relationships, your classroom can weather the challenges that will pop up throughout the course and can support student learning in difficult situations. When a student does make a mistake, focusing on calling them into the conversation versus calling them out can support the health of the whole classroom, encourage the student's learning, and encourage accountability (e.g., Bennett, 2020; Woods & Ruscher, 2021). This can also be helpful to include explicitly in your course commitments. Additionally, the suggestions outlined earlier in the book are helpful guidance for students who have committed microaggressions.

What might addressing microaggressions look like in practice? For instance, consider a student who misgenders another student in conversation. Steps to take can include these:

- Gently correcting a student's mistake: "Thank you, John. I also think that what *they* said was insightful."
- Assuming good intentions: "Thank you, John. I believe you meant to say 'they' instead of he."
- Speaking privately with the student to enhance their learning: "John, I wanted to check in about what happened earlier today when you used 'he' pronouns instead of 'they' pronouns when talking about Alex. I wanted to offer a gentle reminder that Alex uses 'they' pronouns. I've misgendered people before, too. One way I better remember pronouns is by looking at students' name tents to double-check before making a comment in class. Is there anything else you need from me to support your learning in this area?"
- If a student may have experienced harm, checking in with them to see if they need additional support: "Alex, I know that John misgendered you today, and I realize that may have felt uncomfortable and painful. I'm sorry that happened in our classroom, and I know John is working to do better. What can I do to support you?"

In addition to these strategies to meet students where they are, we have several other recommendations for the creation of a critical classroom.

Instructor Vulnerability

Another way to support the development of a critical classroom is through measured sharing and vulnerability. What are stories and experiences that you can share about yourself to connect with students and encourage their own vulnerability and authenticity? For instance, can you share about how you have experienced situations through your own social identity lenses? Or describe a mistake you have made and how you made amends? This modeling behavior can both demonstrate to students the kind of authenticity you are looking for and help them feel more comfortable with their own vulnerability. It is important to be careful, in the kind of information you are sharing, to respect the boundaries of appropriate communication for the level of students—consider your position in relation to your students before getting highly personal.

Acknowledge Current Events

Considering that we are now more connected than ever, we are also more connected to current events. On a daily basis, our students (and we ourselves) are confronted with violence, extremism, war, injustice, and brutality occurring close to home and across the world. No longer are foreign wars the stuff of weekly newspapers or faraway radio broadcasts. No longer are a community's murders by police kept quiet within the confines of the local police department. While we can now hold these atrocities to the light of humanity, they are also a part of our daily experiences and all that entails—long-lasting stress, increased anxiety, overwhelming pain, and the feeling that what we do has no meaning.

We do not have all the answers about navigating this tension, as we as humans are still trying (often unsuccessfully) to figure this out collectively. But in the classroom, our advice is simple: Make space. Offer space to discuss difficult events that are dominating the news and your brain space. Create an opportunity for students to process what is going on in the world, and let them sit with their emotions. When an event occurs that is taking up students' emotional lives (and possibly yours as well), let it in.

For instance, being on campus after the 2016 presidential election was a surreal, scary, and vulnerable place. Students came to our office in hysterics, afraid for themselves, their loved ones, and their country as a whole. I (Haley) felt numb, disconnected, and overwhelmed. Rather than pretending that everything was OK, we cried with our students, watched Secretary Clinton's concession speech, and made plenty of space to sit and talk. Attempting to ignore what had happened would be disingenuous and inauthentic, potentially leading to the erosion of trust.

If possible, you may also make connections from what is going on in current events back to the course material. This makes the content less abstract and more real. This also is an opportunity for humanizing—you, your students, and those involved in any social issue. As human rights lawyer Bryan Stevenson says, we must get proximate to those who are suffering if we want real change (Kane, 2020). After all, it is harder to hate close up. You are also giving your students an example of navigating the world after college. What values will they bring with them into the workplace or other educational spaces? How will they show up? What will they demand of their employers, their colleagues, their governments? Staying tuned into the pain of the world is hard and overwhelming. It is far easier (and sometimes necessary) to check out entirely. But ignoring the plights of our world does not make them disappear.

Facilitation

At this point, you likely realize there are significant facilitation duties in developing the critical classroom. Facilitation is a method to guide others in understanding what they may need to change about their behavior or attitudes in relation to themselves, their own work, or their work with others (Marshall & McLean, 1988). Effective facilitation not only promotes productive group functioning but can also support learners in moving toward goals (Harvey et al., 2002). As Harvey et al. describe, "the facilitator's role is concerned with enabling the development of reflective learning by helping to identify learner needs, guide group processes, encourage critical thinking, and assess the achievement of learning goals" (p. 581). Harvey et al. go on to detail characteristics that support effective facilitation, including patience, being empathetic, believing in the worth of people, recognizing the skills and abilities of others, sensitivity, and attending to the whole person. As an educator, your role as facilitator is to make the process of learning, unlearning, and growing easier for your students.

An excellent resource for effective facilitation is adrienne maree brown's *Holding Change: The Way of Emergent Strategy Facilitation and Mediation* (2021, p. 14–19). In Table 8.1, she describes the elements and principles of facilitation.

TABLE 8.1   FACILITATION ELEMENTS

Element	Nature of element	Principle
Fractal	The relationship between small and large	Small is good.
Adaptive	How we change	Change is constant—prepare less and be more present.
Interdependent and decentralized	Who we are and how we share	There is always enough time for the right work.
Nonlinear and iterative	The pace and pathways of change	Never a failure, always a lesson.
Resilient, rooted in transformative justice	How we recover and transform	Move at the speed of trust.
Creating more possibilities	How we move toward life	Be present.

Credit: Adapted from adrienne maree brown. (2021). *Holding change: The way of emergent strategy facilitation and mediation*. AK Press.

Additional principles are listed here:

- Begin by listening.
- Transform yourself to transform the world.
- What we practice is what we are.
- Name what is, make more possible.
- Release perfection, relinquish judgment.
- Create a culture of celebration—pivot towards pleasure.
- Invitation goes further than manipulation.
- Release *your* way to feel *the* way.
- Time can bend. (brown, 2021, p. 14–19)

Each of these has specific facilitation processes attached to it, along with strategies for troubleshooting challenging scenarios. In addition to the earlier points, important facilitation considerations include the following:

- Create a space that is physically inclusive and supports the physical needs of people (e.g., a comfortable space accessible to people with disabilities, breaks as needed, nourishment).
- Attend to what individuals need in any interaction.
- Build flexibility into agendas.
- Let the feelings of participants guide you in determining the next steps.
- Create space where people can show up authentically and know each other.
- Focus on the strengths of individuals.

You may note that these elements and principles map onto many other ideas already discussed in this book. This is a gift and a challenge of this work—it is tangled and interconnected, making it difficult to separate individual strands.

Reflection and Dialogue

Much of what has been discussed in previous chapters can and should be achieved through reflective practices. During self-reflection, students begin to think authentically on past and present experiences of race, oppression, intolerance, and injustice that are inconspicuously embedded within the college classroom as well as outside higher education. Students reflect upon their own development and practices as well as the issues they face in daily life by paying close attention to the process they are going through as part of the course—how they react and what they think, feel, wish they had or had not said, or wish they were able to say (Kim, 2013, p. 154).

For example, as the University of Michigan Program on Intergroup Relations (n.d.) describes, "Through our national leadership and on-campus presence, we are committed to educating students on social justice and intergroup relations, and emphasizing student learning through intergroup dialogue, engaged pedagogies, research, and leadership opportunities both in and out of the classroom. With a focus on the whole student, we work to build opportunities for our students to facilitate, think critically, reflect, build resiliency and lead." This model supports students in learning and working across different identities while promoting productive dialogue. This is an excellent resource for instructors looking to become skilled dialogue facilitators.

The Husky Sport vignette, from a long-standing community-university partnership program housed at the University of Connecticut, depicts the course structure and facilitation style that the instructors use in the early days of the course to cultivate a critical classroom environment and prepare students for engagement in Hartford. I (Cory) am indebted to the program and the many thoughtful leaders and educators who shaped my entry into this work in graduate school, and I admire the brilliance and sincerity this group brings to the task of developing students to be thoughtful partners and learners.

University of Connecticut—Student Training for Husky Sport

Justin Evanovich, Sandeep Dutta, Jamie Morales, Jennifer McGarry, and Kolin Ebron

Overarching Context of Husky Sport

Husky Sport (http://huskysport.uconn.edu) is a campus-community partnership (Parent & Harvey, 2009) that focuses on a ten-block radius in the state capital of Hartford, Connecticut. This neighborhood is representative of the city's overall racial demographics (61 percent Hispanic/Latinx and 37 percent Black). Sustained federal Supplemental Nutrition Assistance Program Education (SNAP-Ed) funding informs community collaborations with one primary public school and four community-based organizations. Husky Sport works to plan, deliver, and evaluate weekly school and out-of-school programs focused on nutrition and physical activity education informed by a sports-based youth development (SBYD) framework (Perkins & Noam, 2007). Collaborative learning is enacted with an average of five hundred youth participants per year along with their families, school staff, and community partners, all dedicated, hardworking, and loving people who continue to navigate the racist, oppressive institutions that largely shape the concentrated poverty that limits access to resources and opportunities in Hartford.

At the University of Connecticut, a PWI, SNAP-Ed funding has allowed Husky Sport leaders to build a diverse and talented staff (faculty, staff, graduate assistants, interns, and undergraduates). Through participating in consistent professional development as a community of practice (Wenger, 1998), Husky Sport staff build relationships and lead collaborations to engage Hartford residents. Service-learning courses are another key aspect of Husky Sport. University students are positioned in supplementary roles to support Husky Sport's funded and trained staff and community organization leaders to create learning and engagement opportunities. In class, critical examinations focus on the importance of relationships, being relevant, and the power of representation while also working within the community to be present, participate in a shared learning process, and have fun together.

Service-Learning Courses—Foundations for Student Orientation and a Critical Classroom Culture

Husky Sport–affiliated courses have become more explicitly aligned with the framework of critical service learning over time. Course content and facilitation emphasize the need to examine power dynamics across pedagogies, practices, and partnerships, with specific attention paid to authentic relationships, social change orientation, and redistribution of power (Mitchell, 2017). While not an exhaustive list, the following are a few critical examinations we have engaged in through service-learning courses:

- What are the power dynamics associated with collaborations between community partners and university students?
- What are the social identities of the community participants and partners, lead class instructors, and enrolled students?
- How do these identities and positionalities impact connectivity, engagement, and learning as part of the service-learning course?
- Who is centered in the learning process within community-based engagement spaces?
- Who benefits? Who is harmed?

In addition to these reflection questions, the following sections unpack the intentional pedagogies and specific practices utilized on the first three days of the advanced Husky Sport service-learning course.

Day One—Relationships

The first image shown to the class is one word on a PowerPoint slide—"Relationships." The importance of relationship building is framed as an ongoing process and skill that can be transferred into all areas of students' lives. Relationships are then highlighted as a priority in the work of Husky Sport. The instructors work through fourteen different prompts asking for students' favorites and rationale related to music, books, television, movies, meals, social media, travel, desired superpowers, past teachers, and past coaches. Students briefly jot down responses and demonstrate active listening as the class shares these with each other.

Instructors emphasize the opportunities available to be intentional in learning about other people and share about themselves in building authentic relationships. The exercise frames relationship building as a means to emphasize strengths instead of deficits while celebrating aspects of culture, identities, and lived experiences rather than engaging in superficial conversations. Day one sets the foundation for how we will value and celebrate ourselves and others across similarities and differences and serves as a model for the ways university students can begin to engage with people as part of their work with Husky Sport. Relationships and the process of relationship building become one key theme and practice that we revisit throughout the semester.

On day one, we focus *solely* on relationships. We do not review the syllabus or class logistics. This session is effective in establishing the foundation for classroom culture, engagement in communities, and relationship building as a life skill. Additionally, every student speaks multiple times, which we have found to be unique, as a majority of students have shared that they often go entire semesters in other courses without speaking as much as their first day here.

Day Two—Intergroup Dialogue Model and Striving for Accuracy

The Program on Intergroup Relations is our model for day two. We introduce intergroup dialogue (IGD) to inform in-class participation and learning. IGD is unpacked with students by highlighting the tenets of IGD courses. The principles of IGD are discussed to establish the foundations of our own critical classroom.

Following that conversation, a closing discussion is facilitated, including time for self-reflections and small group conversations to reiterate the expectations for students' participation in the course. Building on day one, the instructors reemphasize the need to see strengths, celebrate cultures, affirm shared humanity, build relationships, and critically examine our larger social world. Acknowledging how difficult this will be in practice, the class focuses on the concept of accuracy and the process to become more accurate. To close out day two, the following prompts are shared with the class with a request to reflect and examine what is meant by "accuracy" as a means to prepare for day three and the semester ahead:

- How accurate are we in our thoughts and speech about people different from us?
- Do we use wide-sweeping generalizations about people different from us?
- Do people in our lives use wide-sweeping generalizations about people different from them?
- Can we work to be more specific when thinking and discussing people and our society?
- Are we willing to strive toward accuracy, even though we will never actually achieve it?
- How can we work to hold each other accountable as we collectively strive toward accuracy within our class?
- Though it is early in the semester and we know very little about the work of Husky Sport, how do we foresee "accuracy" as an important component for our approach to relationship building and engagement with the community?

Sharing specific components of IGD highlights the important distinctions around engaging in a discussion, a debate, or a dialogue and fosters good classroom culture. Instead of trying to win a debate or waiting for their turn to speak during a discussion, students are encouraged to consider engaging in ways that celebrate active listening and understanding of others' perspectives.

Day Three—Perspective Building to Combat the Savior Mentality and the Myth of Meritocracy

For day three, students are assigned the first reading of the semester. The reading, a selection from Ivan Illich's (1968) "To Hell with Good Intentions," is foundational to the course.

As the class session begins, the instructors share a prompt for student reflection: "Out of 100 percent of possible credit, what percentage of credit do you deserve for where you are in life today?" The introduction emphasizes that "the prompt is a low stress exercise" and "a hypothetical consideration." The instructors affirm that students have many different life stories and that their experiences are to be celebrated. From there, each student reflects on the prompt for sixty seconds, aware that they will be asked to share their response with the class.

Next, the following questions are posed related to youth sport participation, as the course is grounded in SBYD:

- When you were nine, and if you had the access and resources, did you play youth sports?
- If you were able to, since not everyone is, did you sign yourself up?
- Did you pay the registration fee?
- Did you buy the equipment?
- Maybe you played *fútbol*, otherwise known in the United States as soccer. And even if you did not have the opportunity to play *fútbol/soccer* as a kid . . . maybe you still know about those oranges that got cut up in slices and were provided at halftime for the kids. If you played soccer and you ate those oranges at halftime . . . did **you** slice those oranges?

Then we go beyond youth sport, still hitting upon specific ages and perceived levels of control:

- When you were five, did you choose the school that you attended?
- When you were thirteen, did you purchase the clothes you wore?
- If you had a stable place of residency, did you support paying the bills?

The instructors encourage students to "reflect on these questions, continue to look at our class average that says we believe we deserve 63.7 percent (note: example here gives results from one semester; average between 40 and 70 percent across semesters) of the credit for where we are today, and consider referencing these discussions in our written reflection papers." The class will usually do another minute of reflection and ask to share a new percentage. Proactively, the instructors celebrate them if they choose to keep their percentage the same or choose to change their number following the conversation. Most often, students provide a lower percentage in the second round. The instructors work to collect insights on why students changed their percentages and allow the class to reflect on their peers' reasoning.

Following the percentage-of-credit dialogue, the class engages in personal reflection and small group conversations focused on content from the Illich article. Specific content in the article is shared and examined in these groups, with a focus on power dynamics within volunteerism. A review of student-identified content from the Illich article in combination with the individual reflection and collective examination of meritocracy within the percentage-of-credit exercise is an immediate installment to explicitly combat the savior mentality. Day three closes with one specific Illich (1968) quote:

> I am here to entreat you to use your money, your status and your education to travel in Latin America.
> Come to look, come to climb our mountains, to enjoy our flowers. Come to study.
> But do not come to help.

This quote is chosen to inform the students that they need to maintain a humble approach to engagement and relationship building with talented, smart, resilient, hardworking Hartford residents. We all are at risk of perpetuating injustice, but the message remains that the students will not default to the savior mentality. Instead, through sustained, critical examination, we will actively work to combat this all-too-common and harmful notion of charity.

Closing Context and Appreciation

These insights have been presented to serve as a stimulus for self-reflection and shared examinations among new and invested stakeholders interested in an authentic and positive impact on student development and sustainable community partnerships. While we only provide a small window into the course, we want to stress the importance of establishing the foundations for a critical classroom culture early in the semester so to empower impactful teaching, learning, and engagement among students throughout the entire semester. This service-learning course is designed to explicitly combat the savior mentality. This examination requires a systemic awareness rather than a reliance on meritocracy-driven, individualized narratives of hard work. The students are asked to be willing to engage in continuous learning while striving for accuracy, despite what we are mis-educated and socialized to believe about others in our communities. In closing, as we so often share as feedback with the students on their written reflection papers: We appreciate your willingness to reflect, examine, and share.

Troubleshooting

Inevitably, things will go wrong. People will make mistakes, have disagreements, and experience tension. In this section, we go over some common challenges that arise in the classroom and describe some strategies for working through them.

Different Political and Ideological Views in the Classroom

There will undoubtedly be different political and ideological views in the classroom. However, if you have laid the groundwork of developing a productive critical classroom (front-loading self-reflection, classroom commitments, focusing on listening, practicing humility), students will be poised for greater success in discussions across political difference. Contrary to what some critics of HEIs seem to think, the point of any college education is not indoctrination into any particular set of views; it is to support students in their own identity development and critical thinking skills so they can gather and assess evidence, think critically, and continue to update their ideas as they gather new information. Politics will inevitably be part of the classroom. Political issues map onto social issues in a variety of ways. Political neutrality is not the goal, but critical reflection about our choices is. As Freire (1985) explains:

> Political events are educational and vice versa. Because education is politicity, it is never neutral. When we try to be neutral, like Pilate, we support the dominant ideology. Not being neutral, education must be either liberating or domesticating. . . . Thus, we have to recognize ourselves as politicians. It does not mean that we have the right to impose on students our political choice. But we do have the duty not to hide our choice. Students have the right to know what our political dream is. They are then free to accept it, reject it, or modify it. Our task is not to impose our dreams on them, but to challenge them to have their own dreams, to define their choices, not just to uncritically assume them.
>
> Many teachers unfortunately have been destroyed by the dominant ideology of a society and they tend to impose that way of seeing the world and behaving on kids. They usually view it as "saving" kids, as a missionary would. This tendency stems from a superiority complex. . . . We often believe the ideological words that are told to us—and which we repeat—rather than believing what we're living. The only way to escape that ideological trap, to unveil reality, is to create a counter-ideology to help us break the dominant ideology. This is accomplished by reflecting critically on our concrete experiences, to consider the raison d'etre of the facts we reflect on. (pp. 17–18)

Community-engaged courses and programs are particularly well suited to welcome politics into the classroom. Students are already involved in some kind of social action and are learning about root causes of different issues and more complete histories of issues, and they are learning from those with lived experience. Their preexisting political beliefs are likely going to change and be updated as they incorporate new information and experiences into their existing mental models.

As students encounter beliefs that are counter to their own, several strategies can be useful:

- **Rely on your common commitments:** These will support respectful dialogue and encourage students to speak thoughtfully and with care.
- **Hold students accountable for harm they cause:** If students harm each other, support them in their own accountability without shame. These are learning opportunities for students. For many, this will be the first time they have thought deeply about these topics or had any experience with them. As they develop their thinking and conversational skills, a focus on harm accountability will serve them well in future dialogues while also supporting civil discourse.
- **Encourage respectful listening and disagreement:** At the time of this writing, this is antithetical to many mainstream political dialogues as well as local political action. We are disgusted by the outrage, degrading and dehumanizing language, and flat refusal to discuss political issues. Your classroom can be a space to learn these crucial skills. Set up activities to encourage respectful discussion. For instance, you can set up classroom debates about low-stakes issues, such as whether cats or dogs are better. However, students have to adhere to respectful dialogue rules—listening, not interrupting, asking questions, and using respectful language.
- **Focus on disagreeing with ideas rather than dehumanizing people:** When students inevitably disagree, focus on the conflict between ideas, rather than the people. Agreeing to disagree is always an option.
- **Focus on the importance of life, especially human life:** As students learn about different issues, insist on a focus on the dignity of human life.

Challenges at the Community Partner Site

Another inevitable part of a CE course or program is a challenge that arises at the community partner site. Common issues include partner communication, students doing a task that is different from what they thought it was, personality conflicts, or encountering an awkward situation (for instance, one student in our program contracted lice at her community partner site).

We have found the following strategies to be helpful in supporting students in working through these challenges:

- Remind students of the reality of being a nonprofit organization and the reasons these organizations exist. Staff in the nonprofit sector often work long hours responding to real-time crises and big problems. Student requests may be lower on the priority list. Often, nonprofit organizations exist to support services that the government used to do or could do. A student's role is often to free up staff capacity to focus on bigger issues, which may result in students doing tasks that feel less fulfilling.
- Remind students of the larger picture of the relationship between the organization and the university. The students are part of that relationship and should focus on maintaining it if it is generally productive for both parties. Students' actions can be damaging to the relationship, even if they did not intend them to be that way.
- Reflection! Could this just be the answer to everything? In essence, reflection offers students a pause between the stimulus and their response.

In some circumstances, students encounter situations at community sites that are actively harmful to them. Students may experience microaggressions, unprofessional conduct, or inappropriate situations. In these cases, it is most useful for you to speak directly with the community partner to see what is going on, describe what the student needs, and see if this is a good fit after all or if it would make sense to place the student somewhere else. Although other challenges not mentioned may occur at community sites, we hope these will give you some tools to work through the main issues that students may encounter (see Chapter 6 for more resources on this).

Different Levels of Engagement from Students

As in any course, students will have differing levels of engagement with the course and the course material. In the context of CE work, disengaged students can be particularly disheartening. Checking in with partners can give you information about a student's work in the community and can offer direction for the kind of support a student might need to do better community work there. You can seek out information from their reflections to learn more about them, including their motivations, interests, and backgrounds. What connects them to this course? What makes them tick? How can you build stronger connections to the course material for them?

Doing work in small groups is also an extremely helpful tool, especially if there are peer leaders you can lean on to support those who are less engaged. Our CBL intern model is helpful for this purpose, as students are often more likely to engage with other peers. CBL interns also facilitate one-on-one check-ins with students to get a better sense of where students are and how to help them engage.

And of course, there is just the reality that students will engage with your course differently, and not all students will be energized and engaged in your course. For some, this is a result of circumstances far outside your control. For others, this is simply because they are not as drawn to these issues. In the end, we do what we can with what we have.

Navigating Uncomfortable Situations

Navigating uncomfortable conversations in the classroom could fill a graduate thesis. Our goal here is not to outline every situation and corresponding strategy, but rather to give you support in some common situations that will arise. We direct you to other works that outline this in greater detail, such as *Difficult Subjects: Insights and Strategies for Teaching about Race, Sexuality, and Gender* (Ahad-Legardy & Poon, 2018), which goes into great detail around navigating challenging conversations in the classroom.

Taylor and Reynolds (2019) suggest that dissonance impacts students differently depending on their identities. Its value within higher education is often predicated on dominant assumptions about who college students are: young adults who have moved away from home and have had few experiences encountering difference. This dominant view of discomfort tends to perpetuate the idea that CBL is a pedagogy of whiteness—an approach to community-engaged teaching that tends to focus on the development of white students and the promotion of tolerance through exposure to the "other," typically in the form of interaction with poor communities of color (Mitchell et al., 2012). As such, the development of students of color or other marginalized students is discounted in favor of developing the white students. Taylor and Reynolds (2019) suggest that instructors can make productive use of dissonance by making space for students, especially students of color, to process the dissonance they may encounter.

For white or otherwise privileged students as well, the role of discomfort must be explicitly acknowledged. Frequently the fear of unintentionally causing harm can create barriers to authentic engagement. Often this results in students being more guarded in their interactions with the community (Vaccarro, 2009) and feeling immense guilt when they inevitably end up making a mistake. Instructors can offer additional support by cultivating a learning environment where students can hold each other accountable for their continued learning and improvement as it relates to working with others in culturally informed and respectful ways. For example, if an unintended microaggression slips from a student in the classroom, consider how the event can be used as a teachable moment and learned from.

We again emphasize the importance of comfort with discomfort. We may fear discomfort because it is literally uncomfortable, but remind your students about what is actually going on: They feel something and it will pass. They are not in any actual physical danger. There is not a threat to their safety. Their humanity is not being questioned. They may need to adjust their behavior, but they will be no less worthy of a person or less cared for after their discomfort subsides. Rely on your ground rules, your dedication to listening and reflection, and your focus on relationships.

The Importance of Hope

When talking about social change, it seems overwhelming. Systems are huge and change at a glacial pace. Oppression has been around for as long as we have been here and is unlikely to disappear anytime soon. The academy is an often-ineffective tool for justice and change. Regardless of our efforts, millions of people are suffering and dying around the world. Frankly, doing work for justice can be dispiriting and disheartening. It can make even the most tenacious soul tired, burned out, and hopeless.

So let us make the case for hope. And let us support you in creating a hopeful classroom for your students.

In your classroom, you already have an important piece of the puzzle: a community that is interested in collective change. Positive change is indeed a purpose of your course. Focusing on what a community can do together can cultivate hope. There are numerous examples of this kind of collective change, such as the women's suffrage movement and civil rights protests, and there are likely those in your own community that you can share. For instance, protests and outrage led by the Black Lives Matter movement following the murder of George Floyd in 2020 sparked numerous changes in local communities and the country as a whole, including the removal of Confederate names, statues, and symbols (Ankel, 2020).

By the end of your course or program, your students may feel a bit adrift about their community and civic engagement. What lies ahead for them? One source of hope might be to determine next steps for their own path. The Haas Center's Pathways of Public Service might be helpful (see Chapter 1 for list). These pathways can help students identify their own priorities and values and determine what will fit into their current lives. One particularly useful part of the pathways is that there is not a path that is better or worse; they are presented as simply a variety of ways to engage in public life.

One message that has hopefully resonated throughout this volume is this: Your response to what is happening is under your control. Allowing space and time for processing and reflection can support a productive response. Create room for emotions to show up and be processed without judgment. And then ask your students: What can you change? What is under your control? They can control where they direct their time, energy, and attention. They get to decide what to focus on. This can require "audacious hope," as the scholar Jeffrey Duncan-Andrade (2009) argues. Audacious hope is not burying your head in the sand to ignore what is going on and just looking at the bright side; this "hokey hope" encourages you to ignore injustice and pull yourself up by your bootstraps, no matter if you have boots at all. "Mythical hope" seeks to make grand proclamations about the end of injustice because of one individual's luck. And "hope deferred" makes the case that our circumstances are too overwhelming for hope to be at all possible in our current times. Instead of these three kinds of hope, Duncan-Andrade asks that we believe in critical and audacious hope. As he describes to fellow educators:

> At the end of the day, effective teaching depends most heavily on one thing: deep and caring relationships. Herb Kohl (1995) describes "willed not learning" as the phenomenon by which students try not to learn from teachers who do not authentically care about them. The adage "students don't care what you know until they know that you care" is supported by numerous studies of effective educators (Akom, 2003; Delpit, 1995; Duncan-Andrade, 2007; Ladson-Billings, 1994). To provide the "authentic care" (Valenzuela, 1999) that students require from us as a precondition for learning from us, we must connect our indignation over all forms of oppression with an audacious hope that we can act to change them. Hokey hope would have us believe this change will not cost us anything. This kind of false hope is mendacious; it never acknowledges pain. Audacious hope stares down the painful path; and despite the overwhelming odds against us . . . we make the journey again and again. There is no other choice. Acceptance of this fact allows us to find the courage and the commitment to cajole our students to join us on that journey. This makes us better people as it makes us better teachers, and it models for our students that the painful path is the hopeful path. (p. 191)

Be the bearer of audacious hope for your students. Stare down injustice and oppression. Bear witness to the overwhelming grief and sorrow of the world.

Feel that heartbreak. And then pick up and begin again, doing what you can, with what you have, where you are.

Concluding Thoughts

Community engagement, regardless of its form, is most impactful when supported by a critical learning environment that makes space for interrogation, creates interdependence among all learners, and fosters multiculturalism. In this space, students can develop critical consciousness of themselves and the world around them. Structures are created to acknowledge and overcome oppression in the classroom. CEPs can create critical learning spaces by meeting students where they are on their journeys, clarifying the approach to CE early and often, front-loading reflective work, sharing useful resources, holding students accountable, creating classroom commitments, inviting sharing, and calling students in. CEPs can also support learning by modeling vulnerability and acknowledging current events. This work is best done when the CEP is an experienced facilitator who feels comfortable working with a wide variety of people. Inevitably, things will go wrong, but the groundwork you have laid in setting up your learning environment will support you and your students in overcoming challenges. Last, a crucial piece of developing a critical classroom is cultivating in your students a sense of hope and a belief in their own self-efficacy to create change.

9

Relationship-Centered Systems

Developing effective systems is crucial for supporting student preparation. This chapter acts as a complement to direct student preparation but feeds into the CE "ecosystem." We discuss policies, programs, and university-funded place-based CE centers that foster good relationships. We also share individual instructors' stories of relationship building through their practice of cultural and intellectual humility.

The previous chapters focused mainly on topics directly related to theory, curriculum, and resources for training and preparing students. However, this book would not be complete without a discussion of two other topics that lay the groundwork for a better CE environment that prepared students will enter: how instructors build successful relationships with partners prior to student involvement and various relationship-centered system changes to support equitable engagement that CEPs and students can advocate for and work to actualize at their campuses.

An analogy for a relationship-centered systems approach to CE might be a vegetable garden, which seems appropriate for building a good ecosystem in applied work. Every experienced gardener has learned (sometimes the hard way!) that they cannot just scratch feebly into hard rocky clay, dump seed packets in, water haphazardly, forget to weed and thin, and expect to be eating a bounteous harvest come fall. They have not attended to the relationships that exist in all of nature. The first step to a healthy garden system is always the soil, which we could think of in CE as the foundational, fertile "growing environment" a good partnership needs. Soil must be tested and analyzed to know what it contains and lacks; likewise, CE professionals can organize community meetings, listen to issues discussed at an organization's regular gatherings, host focus groups or interviews, and collate the data to understand community priorities.

Then, the soil needs to be amended in ways most conducive to growth of the particular plants. Whereas blueberries like sandy soil with acidic amendments (as some community partnerships may need specific training or personnel), other plants will fail to grow well in that mix, so you need to research each type of plant—or know what each organization needs. If you only dig out any clay in your soil a couple inches under a kale seedling, you will get roots that go straight down to that depth and then grow sideways, creating a puny plant that never matures. Compare this garden requirement to the unique, discrete priorities of people in different communities or even different blocks within the same neighborhood. A good understanding of what "soil" is needed in each setting is key to everything that comes after.

The seeds are crucial, too—organic may give you a good variety of robust healthy options, while the four-year-old leftover seed packets you found at the bottom of the garden basket may not germinate. You must water daily until they sprout, and seedlings started in a greenhouse need to be coddled during transplanting so they do not go into root shock. This could be compared to CEP work building and nurturing community partnerships through careful tending, funding support and policy changes that make the relationships easier to build and maintain. HEI infrastructure is like the whole orientation and secure setting of the garden plot—where the sunlight is, how much space there is, and where taller plants should go so they do not crowd out or shade smaller plants, depending on the track of the sun (side note: some plants are "deer candy"—your fence must be at least eight feet high! Think of this like you would the protection of community partner data and privacy).

This chapter details several different types of what Jamilah Ducar at the University of Pittsburgh describes as "holistic ecosystems" to create that fertile environment for CE (see her vignette later). Striving toward a comprehensive approach from the institutional viewpoint as feasible prepares the student to enter in an equitable way. Only then is this garden ready for amateur volunteers—undergraduates, if you will—to come in, enthusiastic and armed with hoses, hoes, and cultivators, after having been trained in how to water without drowning seedlings and weed without damaging or destroying the intended harvest. The main thrust of most of the previous chapters has been to address these "student contact" aspects of CE "garden tending," but here we focus on ways to support those efforts at a campus level for greater success in student learning and community outcomes.

Infrastructures That Support CE

There are some models in use today that serve to organize community engagement within an HEI to achieve equity, efficiency, and scalability, and they are improving constantly with knowledge sharing and experience. Our work on this book has centered on educational institutions in the United States, but HEIs all over the world are creating innovative structures that we can learn from and tailor to U.S. frames of reference. Neighboring Canada has many ways of operating in HEIs similar to ours and also some exemplary practices and programs that appear to have evolved earlier and more robustly than the typical U.S. ways of organizing CE. There are several active networks in Canada, including one called simply CBRCanada. A well-funded federal grant cycle called SSHRC has supported equitable partnership projects across the country for years (Social Sciences and Humanities Research Council, n.d.), and Canadians were instrumental in the beginnings of the Community-Campus Partnerships for Health organization before the turn of the millennium (Seifer & Sgambelluri, 2008).

The Science Shop Model

One concept that has been around in Europe from the 1970s and since spread across the globe is the Science Shop model. In addition to a robust participant list in the EU, countries like South Africa, Cameroon, Haiti, Australia, Indonesia, India, Brazil, and more* now have well-developed and funded Science Shops—centralized research and action hubs that community members approach with ideas or questions that might be answered by professional researchers or a transdisciplinary team of students, faculty, and staff researchers. Some countries require hard proof of community decision-making and approval in their national ministry's priorities before granting government funding, using the term "Responsible Research Innovation" (Hall et al., 2015). CEPs in North America and beyond come together biennially in a conference, organized by members of the CBRCanada network, called the C2U Expo. Their EU counterpart, the International Living Knowledge Network (Leydesdorff & Ward, 2005), holds a conference and summer school on the alternate years in the EU. In the past meetings on both sides of the ocean attended by these coauthors, we have only seen a handful of Americans along with many participants from the rest of the globe. Witnessed at these meetings is the overarching philosophy of prioritizing the "co-creation of knowledge" principle that honors community wisdom and participation. Relationships are key to succeeding in this way of doing CE.

---

* For paper on creating Science Shops in Africa, see Africa Knows! Conference, n.d.

One Canadian Science Shop is at Trent University in Peterborough, Ontario:

> Trent Centre for Community Research (TCCE) is separate from . . .
> but funded in part by Trent University, as well as a multi-year foundation grant, and *Service Canada*. TCCBE is an "independent third-party broker." Community organizations submit project proposals to [the centre]. Once projects have been reviewed by research staff, faculty and community experts, these opportunities are promoted to students and instructors. Centre staff work alongside faculty to support students in their work and help guide projects toward successful outcomes for both the local community and students. (Trent University, n.d.)

It is interesting that this movement did not take root more broadly in the United States, and several fledgling shops did not survive their pilot phase. A Science Shop we consulted with at its inception in 2013 was at the University of California, Berkeley (Andrade et al., 2018). It no longer appears to exist in that form, as is also the case at UW–Madison, as we describe later. One American Science Shop still thriving is the Center for Urban Research and Learning at Loyola University Chicago. A brief history is included here:

> The CURL Center opened in January 1996, with a $1.5 million grant and endowment from the McCormick Tribune Foundation. In 2000, the Foundation awarded a $2.5 million challenge grant to guarantee that CURL would be a permanent part of Loyola's research, education, and linkage with Chicago communities. (Loyola University Chicago, n.d.)

While deserving of further exploration, a larger discussion of this model and why it seems less prevalent in this country is outside the scope of this volume. Other types of models in the United States, including the Educational Partnerships for Innovation in Communities Network (EPIC-N, see https://www.epicn.org), a "national network of more than 30 educational institutions partnering with cities throughout the United States and world," have some similar characteristics to the Science Shop model, in that they work to streamline and scale projects with efficient organizational strategies, but do not recognize themselves as such. Hopefully, more of these types of models will proliferate here again. The Science Shop model creates an ecosystem that inherently supports CE partnerships grounded in solid relationships of mutual benefit and justice, a fertile garden plot for students to enter.

See Appendix B for a short list of other networks beyond the United States for further exploration, and read on for more and other types of infrastructures that support effective and equitable CE.

Creating New Infrastructure at UW–Madison

A category of the recommendations from community participants in the *Community Standards for Service Learning* (Stoecker & Tryon, 2007) was "infrastructure." This was bulleted as a suggestion to "streamline the process of finding matches through either service-learning offices or departments." At the most basic level, that could mean creating a database for both campus and community to search for people and places that fit the parameters of a project, and indeed, UW–Madison and several other schools have such a searchable web interface. But something we heard, loud and clear, while creating the *Community Standards* was this: "A website is fine, but we want to be able to get to a real person pretty fast!" (focus group notes, 2007). How could we maximize the reach of those real people at HEIs to serve more community partners? The Science Shop model seemed like an efficient way to streamline the process, create sustainability, and share decision-making in resource allocation and research design.

Our Science Shop Project

In 2010 our center provided three years of funding for a Science Shop pilot as the umbrella for bringing together projects that had been operating in isolation; the goal was to increase efficiency on campus and maximize community benefit. Several place-based CBR projects were organized in an economically challenged area where research and CBL were concentrated. Community mentors received honoraria for becoming coinvestigators alongside the university students, and everyone completed the Human Subjects Protection training together. This work spun off organically into multiple transdisciplinary projects to encompass, at one point, nine graduate students and a plethora of CBL courses that responded to a coordinated set of community priorities.

But the organizing arm was still centered on campus, and our community feedback had suggested that to welcome community members more fully in places they felt more comfortable (and where they could find a parking spot!), we needed to make it a real infrastructure—a place-based, funded, community research and outreach site. We explored models at several other schools, and a pilot version of a place-based site morphed out of the previous campus-based work at UW–Madison.

Place-Based Centers

Around several HEIs across the United States, off-campus centers for CE are popping up that do not identify as Science Shops but share some of those characteristics. We share contributions from two: an urban research center funded by the University of Minnesota called the Urban Research and Out-reach-Engagement Center (fondly christened UROC) and Jamilah Ducar's description of the University of Pittsburgh's "ecosystem," conducive to authentic, equity-based engagement for students at their neighborhood Community Engagement Centers.

We are aware that not all HEIs have access to the monetary resources these programs require or a champion at a high administrative level, both factors that make large-scale infrastructural change possible. Both of the universities highlighted in the coming vignettes had chancellor's office or provost-level support for CE to help make the case for funding a robust, off-campus research and engagement site. We hope that hearing their stories will be inspirational for beginning to lay the foundation for long-term change. Some changes, even minor ones, have taken years or decades to accomplish, much like the "cruise ship" analogy to HEIs—pushing the stern just one degree toward a different course may not look like a change in direction, but in a thousand miles, the ship has landed at an entirely different place.

UROC

At the University of Minnesota, an off-campus center was created in 2009, after then senior vice president for academic administration Robert J. Jones, North Minneapolis resident himself, helped establish an urban outreach center on the city's northside. Along the path to its creation, a series of talks with African American members of the North Minneapolis community (as interviewed by UROC staff, Jones said) challenged the university to

> change how we thought about outreach and partnership. Rather than having academics going out into the community doing research that was based on their own interests, we needed to be a part of the community and tap into their knowledge. We needed to be asking what they needed, and we had to find out what was important to them. It couldn't just be research for research's sake. That was the old model. I didn't understand that when people said it at first, but I finally realized that what they were saying to us was: "What is the point of your research in our community if it won't bring about change?" (UROC website; https://uroc.umn.edu/news-events/living -promise)

UROC operates in a condominium model, with faculty applying to be stationed, at least part-time, in the community location for the duration of a research project. They use a standardized proposal form, and faculty must prove their research has been designed with community input/feedback or co-design and must outline the role of partners throughout the project. The form also collects information about decision points up front with questions like "Who owns the data?" and "Where is it disseminated and in what format?" The research design is submitted to UROC as a written contract with the roles and responsibilities clearly delineated. In order to have a solid proposal that will not be pitched out, faculty or graduate students may need to negotiate with their potential partners to come up with the written agreements or "rules of engagement." UROC instituted this model after learning through experience that some faculty saw the center as a convenient and attractive location to set up "studies on the community."

The Makeda Zulu and James DeSota vignette shows the story of how this neighborhood-involved model, now past its ten-year anniversary, has added value in preparing students to work in communities and increased their personal growth as well as community impact.

Seeds Planted Will Grow

Makeda Zulu and James DeSota

Background

The University of Minnesota Robert J. Jones Urban Research and Outreach-Engagement Center works to find breakthrough solutions to challenges facing the urban cores of Minneapolis and St. Paul, Minnesota. Preparing students, staff, and faculty to collaborate with our communities is crucial to the work that we do at UROC and something that we take very seriously. Being a good neighbor; building relationships through trust, authenticity, and transparency; and honoring the wisdom in both nonacademic and scholarly communities are foundational parts of UROC's work and key reasons why UROC can maintain and strengthen its external and internal relationships.

Proximity Matters

North Minneapolis—and its African American community in particular—has been underserved yet overstudied by academia for decades with little to show for the community's participation. As a result, the community has a healthy skepticism of university research, which is a major reason that authenticity and transparency are UROC's keys to university-community partnership. We believe proximity matters, and as a result, one of our most powerful tools for coaching our academic colleagues is through dialogue here at our building. As part of their introduction to affiliation with UROC, faculty and student scholars are required to first meet with our team to learn about UROC's history as a research center, as well as the broader history of the university in North Minneapolis. Faculty and staff attend an orientation during which we discuss not only their interest in working with communities but also how their interest impacts our communities and our partners. We encourage students to move through our neighborhoods physically, to explore the area around UROC and engage with the local community, because, again, we believe proximity matters.

Student Experiences

At UROC we believe in bringing "your entire self" to meetings and projects. We are convinced that being cognizant of all your roles and identities—both those that you readily identify and those that others will perceive you as having—is critical to being authentic and building trust. As an example, during survey fieldwork for a UROC research project, one of our students was struggling with her lack of exposure to diversity. Our team met with her and encouraged her to express herself—allowing her to talk about how her rural upbringing made her feel and what she thought was going to happen as she was knocking on doors in the neighborhood. We also explored with her about how neighborhood residents might view her and what their assumptions of her might be—a young, white, female university student knocking on their door asking about their children's school experiences. As a result of our conversations, she felt much better prepared to conduct her surveys. Despite her early hesitancy, this student ended up being one of UROC's most successful research canvassers—and she felt she had a transformative and valuable experience that summer.

UROC's group community tours offer potential service-learning university students a chance to visit with UROC staff, as described prior, as well as a guided visit to local nonprofits and community centers. The tours include before and after surveys of their experience to address preconceptions and observances about communities—both in their home communities and in North Minneapolis. We recognize that service learning can be a valuable tool for students to learn from community organizations. The community organizations benefit from having a student who is skilled in the latest technology and has a university advisor to guide them during the placement. One service-learning student, Ashley, who later approached UROC to provide coordination on a three-year project, aspired to be an urban-focused physician who authentically partnered with her patients. The role she played at UROC—as the coordinator of a very nuanced project with five vastly different affinity groups—gave her the chance to see many points of view and recognize how to satisfy needs using multiple paths. During this project, the focus was African American children. A partner organization provided opportunities for cultural exploration for both African Americans and European Americans. Staff participated in these learning opportunities and shared their learning with one another. Ashley built trusting relationships and irreplaceable knowledge as she learned more about her culture, and engaged with others doing the same. Her willingness to engage authentically served her long-term goals. The discussions with the UROC team about the myth of race were critical to building strong relationships. Today, she is a much-sought-after hospital physician in the urban core.

Staying Connected and Learning Together

After any orientation or training with these students, called Josie R. Johnson Fellows, the UROC staff remain connected to their university partners and community collaborators. Our methods can be as informal as stopping by students' UROC project offices to check in and listen to their challenges and successes, attending a community meeting with their partners, or hosting a dissemination event for them as part of UROC's Critical Conversations discussion series. We have monthly meetings with our fellows to ask how they are doing and answer their questions because our focus is on keeping them engaged with their community partners and completing their dissertations. We are there for them. We answer their questions honestly and remember that we all have a host of identities and roles that embody our interactions: instructor, mentor, supervisor, employer, colleague, student, and, hopefully, friend. We at UROC believe we should always be learning together. For a complete list of UROC's projects and affiliations, visit http://uroc.umn.edu.

University of Pittsburgh's Polices to Support CE Centers

We have talked about how overwhelming infrastructure change can seem, especially the large-scale changes needed to bring about an entire physical structure off campus, but it can be an aspirational goal. Chipping away at seemingly intractable campus politics and protocols a little at a time by finding allies and exerting influence at pressure points can lead to long-term growth of equitable CE and eventual off-campus CE centers.

Jamilah Ducar's essay describes the process by which the University of Pittsburgh's administration, faculty, and staff have worked for years in consultation with community organizations to build structural backdrops for long-term, deliberative partnerships that are staged and sequenced for students to be introduced to appropriately. Their intentional community-based infrastructure combined on-campus policy and program change to accompany investments in community place-based centers. Coupled with good class preparation in CE, including a civic advisement office where staff consult with students on better understanding of civic pathways and preparing to work in community, this "ecosystem" has resulted in both successful student learning and community outcomes at the Community Engagement Centers in Pittsburgh neighborhoods.

We're in This Together: Willing Your Own Engagement Coalition Ecosystem to Fruition

Jamilah Ducar, Ed.D.

Sometimes it is easy to miss the forest for the trees. Community-engaged praxis is rewarding, at times isolating, and can mean some missteps along the way. How nice would it be to have a system of support, positive reinforcement, or critical friends for re-visioning? It is possible and (hopefully) easier than you expect, if you have the time and orientation to listen to your colleagues. This vignette focuses on finding "your people" and using the power of networks to advance your institution's understanding (and resourcing) of community-engaged teaching and learning, research, volunteerism, and programmatic initiatives.

I serve as the executive director of the Engaged Campus for the University of Pittsburgh, a position that provides our campus community of students, faculty, staff, and administrators—and our external stakeholders and communities of place, interest, and action—the tools they need to be successful. I came to higher education as a midcareer human services professional; my natural inclinations are to seek systems-level interventions and shared theories of action across interrelated organizations. I am what I like to call a "middepth generalist," both capable across a variety of functions and conversant enough across most nontechnical disciplines to understand and translate aspirations colleagues have for their practice. I am housed within the Office of Engagement and Community Affairs (ECA), an administrative unit that reports to the Office of the Chancellor but has no curricular connections to community-engaged learning. Consider the following elevator pitch for our work:

> ECA champions community engagement efforts across the Pitt system. ECA facilitates strategic community initiatives, leads the university's place-based engagements in the city of Pittsburgh, collaborates with the Provost's Office to support engaged scholarship, maintains

positive relationships with the neighbors and organizations closest to our campus footprint, and ensures that Pitt is a partner and asset to communities, locally to globally.

This means that we are a bit of a Swiss army knife of a team, consistently listening across our university system and communities for ways our institution can be relevant, responsive, and connected to the lived experiences of individuals, neighborhoods, and coalitions outside the academy. In order to be successful, we convene, collaborate, orient, and elevate the voices of others as internal consultants. To that end, an important part of my skill set is a broad awareness of what is happening across our campus and within the region. This is the first and most critical predecessor to shared action. It takes a bit of homework to get to know your institution in a deep dive from the perspective of someone new to it. As part of my self-prescribed orientation to Pitt, I signed up for every internal newsletter that could possibly have content that intersected with my work. I learned about specialty academic centers as well as the unique priorities of each discipline or professional school by looking for the cues they communicated broadly to students and partners. Once in routine communication with university artifacts, key assets (both people and programs) became more visible to me.

After feeling like I understood the landscape a bit better, I looked to my engaged mentor/sponsor for additional context. If you do not have one, please seek one out, preferably outside your own discipline if possible. In this case, it was my supervisor, a man with decades of institutional knowledge and steadfast relationships across campus. He offered me a brief history on what has changed or remained consistent throughout his tenure at Pitt. John introduced me to the small, informal group of faculty and staff that seemingly held the torch for CES to be considered on campus. As individuals, the group was quite well connected and respected. Being a part of this group quickly accelerated my ability to see community engagement in new ways and have my own praxis visible in turn. Despite that, as a collective, their shared purpose was muddled and limited to a single annual event. I volunteered to lead a strategic planning process for the group, leading to concrete goals that could eventually be used to ask the university for organizing resources when the time was right. We harnessed the energy of the annual event the group produced and bootstrapped it into a larger, formalized Community Engaged Scholarship Forum.

We were lucky. Civic and community engagement became a visible point of inquiry across campus, and what began in our small informal committee grew. Our Carnegie Classification for Engagement application process and resulting self-study recommendations were the catalytic spark that led to the institution strongly considering what infrastructure support for community engagement should look like. Our Student Government Board engaged their peers on what tools they needed to feel successful in community contexts. They launched a student survey, advocated for additional civic life support with high-level administrators, and proposed that the Office of the Provost consider "Year of Engagement" as its 2020–2021 focus. The result of these actions are as follows:

- The office of the student home for service and cocurricular community-engaged programming agreed to go through a strategic planning process that would broaden its mission.
- A Civic Advising Program (CAP) was launched, which deploys the Haas-developed Pathways of Public Service and Civic Engagement Survey and advising protocol with students. CAP leverages a cohort of students, staff, and faculty as informal advisors across all six pathways, trains interested students, and offers paid student fellowships for peer-mentored civic engagement.
- The Year of Engagement launched, providing internal funding of up to $8,000 per project for engaged initiatives that reach across scholarship, practice, and capacity building.

I was also given permission to serve as co-convener of our Engagement Community of Practice (ECOP) with our associate vice provost for academic innovation. Our collaboration is a practitioner-scholar lens that provides campuswide leverage for community-engaged scholarship and action. ECOP is now over three hundred practitioners strong and has an internal SharePoint site and email distribution group.

Faculty were an interesting stakeholder group, as even though Pitt has a large apparatus that engages with local and global communities quite deeply, there is limited formal centralized infrastructure for community-engaged learning. Through funds provided by the Year of Engagement, Dr. Lina Dostilio, vice chancellor for community engagement, was able to pilot a professional development program called the Engaged Scholarship Development Initiative, covering the basic elements, ethics, and outcomes of engaged scholarship.

The resources and programs detailed here took almost five years of consistent community building, but it is paying off. The conditions for engagement have changed significantly, and there is a growing culture that considers societal impacts within, and as a result of, institutional actions. Our team has shifted our own praxis to better incorporate critical, reflexive lenses. We worked across our volunteer management functions for students, faculty, staff, and researchers to develop a campus-wide theory of action and call to action for public service and volunteerism. This theory of action is grounded in the realities of lived experiences, research insights, and our institutional capacity embedded in people power. We developed resources (which can be viewed on the TU ScholarShare website: https://scholarshare.temple .edu/handle/20.500.12613/8178) that can be used to teach volunteers and volunteerism champions how to engage in community-facing work with an orientation we would consider to be necessarily ethical and compassionate.

This shift has run parallel to the growth of Pitt's Community Engagement Centers (CECs), the university's set of investment, infrastructure, and programming strategies to anchor long-term place-based partnerships. The CECs also take a significant leadership role in reorienting the aspirations of the academy toward community-centered priorities and values. As part of an ongoing CBPR project led by the School of Social Work, the CECs have developed a set of exploratory orientation modules, compiled preexisting neighborhood reports, and created playbooks for equitable development that were directly informed by resident conversations. These resources allow our campus community to gain a better understanding of community contexts without asking residents to continue to take on the labor of being surveyed, interviewed, or otherwise tapped for their cultural wealth. CEC directors also serve as technical advisors and guardians of neighborhood assets by serving as the first point of contact for those who are interested in community-facing work but do not have the prior relationships necessary to advance their ideas to fruition. Part of the shared governance structure of the CECs are neighborhood advisory councils, groups composed of residents, nonprofit staff, and elected officials all with a vested interest in the future of the places we share.

In such a large place, it is easy for all the components to feel piecemeal and disconnected. It is my work every day to bring the threads closer together to knit an ecosystem that can truly be interdependent and conversant no matter the point of entry. It is important to realize that it is OK to start small and stay within your sphere of influence. Eventually, with enough overlapping networks, a magnetic center emerges that can catalyze and elevate community-engaged pedagogies and praxis. The potential in full participation is that students, faculty, staff, and communities all have the self-efficacy and resources to effectively situate their priorities, assemble allies, and encourage shared action. If you are looking to encourage that on your own campus, take the first step by going on an intentional mission to *listen*. You might be surprised at what you are able to discover. Our students rely on the interlinkages that we as faculty, staff, and administrators are able to weave together to support their civic lives. With a network of their peers for support, clear pathways for involvement and growth, and trusted relationships within the communities they are expected to partner, we provide them the strongest foundation possible for community engagement to thrive.

UW–Madison's New Place-Based Center

Because of site visits our staff and campus administrators made to UROC over the course of several years, UW–Madison created a fledgling presence for CE in our community, beginning in an empty strip mall storefront and growing to take over a former community college satellite campus in 2020. Due to the pandemic, programming could not expand immediately to fill the new space, but that respite helped staff ensure that good principles and policies would be in place by the time people were allowed to enter and begin new CE partnerships. Our community advisory committee believes the infrastructure is key to providing the foundation for well-prepared students to succeed. It also models for students the values the university espouses: the importance of relationships, equitable investments in CE work, and co-

UW South Madison Partnership

Provided by Merry Farrier-Babanovski

O pened in 2015, the UW–Madison South Madison Partnership (UWSMP) connects UW–Madison with the South Madison community and works to foster mutually beneficial partnerships that reflect community-identified priorities. The shared event and program space on South Park Street promotes an environment of belonging, access, and awareness of both community and university resources and provides opportunities for building quality relationships. We promote excellence in the areas of teaching, research, and outreach to foster purposeful partnerships for the betterment of our local community and beyond. We invest in building and sustaining quality relationships grounded in shared power and mutual benefit.

The UWSMP brings together university programs and initiatives with a solid foundation in South Madison and long-time relationships with community members. Partners like the UW Odyssey Project, the Neighborhood Law Clinic, and the Wisconsin Alzheimer's Disease Research Center have been involved since the initiative's start, and others, like the Richard Dilley Tax Center, are new this year. A variety of campus and community partners host meetings, events, and programming in the space spanning the areas of health, economic empowerment, and education.*

---

* Links for these programs: https://morgridge.wisc.edu/2015/02/13/open-house-offers
-warm-welcome-for-south-madison-partnership/; https://odyssey.wisc.edu/; https://law
.wisc.edu/eji/nlc/; https://www.adrc.wisc.edu/; https://fyi.extension.wisc.edu/danecounty
financialeducationcenter/tax-assistance/free-tax-help/the-richard-dilley-tax-center/

creating partnerships. Merry Farrier-Babanovski's vignette has a short description of what that looks like as of 2022.

Community Campus Connectors

Additionally, we have created a robust support network for CEPs at our university through a group called the Community Campus Connectors (C3), a network of community engagement practitioners across UW–Madison. Our units support CE in a variety of ways in different disciplines. We connect directly to community partners and often act as a "front door" to the university. We care about promoting good practice. The C3 group connects quarterly to share updates, collaborate, and discuss the news in our respective units and areas of campus. This group provides support, thought partners, and a ready network of connections as we talk with community partners so we can do the following:

- Have awareness of the work our units are doing
- Collaborate on projects as needed
- Advocate for institutional support for quality community engagement across the university

In practice, our work involves keeping an inventory of community-campus partnerships, coordinating intake processes across units, exchanging information about the work we are doing, and communicating best practices for community engagement to the broader campus community, among other tasks. The C3 group is a crucial piece of infrastructure for supporting excellent student CE. We are able to share community inquiries with our units, advocate for greater institutional support, and create campus momentum for initiatives, such as our student preparation work.

Advocating for Other Types of Institutional Change

Infrastructure is one piece of an agenda for changing the way CE happens in higher education, although, as we stated earlier, it can be financially intensive to create an actual physical community presence, and even a Science Shop located on campus requires a large time commitment to continuously coordinate across disciplines. Another route, not mutually exclusive to that long-term goal as illustrated by Ducar's story at Pitt, is working toward changing some of the policies and practices of the HEI's administration to make it easier to participate in high-quality, equitable CE.

Tenure and Promotion

At many research universities, tenure pressures on junior faculty fall under the category of "harder," sometimes "impossible," as pertaining to capacity for doing CE. This book is not meant to catalogue all the various issues within that struggle—let it suffice to say that some pre-tenure faculty cannot even consider teaching a CBL course or doing CBR without encountering a very strong, occasionally insurmountable headwind or, worse, being denied tenure because they disregarded their mentors' advice to "stay out of the community until after you get tenure."

Some HEIs are beginning to address this conundrum as more and more new faculty come in with a strong desire for more meaningful research and teaching—and some even come in with established community research partnerships (and grant money!). We studied one HEI in particular as a potential model for making changes to tenure review at UW–Madison: the University of Minnesota Twin Cities. After consulting with Dr. Lorilee Sandmann, former cochair of the National Engaged Scholarship Review Committee, the University of Minnesota Twin Cities created their own review committee on CES (University of Minnesota, Office for Public Engagement, n.d.), composed of engaged faculty across disciplines who not only review tenure portfolios and write recommendation letters to be included in tenure files but also mentor junior faculty in ways to achieve tenure while doing CES.

Simultaneously, we had begun having monthly events at UW–Madison, gathering CEPs from across our large campus to discuss ways to support each other's work and advocate as a group for policies that would help improve CES. This corresponded with increased support flowing from our Civic Action Plan—and, in particular, Recommendation 6: "Increase support for quality CES across campus." Two faculty members focused on the objective of making tenure and promotion guidelines more inclusive of CES agreed to co-chair an ad hoc committee to discuss the models and changes we had researched and decide on a course of action. A perfect storm occurred—one faculty was already on the campus governance committee, and the other had become a vice provost. Having or cultivating champions on your campus really helps achieve these changes. Our tenure and promotion committee reviewed the existing tenure guidelines for our four divisional committees and then made recommendations that would reflect the type of CES done by faculty in those disciplines. Our center's faculty director and the co-chairs then took those recommendations to each divisional committee meeting, where each of the four committees approved at least some language change in support of CES.

Programs to Support Good Instructional Practices

Many universities have created faculty development programs specifically geared to CES, such as the University of North Carolina at Chapel Hill's Thorpe Faculty Engaged Scholars, the Faculty Fellows in CBL at the University of Colorado Boulder, and Seattle University's Community Engaged Justice Fellows. The purpose of the like-minded Morgridge Fellows program at UW–Madison is to further institutionalize and support CES. Faculty, academic staff, and Ph.D. students apply and are selected by a committee to create a well-rounded, cross-disciplinary cohort that meets monthly to discuss readings, develop new courses or add community-based learning to an existing course, plan community-based research projects, or work on other CES activities. Readings are chosen that highlight techniques for creating equitable partnerships and strategies for teaching intellectual and cultural humility. Fellows are asked to share things they have learned from their cohort experience with future fellows and a broader audience (e.g., teaching and learning symposia, lecture series) and to act as champions for CES in their discipline. As of its fifth year, several former fellows have informally mentored incoming cohort members, and some cross-year collaborations have occurred. The fellows themselves report that the experience has helped them improve their teaching and ability to give students the background they need before approaching community partners. Here are a few reflections they have sent:

> There is absolutely no question that the multiple opportunities that I have been offered through the Morgridge Center—the course development grants and the Fellows Program—were pivotal in my ability to secure this specific type of faculty position. The work and support that you all provide to our campus was one of the main reasons I chose to do my doctoral training at UW–Madison, and I just feel incredibly lucky to be able to carry that work forward in this new faculty appointment.

> I found connecting and learning from others doing community based work was incredibly energizing and inspiring. I came from decades of community-based work into an academic environment and the disconnect with the community stood out immediately to me. What I realized clearly in the fellows program was that I was also "out of the loop" on all the amazing community based work on campus in different departments. I think we are at a point where the UW has tipped toward valuing this work. The program increased my ability to effectively communicate this to others and play a role in expanding support.

Instructors and Other CEPs Building Relationships

Every campus has several "community-engaged faculty heroes" or "rock stars" who are often written up in local and campus press releases or invited to keynote campus-wide events to inspire other faculty. At our university there have been many such champions through the years, and we have noticed that they have special, deep relationships with community partners. One of the faculty associates, a white woman we have worked with on many projects, is so embedded in a place-based model that one of her long-term community partners, a Black man, regards her as family. Another has held the same partners since the year she arrived as a first-year assistant professor and has remained deeply committed to them despite the challenges of preparing for tenure while doing CES. When our center holds events for CEPs across campus to come together and share their strategies, we often highlight these exemplary "CE champions" as role models. Some of the qualities and factors that make these exemplary instructors so successful have been described by community partners as the following:

- **Patience:** Understanding the challenges nonprofit staff face and why they need plenty of advance notice to plan a CBL project; flexibility when things come up and timelines are postponed
- **Relationships before ideas:** Getting to know people and issues at a community site before asking or offering to design a project
- **Clarifying roles/goals:** Using an MOU or other short written document that everyone contributes to and approves to prevent confusion or unrealistic expectations
- **Multiyear projects:** Phasing in chunks of work in sequential semesters so that each course scaffolds with the next and ultimate long-term impact can be created

Relationships in Indigenous Scholarship

The primacy of the relationship is crucial to working in Indigenous cultures. We have talked a lot about people of color, including Native Americans, as victims of oppression and discrimination. However, many groups are developing to reframe those issues and reclaim power (e.g., Jolivétte, 2015; D. A. Smith, 2021). A body of literature is also beginning to pay more attention to Indigenous researchers, and some have coined the term "warrior scholars" to refer to them. Jeff Corntassel and Adam Gaudry, in *Learning and Teaching Community-Based Research* (2014), propose the term "insurgent education, a way of challenging the injustices of colonialism, dispossession, and racist oppression, while re-affirming the work views of our ancestors" (p. 168).

In the same volume, Indigenous scholar Linda Tuhiwai Smith noted that the word "research" itself "is probably one of the dirtiest words in the indigenous world's vocabulary." However, the work of indigenous scholars now includes a focus on taking back the term. In Tuhiwai Smith's words, "I did not know there [were] Indigenous ways of doing research. I am delighted to learn how to do research 'in a good way'" (p. 105).

The following are two stories of academic partnerships that are inclusive of Indigenous knowledge.

CBL with Wisconsin Tribal Nations

As a young non-Native mother, Dr. Jessie Conaway became involved as a volunteer worker in watershed and environmental advocacy with several reservations in Wisconsin. Because she presented herself with an ethic of "humility is key," spiritual and cultural leaders in the tribe took her under their wing and taught her more about Native culture. She had previous knowledge of wildcrafting and plant medicines that she could share with them too, which solidified her relationships with tribal elders. This set the stage for her to be successful in bringing students into projects on the reservations.

Conaway has now taught a CBL capstone course at UW–Madison since 2012 in partnerships with tribal nations in Wisconsin. She utilizes one of our center's CBL interns to develop activities for training the undergraduates in cultural awareness, with the main theme being "listening and responding." First, students learn about the contemporary issues and historical background of the tribe they will be working with before training in communication and cultural protocols of that tribe. As an example, students are taught to approach potential Native speakers or panelists in a way that they will be more receptive to. According to Conaway, "If you want to invite a tribal ally to speak at your event, they will need a formal invite about what you are asking for, who is the audience, when it is, where it is, what type of info that you want shared, and what the honoraria and travel budget are" (J. Conaway, personal communication, May 6, 2022).

The objective of the training, according to Conaway, is to create "good listeners that are informed about the culture," and the "end goal is for students to engage with the community on its terms, not the students', as much as we can understand about their culture." Through active listening, elder epistemology, awareness of the tribal leaders and deference to their position, local knowledge is centered. They discuss the recognition of power that comes with representing the university but then learn to set that aside and learn the principles of being a good human being—respect, manners, humor, generosity, and willingness to serve. There is a very deep commitment to continual improvement in the student preparation. Conaway and the CBL interns meet weekly, and they bring activities to the meetings that can be adapted for use with Native American culture, such as the privilege walk and one she calls "walking in two worlds."

This training enables students to complete projects that are immediately relevant to the tribal communities. Some projects have included AutoBio-Mapping and an ArcGIS story mapping that fits in with tribal understandings of spatial knowledge. When the projects are in rough draft form, they enter into the "listen and respond" feedback loop with the tribal partners. First, students share the work they have done and then receive feedback from the partners, incorporating that into the draft so it is validated by the tribal members (J. Conaway, personal communication, May 6, 2022).

A Programmatic Perspective
CEPs Maria Moreno and Cheryl Bauer-Armstrong created a course at UW–Madison in 2019 to prepare students for engagement as a prerequisite to the CBL class that works in one of the community sites.

Planning and Landscape Architecture's Earth Partnership: Connecting Students with Tribes and Other Community Partners Using Land-Based Learning for Reciprocal Community Relationships

Maria Moreno, Ph.D., and Cheryl Bauer-Armstrong

The Earth Partnership program offers students opportunities to engage with diverse communities and have experiences outside the classroom. The program frames restoration as a learning process, a hands-on way to deeply connect to place and enact ecological values. Ecological restoration transforms people's relationship with the land so they begin to see themselves as "plain members and citizens" of the ecological community. As they transform themselves and their role, they learn to care for nature and become stewards in their own communities, providing them competency and purpose to make a difference in the world.

In an effort to reimagine an Indigenous-academic partnership based on mutual respect and shared interests, in 2011 the EP-IAS (Earth Partnership–Indigenous Academic Studies) initiative began in response to Indigenous community-identified needs for water stewardship, protection of subsistence harvest, resilience in the face of climate change on cultural practices, and Native youth access to higher education and natural resource careers. The development of the EP-IAS program provides a model for Indigenous-academic partnerships that recognize, respect, and include sovereignty of tribal nations through collaborative design and planning. The collaboration is creating new possibilities for integrating Indigenous traditional environmental knowledge with Western science-based land stewardship practices. Current funding from the National Science Foundation is allowing us to deepen our understanding of this process of collaboration and how a university can authentically and honestly engage in this process. EP-IAS was codeveloped with Indigenous partners in Wisconsin, including the Mashkiiziibii (Bad River Band of Lake Superior Chippewa), the Ho-Chunk Nation, the Lac Courte Oreilles Band of Lake Superior Chippewa Indians, the Waaswaagoning (Lac du Flambeau Band of Lake Superior Chippewa Indians), and the Miskwaabi-kaang (Red Cliff Band of the Lake Superior Chippewa).

According to Moreno, the course approaches learning about Native communities from an asset-based lens:

> The essential [thing] they're learning is that Native communities are here, they're resilient, they're thriving, engaged; some provide the most jobs in their region. They have the gamut of educated people, lawyers, professionals . . . [giving them a] greater appreciation for the humility that is required . . . [learning] that there have been issues historically and we're trying to change them one class at a time. (M. Moreno, personal conversation, April 20, 2022)

Moreno shared some written reflections by students toward the end of the course that showed much transformative change:

> I need to step back and *listen* to where my support and energy is needed. I think that will help me to form genuine partnerships and relationships. To approach these relationships with patience and humility in order to form long-term collaborations and continue to grow individually and collectively. Moving forward, I want to continue to take these intentions and realizations I've been given and challenge myself. To use my privileges to support change that tears down my privileges. To be a white ally. To follow where I am called to follow, and to lead if and where I am called to lead. This class has been an integral part of giving me humility, knowledge, and clarity for the unknown of the future and what my place is in it. (M. Moreno, email conversation, April 20, 2022)

Moreno and Bauer-Armstrong also recounted an exchange regarding Native spearfishing with a white UW student from near a reservation in northern Wisconsin who has family who are fishermen. Tribal communities have spearfishing privileges as part of the "hunting, fishing, and gathering rights reserved in three mid-nineteenth-century land cession treaties the Ojibwe negotiated with the federal government" (Loew & Thannum, 2001, p. 161). Fishing members of the student's family constantly griped, "Native people are taking all the fish," and he accepted this knowledge as fact. After hearing from tribal elders in class, he now knows that is false and that, in fact, the tribal communities are doing more stocking of fish in the lakes than white people. Moreno stated, "It's been an eye-opener and really inspiring to see how the students are transformed by giving the elders the space to discuss the real situation in their communities" (M. Moreno, personal conversation, April 20, 2022).

From these stories, the need to prioritize cultural preparation becomes clear, lest CE projects in some areas be refused or disbanded, leaving instructors and students with fewer options for the real-life experience they desire. In different community contexts, learning from experts and community members prior to engagement is crucial.

Concluding Thoughts

Whether your institution is in a position to consider or implement any of these or other infrastructures or policy changes, we hope that their stories are food for thought and give a compass point to what is possible in a long-term horizon. Perhaps more immediately useful will be some of the ways that exemplary instructors have organized their coursework and community relationships we have described in this chapter, as you consider practices that lead to authentic and equitable community partnerships and how to prepare your students for that work.

10

Context Matters

Reflections from HBCUs and MSIs
and Working beyond the United States

The bulk of this book is aimed at preparing students who may be culturally disconnected from the communities engaging with HEIs, including white students, students from out of state (or country), and students from rural areas. Our institution's Civic Action Plan, as well as findings from CBR projects mentioned earlier, identified this as a primary concern our community partners had around CE. That means we have not explored the experience of students of color as fully due to the scope of the charge our community set, although such a study is currently underway at our campus. This chapter contains contributions from CEPs at other types of institutions or other demographic areas of the United States.

We co-authors are positioned at a large research intensive (R1) institution, meaning that we typically interact in national networks of our peer institutions, giving us less expertise in other types of institutional landscapes. Many of these R1s—especially private ones with huge endowments—have dedicated centers for engagement with anywhere from three to more than fifty staff, funding for graduate program assistants, and sometimes up to forty or more undergraduate intern positions. Steeped in this environment, one can consequently fail to appreciate the challenges that some HEIs face.

Although there is new, ongoing work at our institution to support BIPOC students doing CE, we know we have less experience and knowledge of how CE is different for students of color, and we want this book to be useful to HEIs who already have more diverse demographics. Luckily, thanks to referrals from Campus Compact, several CEPs around the country at different types of HEIs were willing to share their perspectives. Others whom we invited were interested but unable to provide a contribution due to having oversubscribed work portfolios. They shared common situations—lack of funding, campus restructuring due to leadership, and priority changes and resultant staffing shortfalls that precluded their participation. Some felt they were covering at least two full-time positions, if not more, as well as being the people that BIPOC students came to for academic, financial or emotional support. This gave us a heightened appreciation for their challenges and a better understanding of the difficulty of getting students the support needed to engage in CE, including any preparation required. In this chapter we share several stories from HBCUs and other MSIs that illustrate the resource disparities and special strengths and challenges in implementing CE at those campuses.

Dr. Lena Jones's essay shows one perspective from an urban community college, illustrating the issues created by lack of funding but also the strategies revised from the necessity of "working in the margins" to help students gain support and access to CE.

Community Engagement Challenges and Opportunities at an Urban Community College

Dr. Lena Jones

For over twenty years, I have been a political science faculty member at Minneapolis College, an open-enrollment community and technical college in downtown Minneapolis. Like many of its peer institutions in urban settings, it is a commuter college with a student body largely from our city. The average age of our students is twenty-six, and more than 70 percent of the student body identifies as "people of color, American Indian, two or more races, international, low income or first generation" (Minneapolis College, n.d.).

Unlike many of our research university peers, our college does not have a civic engagement office or an institutional budget to support such work. With a student body that is largely from the zip codes surrounding the college, the issues related to sending students "out in the community" are a bit different than those that exist in many residential colleges and universities. However, I hope that anyone grappling with the issues explored in this volume will find aspects of my personal story and my account of the evolution of experiential learning at my college useful.

There are times when desperation spawns innovation. During my first semester at the college in 2002, one of my classes was a state and local government course that I felt ill prepared to teach. A fateful conversation with a dear friend birthed the idea of incorporating Public Achievement, an initiative and framework that uses community organizing principles to increase the civic capacity of students, into this course.* This choice, driven by my insecurity and because it sounded fun, connected me with people who changed my life. Public Achievement's founder, Harry Boyte, and Dennis Donovan, the national organizer for Public Achievement, provided invaluable mentorship and support inside and outside the classroom. However, the people who changed my life most were my students. While using this approach and having students share their stories and passions early on, I realized that many of them had a deeper knowledge of the local context than I did, as well as life experiences that enabled deep and nuanced discussions about their own power and the effects of political institutions on their lives and communities. I also saw the transformative potential of intentionally creating spaces for their knowledge to be affirmed, shared, and utilized while collectively working on issues that they cared about and utilizing the resources available to them as students.

During this time, I connected with other faculty and staff members at the college who incorporated Public Achievement and other forms of experiential learning into their work with students. Our group grew to include students and our college's service-learning coordinator, and we met regularly for several years to brainstorm, troubleshoot, share resources and relationships, explore ways to connect students in our courses with one another, and collaboratively organize public events. In 2006, our group received a grant to deepen our work,† and we began to call ourselves the Center for Civic Engagement. Our name was definitely aspirational—we did not have (nor did we ever acquire) an actual "center." However, the faculty release time covered by the grant, along with the expertise and institutional resources of the service-learning coordinator and resources to pay community partners to work with our students inside and outside the classroom, led to some transformational experiences inside and outside our classes. At some point we became an "official" group, recognized in college documents and promotional materials.

Interestingly, this recognition and the bureaucratic demands that accompanied it seemed to drain our energy over time, and eventually, the official

---

* That dear friend was Roudy Hildreth, a fellow student in the University of Minnesota's political science Ph.D. program and lead author of the *Coach's Guide to Public Achievement* (posted by the Center of Democracy and Citizenship, Augsburg College linked here: https://web.augsburg.edu/sabo/PublicAchievementDigitalManual.pdf).

† This was a grant from the Minnesota Office of Higher Education and Minnesota Campus Compact.

community that was our "center" withered. Other contributing factors include the absence of some of our core members due to sabbaticals, the resignation of our service-learning coordinator, the college's decision to eliminate that position, and our inability to acquire more grant funds or hard money to support the work. While we maintained strong relationships with one another, many of us became less interested in devoting (mostly uncompensated) time and energy to drafting the community engagement section of the latest institutional master plan or promoting our vision for a center that had no chance of manifesting in a campus climate affected by retrenchment and an increasingly contentious relationship between faculty and administrators.

To quote from a paper I wrote for the Civic Reconstruction of Higher Education Conference (Jones, 2018), some of the most powerful educational experiences have been the moments when we have collaborated with students to create curricular and extracurricular spaces for students to "build meaningful relationships with one another, faculty, and community partners, to collectively think about their vision for their campus, city, state, and country, and to craft a career and life journey that feeds into that vision." Practically speaking, these are spaces where students can "identify their talents and passions, explore vocations that would help them make a living and work towards their collective and individual goals, identify specific skills that they need to develop, and devise strategies for developing those skills inside and outside of the program." Relying upon an advisory committee of nonprofit and government staff and other four-year institutions "to help shape the curriculum, identify potential field placement and employment opportunities for students, raise money for the program and its students, and advocate for the program within and outside of the college . . . partnerships with organizations outside of academia have been central to this program from its outset."

What would I want in an ideal world? Perhaps I have become used to working the edges and margins for the resources to do the work I have described, but that is a hard question to answer. Most of the work I see as having the greatest impact on our students and the community beyond the walls of my college would not have happened without significant monetary and other forms of support from outside organizations that appreciated our vision and the work we were doing. I guess the simple answer is a line in the college's budget that would provide enough resources for faculty to do this work without constantly hustling for outside money and support and that would support deep, lasting, nonexploitive collaborations with community partners. Whatever the amount, it would need to be enough to create and staff a community-based learning center with more than one full-time employee that would provide training and support for our faculty, students, *and* our community partners as they develop and implement impactful work that equally benefits the community and our institution. It would cover release time for faculty members to build and develop that impactful work, and it would provide a reliable and consistent pool of funds for guest speakers and deeper collaborations with our community partners within our classrooms (particularly those who do not have the "credentials" to officially teach at our college).

In the absence of that important institutional support needed to do meaningful CE and its corresponding preparation, Jones and her colleagues have done the heavy lifting essentially in isolation. In follow-up correspondence, she shared more about the types of relationship skill-building her program has done with students prior to CE:

> Training students to do power-mapping, community organizing-style one-to-one interviews and other relationship-building activities with one another, their instructors, and those outside of the college; collaborating with student life and community organizations to do assessment (surveys, organizing discussions); and addressing basic needs issues such as housing and food insecurity (Ex: working with Students Against Hunger and Homelessness (SAHH) to help with the student-run food pantry on campus). As far as popular education, that broadly entails creating learning spaces inside and outside of the classroom that honor the knowledge, experiences and wisdom of the students and challenges the divides between students, faculty, staff and administrators. For example, after the shutdown of the college in March 2020 due to the COVID-19 epidemic, SAHH and Community Development students facilitated several conversations between students, staff, faculty and administrators that helped lead to the creation of a student laptop and hotspot rental program and the decision to continue operating [the] campus' other food pantry. (L. Jones, email correspondence, April 20, 2022)

Funding challenges play a part in the next vignette but do not make up the whole picture. There may be assumptions at PWIs that if the student body were more racially and ethnically diverse, CE would magically become ideal for all parties. For example, we have heard parents of BIPOC youth in after-school programs say, "Please send us some students who look like us" and we wish we could, if only there were more in the course. Indeed, doing CE with those of similar identities has advantages, and when students of color have time, capacity, and interest, they are a valuable resource to the community.

A common assumption is that they come in with more affinity with the typical population demographic in many CE partnerships, but that is only one layer of self-identity and does not account for student capacity. There is much more to community context than simply pairing students and community partners with similar racial identities together. The reality of how college students and community members relate to each other is much more sophisticated, as we discussed in Chapter 5 and as Del M. N. Bharath's essay describes. She shares valuable lessons drawn from an initial failure, told with honest self-assessment and wisdom.

Why Didn't It Work? When Preparation and Practice Do Not Lead to Success

Del M. N. Bharath, Ph.D.

In the fall of 2020, I accepted a tenure-track faculty position at Savannah State University (SSU), the oldest HBCU in Georgia. I was living in California, where I was a faculty member at a Hispanic-serving institution while finishing my doctoral degree from a midwestern PWI. I had trained extensively in planning and implementing service-learning projects, and I used these experiences to conduct research and write/publish about service learning as a pedagogy. However, this academic knowledge and practical experience did not prepare me for the reality of using a community-engaged pedagogy at my new institution.

Advantages of Being an HBCU

HBCUs have a unique promise for community-engaged work. One of the more exciting aspects of HBCUs is the passion and awareness that students bring to the classroom. There is an unmatched HBCU culture and pride that are vastly different from other institutions. Students are predominantly Black and are aware of the systematic challenges they face socially and professionally. A student once asked me, "How are you preparing us to work in systems that were not built for us?" This question stumped me then, and I doubt I will ever have an adequate response. HBCU students are more aware of the societal issues experienced by underserved populations, especially Black populations, than more privileged students. Many times, HBCU students are part of the community we seek to serve. They desire to help improve and empower their communities instead of fixing communities for the residents. This may differ from the "savior" perspective, which is more prevalent in other types of students who may not be as connected to the communities served. Many HBCU students are, or personally know, service recipients of community partners. They understand the service needs of the community and the impacts of the work being done—things other schools might have to prepare students for. There is decreased town-gown tension as community members are connected to students.

Disadvantages of Being an HBCU

Conversely, there are pitfalls to implementing community-engaged research at an HBCU, lessons I learned the hard way. HBCUs are notoriously under-funded and may lack necessary resources due to budget constraints. For example, SSU does not have a dedicated community engagement office, and there are limited resources to connect faculty/students to community partners. Data has shown a disparity in endowments per student between public HBCUs ($7,625) and public non-HBCUs ($25,390) and private HBCUs ($24,989) and private non-HBCUs ($184,409) (L. T. Smith, 2021). The com-bined value of all 102 HBCUs ($3.9 billion to serve three hundred thousand students) is less than the endowment for *any* of the twenty-five largest PWI endowments, such as the University of North Carolina at Chapel Hill, which serves a tenth as many students with a similar endowment.

Project Plans

I teach in a public administration program, and at my previous campuses, I noticed students were more focused on the administration (how to) than the public (who for). At SSU, it was the reverse. Students entered the program with the desire to help the community but were less focused on the practical administration skills to be developed. While students' high public service motivation was a positive asset, the lack of interest in administration pre-sented a unique challenge. In the spring of 2021, I tried to implement service-learning projects in two graduate courses—grant writing and human resource management—similar to projects had I implemented in undergraduate class-es at other institutions. The plan was to have student groups create grant drafts or human resource management tools for their assigned community partners. Before the semester, I worked with the local United Way to recruit community partners with whom I met individually to discuss roles, respon-sibilities, and expectations. At the start of the semester, student groups met with their community partners to discuss projects and expected outputs and drafted contracts among themselves, the respective community partner, and myself detailing timelines, contacts, roles, responsibilities, and so on. As I was using best practices in the field, I thought we were off to a good start, but I was ill prepared for what happened during the semester.

Challenges

First, I did not expect pushback from students about the projects. The projects felt overwhelming, and students did not think they had the skills to perform them. They contended that they were here to learn the skills I was expecting them to use, which was above the expectations of the class. Despite my explanation that they were learning by doing, not all students agreed with the approach, which was reflected in my course evaluations. I was also not prepared for the preliminary training needed before students could engage with community partners, such as proper communication, teamwork strategies, project planning and management, and so on, even confidence building. Savannah is commonly called Slow-vannah by residents (due to their laid-back nature), and my expected pace of work was not realistic. Timelines were disregarded by community partners, leading to students being unable to complete work or get proper feedback. Projects that were previously feasible at other schools with more resources were unachievable in this new landscape. My ignorance of the students, the institution, and the community, as well as my overconfidence in my skills, did not lead to the success I envisioned.

Lessons Learned

The overall experience was disheartening—students did not feel as if they learned, community partners did not get the promised resources, and I felt as if I failed to connect course materials to real-world experience. This was the moment for me to reflect on what went wrong. As a newer educator, I believed graduate student populations were essentially the same and I could teach as I had been taught as a graduate student at a research-intensive PWI. I did not take the time to learn about the culture of the school or the community. As an HBCU, the school focuses on access and providing a pathway to education, and faculty are expected to "meet students where they are," which varied drastically. I was not prepared for the required amount of scaffolding of assignments and simplifying of learning objectives to help meet students and community partners where they were, instead of where I expected them to be. In my experience as a graduate student, I never imagined challenging a professor on an assignment, but students were empowered to do so (and rightly so). I did not take the time to understand the systematic barriers that students faced. I was not prepared for the additional work that the lack of resources (e.g., the lack of a writing center) created for me. Moreover, I was naive in thinking I could so quickly develop trust as a woman of color but non-Black faculty member, new to HBCU culture and the community. Upon reflection, I realized that I was doing the same thing that I criticized public administration students for doing. As a public administration educator, I was focused on the administration of the project, something I had experience with, instead of the "public" in the students and community partners being taught/served. I have taken a step back from planning and implementation and am instead focusing on developing relationships with community partners and students.

In the future, I plan to use the lessons from the perceived failure to create scaffolded projects with more appropriate timelines and expectations. This means understanding the knowledge base of my students and adjusting project expectations. For example, service-learning projects with final-year students will be more involved than those with first-year students, and requirements will be higher for those about to enter the professional field, though the bar of excellence will be high for all. My main lesson is that there is no one-size-fits-all approach to community-engaged pedagogy. Educators must be willing to do critical self-analysis, learn from mistakes, adapt, and remember the purpose and promise of community-engaged teaching and learning. Planning and practice alone do not ensure success. Educators must understand the landscapes they are functioning in and adapt to meet the needs of stakeholders. It is work, but the potential outcomes are worth it.

Other Issues Unique to MSIs and HBCUs

Not all MSIs have funding gaps as large as the ones described prior. Having more resources seems to improve students' access to CE, and with those resources comes more ability to work with students so they are supported in CE and succeed in it. That still does not mean that students of color in MSIs and the communities they engage with creates an "instant win" by virtue of being in the same affinity group, as discussed earlier. In the following we share stories from other institutions where different strategies have led to good outcomes for both students and communities.

Dr. Azuri Gonzalez's vignette comes from the University of Texas at El Paso, "one of the largest and most successful Hispanic-serving institutions in the country, with a student body that is over 80% Hispanic. UTEP is an R1 research university, and ranked fifth in Texas for federal research expenditures at public universities" (University of Texas at El Paso, n.d.). Gonzalez illustrates how the alignment of UTEP students with the community is part of what makes them successful and how their holistic approach to the symbiotic relationship improves student learning outcomes while creating a stronger community.

Hispanic Servingness and Community Engagement

Dr. Azuri Gonzalez

We are at a time when many institutions are enrolling a larger population of Hispanic students and therefore attaining the Hispanic-Serving Institution (HSI) designation as defined by Title V of the Higher Education Act. This designation is mostly attributed to institutions whose Hispanic student population is at least 25 percent of the total. Earlier studies indicated that the Hispanic population was the fastest growing in the United States (Chapa & Valencia, 1993) and that higher education institutions needed to be prepared to serve this population in a different way if retention is a priority. It has been the experience at the University of Texas at El Paso that to properly serve its student population, we needed to move from Hispanic enrolling to Hispanic *serving* (Garcia, Nunez, Sansone, 2019).

To be Hispanic serving means to understand the assets students bring with them and to serve through culturally responsive practices. It means not categorizing this student population as simply different—or, worse, as at-risk—because it performs differently, especially at PWIs. Viewing this student population as unique, not to be confused with homogenous, is part of that process. One of the many assets that a Hispanic, Latino/a, or Latinx student population brings to any institution is its culture, very often characterized by its familial ties. Family and culture are very much part of who students are and what they bring to an institution. At UTEP, this understanding brought about what we refer to as the UTEP Edge: The acknowledgement of the "talented" UTEP student who is simply offered opportunities to raise their potential to the next level and give them an "edge" in their education, career pathway, and role in society. It is an asset-based approach that builds on what the students bring and works in tandem with them to bring about student success.

When participating in community engagement, a high-impact practice and a principle of the UTEP Edge, Hispanic students' understanding of community is viewed as an asset. They can more easily navigate the nuances of the community from a language, geographical, regional, and sometimes even global perspective (Villalobos, Gonzalez, Nuñez & Sirin, 2022). The majority of students at UTEP hold a part-time or full-time job while attending college and are often caretakers of their own parents or are parents themselves. Many students from UTEP are still the first in their families to graduate, and education is viewed as an avenue for upward social mobility.

Connection to Community While
Retaining Cultural Humility

In the context of education serving as a motivator for overall life improvement for themselves and their families, a sense of service is also part of who students are at UTEP. Being part of a family translates to being part of a larger community, and in that vein, students have an immediate connection to the community they serve. Additionally, while this connection is beneficial, it is still viewed as novel because the community they serve is multifaceted and not homogenous. Students from the community understand this. They know that the El Paso community, with over eight hundred thousand residents, is composed of smaller communities with different dynamics and "personas." They know that to know the Northeast side of town does not immediately mean they know the Segundo Barrio. Having gone to school on the Westside does not mean they understand the Eastside. It is a beautiful thing to see how their El Pasoan credential is not immediately seen as a way to enter a part of the community as an insider, but it does allow them to be aware of what they do not know and still have to learn.

This is a dynamic that needs to be taught to others. Knowing a community and serving a community are very complex processes that require relationships that are not transactional, but meaningful. Students may approach a community as part of their course, but they have the humility to know that they are not entitled to that community knowledge and that they are still outsiders until they know what their role is in that context. They enter as learners, with deference to those who are situated in that space, and they come out as eager advocates for others to experience similar learning.

UTEP as a Culturally Humble Partner

Not all HSIs have a similar student population or are as intricately connected to their region, but at UTEP, we learned early on that we had a student population to serve and that our community plays a significant role in being able to achieve this. We do not operate as the center of a community but as a partner like many others in it. The community serves as an educational ground where many alumni live and where families encourage the next generation of professionals to get an education. The community is a backbone to our students' lives and growth, and community engagement is not just a pedagogical tool. The community offers students an opportunity to build a stronger sense of self and purpose, providing a means to visualize their future, and an affirmation of their strengths, assets, and skills.

In a telephone follow-up with UTEP's community engagement center, we learned their staff are in charge of student orientations and spend time helping students not to make assumptions based on their own experience, even if there are similarities, because, according to Associate Director Jenna Lujan, "there are so many different issues depending on the part of town; you set the stage, and then through the required reflection sessions, students identify some of the preconceptions they had before they [went out into that community setting]." She tries to help them pull out what they learned and document it for their personal growth, as well as to inform future orientation meetings (J. Lujan, personal interview, April 11, 2022).

Another phenomenon affecting CE outside of funding shortages was noted by staff and faculty at several HBCUs and MSIs, as well as PWI community colleges and small private colleges with departments designated to serve BIPOC students. When we asked them to tell us about how they prepare students for CE, they replied that the students first need support for academic success and that CE is aspirational but not a high priority at the outset. However, some of the mentorship programs reflect a desire to support CE as a way for students who want to feel connected and give back, and these programs know that CE is a high-impact practice that will benefit students as they look ahead to careers after graduation.

Harper Community College, a PWI outside Chicago, has not one but two separate ways for students to be mentored and build the foundations that will enable them to take part in community engagement. One can make an argument that participating in programs at community colleges to benefit student success can be viewed as engaging with a "community"—namely, other students who need support from those who received it in the past. Dr. Amelia Ortiz's vignette shows an advisor's perspective, and Aaron Posey's shows the perspective from a staff member in the second mentorship program.

Advising Underrepresented Students Who Participate in a Community College Mentoring Program

Dr. Amelia Ortiz

Working with students deemed a "special population" in a case-management advising system allows genuine relationships to develop with students beyond academic advising. The One Million Degrees (OMD) program prepares low-income community college students to transition into the workforce with the necessary knowledge and support network. In the OMD program, intentional outreach is done throughout the semester to ensure students continue to be engaged and successful, and the program also holds them accountable for their participation. Students are expected to attend a weekly class during their first year in the program and for the next two years must attend monthly Scholar Development Sessions where they meet individually with a coach. Coaches are volunteers from the community who are aligned with the students' academic or workforce goals and work with them on their resumes, cover letters, and so forth.

It is crucial to create a connection and establish a relationship with students immediately. With consistent interactions and intentional communication, students will trust that the information being provided is vital to achieve their goals. Students need to receive holistic support when they are struggling academically and may also need community resources for other issues. The OMD curriculum teaches students real-life skills that they can implement at their current job, at an internship, or in future endeavors because it concentrates on professionalism, financial literacy, and civic engagement.

The first-year OMD students must attend a free weekly class that focuses on developing professional skills, such as creating resumes, engaging in mock interviews, and writing personal statements. In addition, all students are required to attend monthly "Scholar Development Sessions," where they work with their coaches on completing their professional development goals. The coaches are volunteers from the community and ideally are connected to the student's area of academic interest. They work closely with the student to guide them through professional expectations and norms.

The second-year scholars learn aspects of financial literacy, and the third-year scholars discuss how to be leaders in the community. These discussions include developing leadership traits, developing one's core values, and advocating for oneself and others. All OMD students are asked to volunteer at OMD-hosted campus events to help recruit prospective students by sharing their experiences in the program. In addition, OMD students are invited to participate in campus improvement initiatives such as focus groups, surveys, and other activities on campus. Students receive stipends for participation, which increases the amount of engagement. Overall, through their participation in the OMD program, students obtain additional opportunities and begin to acknowledge the value of helping others; they begin to model the behavior of their coaches and want to give back to others.

Programs that provide supplemental support services for students encourage students to later become coaches or mentors. The program has existed long enough for alums to obtain their degrees, enter the workforce, and return to the program as coaches. Students become invested in their community and want to give back to others with similar backgrounds. Mentorship programs are an influential factor in students becoming an integral part of the community and give them a sense of belonging to it because they collaborate with the same local community advisor through-out their time at the institution.

Rise-Up: A Mentorship Program to Help Enable Institutions to Support Minority Students

Aaron Posey

We live in an increasingly diverse society as history progresses. Diversity measures more than just an assortment of ethnic and cultural variations. Students must be prepared to work and serve in all kinds of communities with a general awareness of their own cultural background knowledge, sincere respect for others' cultures, and the modesty to acknowledge the limits of their viewpoints, building intercultural skills to help them work with others in effective and applicable ways. A common theme among institutions should be to provide resources that can be used to prepare students to engage ethically in their community. In the higher education sector, various members sometimes convey that students' lack of cultural awareness and experience with community engagement is a problem that needs to be rectified.

My institution works toward the goal of giving students the chance to participate in community engagement in various ways while supporting their ability to succeed. We started a mentorship program for students of color run by faculty and staff members of color called "Rise-Up" which was intended to help with retention of minority students, faculty, and staff and assist minority students in connecting with minority faculty and staff members to embrace DEI on its campus. This program helps incoming and current minority students acclimate to being in a higher educational institution. Mentors also assist students in determining their vocational aspirations and work alongside them to achieve goals.

Some students need this kind of mentorship support before they can even think about having extra capacity to serve others. As a part of the overall support, the program can help prepare students to engage by acquainting them with resources and information about various organizations in the community. Participants learn from one another as they interact in the program and encourage each other to support their communities outside their campus community. With this support, students partake in various community-engagement practices, some with clusters of comparable people who share similar understandings and social resources while others have branched outside their own community to engage. Mentees are able to participate in community service, with oversight from the mentorship program, which allows students to gain real-world experience and exercise significant habits like leadership, conflict resolution, problem-solving, and time management.

The Rise-Up mentorship program also looks for ways for students to volunteer on projects based on ideas brought up within their group or concerns happening on campus. Various advocacy efforts arose on campus because of mentees who wanted to see change. By looking for opportunities, the goal is to have students be prepared to communicate and network with others who are different from them. This program became successful because minority students learned and had access to other minority professionals across campus in various departments and roles, which helped build community and empower them. The development and implementation of a mentorship program take time, effort, and sincere consideration.

Engaging in the Global Context

All the same issues that students can cause or encounter a mile away from campus are still in play when abroad, with the addition of other unique challenges—language barriers, cultural differences, massive disparities in financial resources/privilege, and traveling in unfamiliar territory—that can put students in a less confident headspace where it is harder to make even the simplest decisions. It is outside the capacity of this volume to go into depth about global engagement, but we would be remiss not to touch briefly on a couple of main issues and provide some good sources if this is an area of interest.

Voluntourism

One issue that has arisen in global engagement is what is being called "voluntourism," or using global volunteering as a form of tourism. There has been a rise in think pieces and op-eds exploring the perils of voluntourism in recent years (McLennan, 2014; Stephens, 2019), and rightfully so. In many ways it can be seen as the epitome of the savior mentality, yet it is a commonly practiced form of international engagement. From mission trips to alternative spring breaks and programs such as Engineers Without Borders, such trips have a history of being rooted in ideas of pity, superiority, and colonization. See Appendix B.4 for some links to illustrative videos that have been used in helping students understand and interrupt this dynamic.

Ethical Decision-Making

Closely linked with power dynamics, as we discussed in Chapter 5, the stakes around decision-making can be even more dangerous in international engagement. In global settings, students may be engaging in practices that would be considered unethical in their home countries but are more or less accepted abroad because of the "othering" of the people they are working with, paternalistic and colonial views, and general disrespect. A good illustration is when underresourced communities offer inappropriate opportunities to students (e.g., and a true story: a student completely untrained in any nursing or health skills being allowed—in fact, asked—to scrub in and assist with a Caesarian section in a rural Ugandan health clinic where no staff are available).

Responsible Research

Introduced in Chapter 9, the International Living Knowledge Network has also examined global engagement at length through several channels. Conversations have been held regarding inequities in how researchers from the Global North were approaching projects in the Global South (Ofir & Gallagher, 2021). In 2008, the International Living Knowledge Network signed a charter for the Global Alliance for Community-Engaged Research (Hall et al., 2013), predicated on principles of equity, mutual benefit and respect, and responsible research. That work migrated into a six-year, €80 million grant initiative funded by the European Commission (n.d.).

Some resources for further exploration of global engagement include the robust Community-Based Global Learning Collaborative, who are working to advance "ethical, critical, aspirationally de-colonial community-based learning and research for more just, inclusive, and sustainable communities," according to the website's homepage (https://www.cbglcollab.org). This group evolved out of a group of scholars—including Eric Mlyn at Duke, Amanda Moore McBride at Washington University, and Eric Hartman, who wrote on 'fair trade learning' (Hartman, 2015)—and hosted biennial events called International Service Learning Summits. Campus Compact hosts a section on both of these resources, with good references to follow for those interested in learning more.

Laura Livingston is a young researcher whose perspective as a doctoral candidate who has done work in Ghana highlights some of the unique considerations of graduate engaged research. She recommends using the principles of fair-trade learning, which is outlined in her contribution.

International Community-Engaged Scholarship

Laura Livingston, Ph.D.

In January 2020, I traveled to Ghana to prepare for a community-engaged scholarship project built on relationships from my prior Peace Corps service. In this preliminary research trip, I listened to agroforesters discuss challenges and opportunities related to climate change and global markets. Working with an interpreter and my adolescent-level Twi language skill, we collectively forged research questions, and I left Ghana inspired to write my dissertation proposal guided by the knowledge and experience of the farmers and farmer educators there. I am not alone in my quest for doing international community engagement. Within academia, there has been a deepened focus on global commitments to equity and anti-racism in community-engaged scholarship, along with intensified funding, publication, and visibility of cross-cultural scholarship—especially in partnership with countries in the Global South, Indigenous people, and people who are marginalized within global and local political systems (Henrich et al., 2010; Purzycki et al. 2018). But with this growth come new challenges, especially around power differentials between academic and community partners (Whiteford & Trotter, 2008), and new opportunities for reflection on responsible methods, practices, and contexts for engaging in cross-cultural and international community-engaged scholarship.

Strengths of Community-Engaged Scholarship for International Research

I chose a community-engaged approach because I knew that the local knowledge and expertise of the farmers I was working with would be indispensable in project design and development. During this preliminary trip, I worked with Emmanuel, a farmer educator I had worked with as a Peace Corps trainer, who could connect me with farmer-based organizations in several communities. He helped me identify current community leaders and how their political interests and goals might intertwine with our scholarship. In addition, Emmanuel translated complicated conversations around research goals and methodologies. The farmers and Emmanuel shared culturally appropriate types of methodological approaches and other aspects of the research process. Working with a diverse research team, we discussed innovative approaches that could lead to greater scientific impact than if I were designing a research study in Ghana alone (AlShebli et al., 2018). Through these discussions I was able to uncover hidden subjectivities and biases and account for those in the research design.

I compensated Emmanuel for his time, which we calculated using his hourly wage at the social enterprise where he was employed. We met the farmers' groups during their regular meeting time, so we did not compensate them. But Emmanuel and I agreed that for future workshops, we would need to provide food, a small stipend, and childcare.

Emmanuel, as my co-lead in the research process, had no university or research center affiliation. However, there are universities and research centers across the Global South that have place-based research projects that might create opportunities for partners in the Global North and South alike. Wright et al. (2005) note that academic collaborations across countries offer opportunities for mutual capacity building, career development, and the potential to support the development of localized research infrastructure.

Challenges to Cross-Cultural Community-Engaged Scholarship

In March of 2020, as COVID-19 was spreading across the globe, I spoke with Emmanuel and the other employees at the social enterprise, and we postponed our project indefinitely. The methods we had chosen and the types of questions we were asking were not conducive to the virtual format. Not only that, but I had not built my own capacity to do virtual engagement, and Emmanuel did not feel comfortable engaging in the research process without me. We had not had enough time to build our collective capacity before this global change. In fact, time is one of the many challenges of international community engagement. As a graduate student, postponing this scholarship project meant changing my entire dissertation and hoping to rekindle this partnership at a future date. If I was a faculty member or researcher, job stability and a longer job tenure might allow for an easier transition back into the research project once travel was permissible. However, with my specific graduation timeline, this would not be the case.

Navigating collaborative partnerships in international scholarship projects takes time and effort, with academics spending months at a time in other countries to build the relationships and contextual knowledge required to engage in collaborative scholarship. As cross-cultural scholarship has been historically rooted in Western and capitalistic ideas and motivations and colonial developmental frameworks (Reynolds, 2022), scholars may find resistance to collaboration or an expectation of passive participation. In domestic engagement, scholars may also be representing their university and its legacy in the community where they are working. In international scholarship, community members may also conflate a scholar's identity with the legacies of international aid and government entities (Reynolds, 2022), increasing the complexity of scholarship partnerships. Scholars from the Global North and South have generated robust scholarship on the negative impacts of cross-cultural engagement (see Easterly, 2006; Grusky, 2000; Tomazos & Butler, 2011). Furthermore, conflict can arise because of different ontologies, epistemologies, cultural views, and goals for partnership or scholarship. Far worse, in my opinion, is when conflict does *not* arise and hegemonic views remain unchallenged and potentially lead to new forms of colonialism and dependency (Hammersley, 2014). A prime example of exploitative cross-cultural scholarship is often called parachute research, where scholars extract information and data from the community without building relationships or reciprocating for time and knowledge (Abimbola, 2019; Jumbam, 2020). A community-engaged approach can increase the chances of building a reciprocal relationship. However, even the methodologies used in research projects, such as standardized cross-cultural measurements, are still rooted in colonial and imperialism practices (Kline et al., 2018) that can entrench and reify power inequities.

Strategies for Cross-Cultural Community-Engaged Scholarship

There is no way to counter the colonial legacies and extractive legacy of scholarship in the Global South. Scholars who want to engage in cross-cultural engagement must continue to reflect on these issues and be accountable in their scholarship practices. Speaking from my experience, graduate students and others with short timeframes should potentially reconsider what is possible within a field season and how deeply they will be able to engage with coresearchers and community members given potential disruptions.

Partnership development is a key component of successful cross-cultural community-engaged scholarship. Partners in the research process should define early in the process how decisions will be made and what an equitable leadership structure looks like. Hierarchy, participation, and power look different across cultures, and collaborators will need to discuss these concepts in depth. Once partners establish decision-making and leadership structures, I suggest spending ample time discussing research goals and goals for mutual capacity building. Community partners may be interested in community development milestones, and they could also be interested in co-authorship and be open to (and excited about!) the opportunity for intellectual collaboration.

Scholars should be flexible and creative with funding. Academic researchers from the Global North often have disproportionate access to infrastructure and financial resources, yet academic institutions that are hosting grants demand high overhead and often restrict opportunities to pay overheads to overseas institutions. I found that grants awarded internally were more flexible and allowed us to use all grant funds on the CBR project. Although the grant sums were smaller, I was able to cobble together four grant awards that exceeded our total research budget.

For instructors planning to take students abroad for international community-based learning, I recommend utilizing the fair trade learning (FTL) (Hartman et al., 2014) framework, which highlights several forms of reciprocity: exchange, influence, and generativity. Core principles include community voice and direction, economic and environmental sustainability, dual purposes, and deliberate intercultural contact and reflection. This framework relies on robust student preparation, which may depend on the program and learning experience but could include culturally appropriate project design and knowledge of the country's political history, cultural customs, and current events. During the international learning experience, instructors using the FTL method provide space to connect course content to student experience and reflect on new knowledge.

Last, these cultural changes need to be supported by structures in higher education that value relationship building and equitable partnership structures. Tenure and evaluation processes should value the time spent to build partnership and the qualitative impacts of scholarship projects, such as mutual capacity building and social change. Without institutional support, it will be difficult to sustain cultural shifts in cross-cultural community-engaged scholarship projects.

Concluding Thoughts

If you are thinking about or already involved in global engagement, we encourage you to pursue the resources mentioned earlier and many others written that target this unique practice and pay attention to the extra layers of complexity in CE abroad. Reflecting on the other stories prior, it is clear that every institution has different strengths and challenges. While UTEP is one MSI that has a robust research portfolio and a dedicated engagement office, the essays from staff and faculty at HBCUs point out that higher education as a whole needs to look critically at how resources are allocated or won in grants, how understanding and honoring community context are essential to preparation work regardless of institution, and how the ability to pay higher tuition plays into access to opportunities. Although beyond the scope of this volume, we feel these are topics for further interrogation. Future national conversations could support CEPs in understanding how to best share resources and program ideas, and how to incentivize collaboration and partnerships between HEIs in the same geographic vicinity to achieve a richer, more equitable future for CE and for all students.

11

Final Thoughts

O ur community partners are the driving reason we developed the curriculum we have shared here. We did not write this book because we thought it would just be a fun thing to do, although it has been a rewarding experience. We wrote it because we had looked for such a resource in the past to recommend to faculty and could not find it, so we created our own. While a fairly robust body of literature has evolved that documents the harms CE can cause in communities (as well as the positive outcomes that can occur when it goes well), one crucial piece was notably lacking: How do we set up students for successful CE work? How can we mitigate harm? What do students need to know? How can we help them learn it?

A starting place is understanding why students do CE and helping guide them toward motivations that are altruistic without being paternalistic. CEPs can support this learning through a focus on relationships, principles of community partnerships, and an asset-based approach. Next, students can better understand themselves and develop better self-awareness. Who are they? What are their social identities? What is their positionality? How do they move through the world? How are they seen by others? What harm might they, even unintentionally, be causing? How can they mitigate that harm? How can they be better collaborators? This grounding helps students understand broader systems of privilege and oppression, as well as how they fit into these complex systems as individuals and why this is important in the context of CE. This also sets up students to understand the unique way power plays a role in CE, including community- university power dynamics and unequal distribution of resources, and how to mitigate this inequity through resource sharing, co-creating projects, and prioritizing community knowledge. We hope that, once prepared through this content and other resources, students understand that they are a part of a larger ecosystem (the metaphorical garden!) and that their job is to be supportive and useful, rather than act like an invasive weed.

The heart of this book—and a key disposition for students—is humility. We want to send out into communities students who understand what culture is and how to respectfully and appropriately engage with people from different cultures and circumstances. Ultimately, we want students to feel empowered to be active participants in whichever communities they find themselves. We hope that students can be open, curious, and eager to learn from and with others. We also want students to understand the many kinds of knowledge in the world and that the best outcomes occur when we can all apply our knowledge and skills and when we can all show up as human beings first and foremost.

This work can be done most easily when a critical classroom or CE setting has been developed. The CEP overseeing students, whether faculty, staff, or student organization advisor, can use common commitments or ground rules, meet students where they are, encourage rather than demand participation, and practice calling students in to hold them accountable versus calling them out. Excellent facilitation will further support student development, as will a focus on hope.

These practices and ideas will function best when relationship-centered systems are developed and nurtured. This may look like a Science Shop, place-based community engagement, or specific positions and university structures in place to support relationship-centered CE. This can include tenure and promotion policies, funding, staff support, leadership positions, and higher institutional investment. Different university and community contexts may need different structures for high-quality CE (e.g., partnerships with Indigenous communities and tribal nations, HBCUs, MSIs, and global engagement).

Prepared students are not those who have all the answers or knowledge but rather those who are reflective, thoughtful, and self-aware. They know to focus on relationships, how to listen, and how to ask the right questions of community partners and themselves to promote trust and mutual benefit. They come to CE from a place of humility, openness, and nonjudgment of themselves and others. They are comfortable with accountability, discomfort, and ambiguity. They are well versed in the art of reflection and are supported by CEPs to continue learning, unlearning, and growing throughout the CE experience.

We realize this book will necessarily be incomplete, and we encourage you to find new resources, including those tailored to your institution and material focused on your specific community context. Our goal in writing this was not to *be right* but to begin a path to help us *get it right*. We found there was information about what characteristics prepared students might have but less practical information about how to develop those characteristics in students. We hope this volume helps bridge that gap in providing the "what," "why," and "how" of student preparation. If you are planning to connect with the online modules on Canvas, we stress that creating your own virtual platform tailored to your institutional setting will make the content most relevant to your student body.

We are also aware that our lenses are limited. While we sought out a variety of contributors from different institutions, our work is focused primarily on those contexts we are familiar with and the student population that our community asked us to prepare. We recognize that our advice may not be useful for those whose context is completely unique from ours, and the vignettes from HBCUs and MSIs may not cover all the situations CEPs face at different HEIs. In any case, we encourage you to keep striving to find resources to complement this book, and we would be very grateful to hear from you about things you discover that will improve our own preparation and facilitation work. We welcome new, and even contradicting, ideas and suggestions.

In the future, we hope that preparation is built into all CE programs and courses and is seen as an essential part of all CE itself. We would love to see a future where a three-credit preparation course is a prerequisite for taking a CBL course or getting a graduate research grant in a community setting. If HEIs are going to tout their CE bona fides, we hope they realize it is their responsibility to send prepared students who are ready to be useful to community sites and to prioritize this preparation. If we continue to send ill-prepared students, eventually we will no longer be welcome in community settings, and a powerful model for student learning and social impact will be lost. HEIs have to do better than they have in the past. Since the time of the study for *The Unheard Voices* in 2006, the findings of the follow-up in our community in 2016 saw that substantial change was minimal over those ten years, except mainly in the discernment of our partners. Since the events of the global pandemic and recent shifts in emphasis on racial and economic justice, the conversation has heated up even more. Our communities are definitely done with the tired excuses of HEIs about change being slow and hard. They are ready to demand what they need from a CE partnership, and they will tell instructors and others to stop calling them if those needs are not met.

We also hope there is a shift in understanding the role and importance of community-engaged work at HEIs and across academia—that it is no longer thought of (or advertised) as a way to pad a résumé or do good in the world, or as a marketing tool of admissions and development offices, but rather is a form of civic responsibility that we all share as global citizens and members of communities. We must remind ourselves how privileged we are in academia, with our resources and luxury of contemplation and study, and how a moral obligation to do useful, responsible research comes with that privilege. In that mindset of academic accountability, we will see well-executed CE that produces rigorous and relevant scholarship that is undertaken to work toward social justice and change, which cannot happen from atop the ivory tower. And ultimately, in that scenario community engagement is thought of as an integral part of higher education and is robustly supported by our institutions and community partners alike. We are encouraged by each cohort of new faculty hires we meet every fall, who come looking for meaningful engagement and are more and more eager to "do it right" than the group the year before, and new CEP attendees at engagement conferences who have actually been able to study partnership practices as part of their education. Someday soon, with added impetus from organizations like Campus Compact, The Engagement Scholarship Consortium, and others, we hope the issues described to us by community partners in 2006 and again in 2016 will be relics of a distant past, no longer a deterrent to full, equitable community-university partnerships.

Appendixes

We have gathered a collection of additional activities and resources that readers might find useful. We include some activities for engaging students to augment the material embedded in the chapters, as well as a list of resources to fuel your continued learning and development.

Appendix A

Activities

A.1. Identity and Inclusion Activities

Visioning Activity

This activity allows students the opportunity to consider how bias may belie our assumptions, as well as how representation may impact what we perceive as "normal."

Prompt: Please close your eyes and envision the different people as I tell you about them:

- African American woman
  - Single mother
  - Wealthy
  - Physician
- Teenage girl
  - Salvadorian refugee
  - Lives in New York City
  - Studies in famous dance school
- Sikh man
  - World-class athlete
  - Wheelchair user
  - Nonprofit executive
- White woman
  - Renowned business leader
  - Mother of three
  - Committed felony tax evasion

Reflect:
- How did your mental images evolve during the process?
- Did anything surprise you about the activity?
- Why might this exercise be useful?

Identity Signs

This activity allows students to reflect on the saliency of different aspects of their identity and consider how identity can influence daily life. Students will move around the room to the relevant sign (see setup below) as the facilitator reads off a series of questions. Note: although students may experience their identities in complex, intersecting ways, they should only select one sign. You might consider asking students to optionally share out any reflections or context on why they selected their place in the room.

- Setup: Place a series of signs around the room corresponding to different social identity categories (race, ability, sexual orientation, gender identity, religion, class, ethnicity, other).
- Prompts:
  - The part of my identity that I am most aware of on campus is . . .
  - The part of my identity that I wish I knew more about it . . .
  - The part of my identity that I think the least about it is . . .
  - The part of my identity that gives me the most pride is . . .
  - The part of my identity that I feel is difficult to discuss with others who identify differently is . . .
  - The part of my identity I am most aware of when entering the community is . . .
- Reflect:
  - What did it feel like to do this activity?
  - What did you notice about yourself or the group?
  - Were there any additional categories you wish had existed as options?

Temperature Checks

This activity could be facilitated virtually and anonymously by using online teaching tools such as real-time polling through sites like Kahoot. Used at the beginning of a meeting or discussion, this tool can help give students a sense of the ideas or opinions in the room before diving into deeper conversation. Instructors can utilize this information to better understand the makeup of the course as well as students' understanding of different topics. This format allows for multiple different activities. We list a few prompts and associated questions here:

- **Understanding harm:** On a spectrum from not harmful to most harmful, where do the following activities fall?
  - Native American mascots
  - Dressing as a stereotype for Halloween
  - Applications that require you to select "male" or "female"

- Assuming students of color are on a scholarship
- Hawaiian luau–themed menus in the dining halls
- Keynote speakers with no interpretation provided
- Assuming that everyone can communicate via a smartphone or personal computer.
- Textbook examples focused on two-parent families
- Fall semester breaks coinciding with Thanksgiving and Christmas
- Unpaid internships targeting first-generation students
- Assuming that anyone can get into school if they just work hard
- **Assessing the course experience:** To what extent do you agree or disagree with the following?
  - I feel comfortable sharing my opinion in this class.
  - I enjoy the work we are doing with the community.
  - I am learning a lot from my experience in the community.
  - I feel that I am being listened to by my peers.
  - I feel that I am being listened to by the instructor.
  - This partnership is valuable.
- **Community- or topic-specific questions:**
  - Rank your level of familiarity with the community/organization.
  - What two to three words come to mind when you think about addiction, poverty, mental illness, etc.?
  - Rank your level of *personal* familiarity with homelessness, food insecurity, tutoring, etc.

A.2. Community Engagement Scenarios

These are scenarios that have actually happened at our HEI or at others that we have heard about through our national engagement networks. Testing your chops on these will help you respond quickly to situations students bring to your class or research project.

Scenario 1

An instructor sent undergraduate CBL students to an alternative high school where a course was devoted to coping strategies for some of the thorny, complex, and extremely private issues the youth were dealing with in their home lives, such as financial problems, health concerns, personal and social relationships, and so on. The classroom teacher had not been asked to explain why there were several strangers in the back of the classroom who did not participate or share any stories of their own. To make matters worse, the college students only attended sporadically, and they sat in the back of the room with clipboards, writing down what they were hearing. The youth balked at appearing vulnerable in front of people they did not know whose intentions were unclear, and they clammed up. This upset the classroom teacher, who called the university instructor and asked to back out of the arrangement.

What would you do? What else could have been done at any phase of this scenario? List the points at which this situation could have been avoided and what you think would work better.

Actual outcome: The classroom teacher met privately with the university instructor and the CEP who was helping coordinate with the high school to institute new parameters for the CE project. The next semester, college students were asked to sign a commitment to attend the class every week, agree to participate in the discussion and share their own vulnerabilities (but not take up all the space in the room!), and not write anything identifiable about what they heard, in advance of the high school permitting them access to the classroom.

Scenario 2

Students in a CBL course develop a kids' science activity series; they send an email announcing their intentions to the place-based community-engagement center a week before they plan to come. The students show up at the center on a random Friday at three in the afternoon expecting a room full of grateful kids eagerly waiting for their "science club," but there is absolutely no one there. They feel affronted after all the work they put into designing the activities, buying supplies, and carting them on the bus to the off-campus location. The students vent to the center's staff, asking to be put on the agenda of the community advisory committee's (CAC) next meeting to register their indignation and demand that someone get some children to show up so they can get credit for their community project.

When the students attend the meeting, several of the community members are very quick and very vocal in their criticism of the students (bringing one of them to tears) for having not done the following:

- Contacting the center's staff to ask what might work best and what help they might need with distributing promotional material.
- Trying to poll some of the parents as they came in and out of the center for other reasons to ask what days or times most people could come. One CAC member, a single working parent herself, was particularly, scathingly brutal in her response to the students that they had no concept that children might have no one to drop them off at the center when their mothers were at work and that the only after-school programs they could attend were ones that happened at their school.

What would you do if this was the first you heard about it? What else could have been done that would have avoided this interpersonal conflict? If you had a class planning a CBL project, what would you advise them to do before starting to design it?

Actual outcome: Once the students stopped crying, the center staff were able to ask them to meet at their office at a later time to help them try to salvage their CBL project. They knew that the idea had merit, if handled properly, because constituents of the center had asked for more kids' activities.

The staff asked them to develop a short three-question survey and offered to display a QR code to link to it along with some material promoting the science club. That way, interested parents could give their time preferences and children's age ranges, as well as brainstorm age-appropriate science activities that would more likely be popular with the youth who regularly accessed the center.

Here are some additional scenarios that we have utilized. Although based on real situations, there are some revisions we have made to make them more accessible to students. As such, we do not list any actual outcomes with these scenarios.

Scenario 3

You are a second-year master's student in nonprofit leadership. For your capstone in the degree, you are required to partner with a local nonprofit to complete a project that meets a community-identified need. You have been working in collaboration with a local nonprofit that focuses on youth education to expand and assess a tutoring program. A month into the semester, your staff partner informs you that he will be transitioning out of his position within the next two weeks to take a job across the country. In your time together, you have established a structure for the project and formed important initial relationships; however, your partner's sudden departure leaves you feeling frazzled and severely alters what may be possible for the project.

Questions: How does this departure impact your project and its original timeline? It is likely the project will not be completed by the end of the semester. What steps might you take to readjust the project in a way that is still useful to the community partner? What information might you want to make sure you can get from your partner before he leaves? What other considerations should be made? Who else should you be talking to/working with?

Scenario 4

You are a third-year undergraduate assisting a professor with a community-based participatory research project focused on the effectiveness of a public health intervention model intended for African American women. Your research team has partnered with a local nonprofit focused on access to health services and with a history of outreach to this population. After one of your early meetings with your research team and the staff of the nonprofit partner organization, you are hanging around in the nonprofit building, waiting for your bus.

A Black woman approaches you, asking if you are from the university. You answer yes and briefly explain your intention to do research with the nonprofit. The woman appears annoyed and begins to explain that you and your research team are not welcome in the community. She says that she is sick of elitist university folks coming into her community and treating her friends and family like lab rats. She explains that researchers are often condescending and rude and never really share the results of the research, just ask their questions and leave. You are in shock and do not know how to respond, but the woman walks away before you really even have a chance.

Questions: What do you do with this new information? Who do you share it with, and how does it shape your project? The woman's concerns are valid, so what will you do to address them? What actions do you think the professor and research team should have taken beforehand to better prepare students and the community for this project?

A.3. Community Engagement Role Play

We have done these as an hour-long role-play exercise for our faculty development program. Here are the basics and an example scenario. You can develop your own based on current events in your area!

Introduction (Approximately Five Minutes)

Hand out the following scenario or one that you create to all participants in writing:

SCENARIO: Housing insecurity is a significant issue in the community of Smithville. Although legislators have tried various solutions, the policy stance seems to be to leave the individuals experiencing housing insecurity to the care of the community they live in and the surrounding nonprofits. However, this solution does not seem to be effective—the number of people with housing insecurity remain the same, neighborhood members are frustrated because they have safety concerns, and nonprofit organizations feel as though they are just providing assistance without contributing to social change.

In this role-playing game, you are given information about the role you represent. Using this information, act as your role at the "neighborhood meeting" about housing insecurity. Throughout the simulation be true to *all* aspects of the character you are given. Think about both what your character wants and would say as well as why they would act in that manner. However, *you should not* reveal information about your character's policy preferences, goals, interests, background, or identity unless you think they would authentically do so in the situation.

SETTING: Smithville is currently in the process of finalizing its budget for the upcoming fiscal year. Recognizing the persistent challenge of housing insecurity in the area, the city council wants to explore ways existing funding for programs and issues related to homelessness might be changed (modified, expanded, reduced) to better address the challenges faced by Smithville residents. To that end, the council has organized a community town hall meeting to hear from stakeholders and issue area experts about the best path forward. The council is interested in both short- and long-term solutions to this problem that many Smithville voters have expressed concern about.

Breakout Rooms Grouped Below by Role or Context (Approximately Ten Minutes)

Allow participants to get to know each other briefly and talk about planning for the meeting. They are told: "You will be attending the town hall meeting together, where you will discuss the proposed community development plan." **Roles to assign participants:** It works best if you have enough people to take each of these, but if not, have them choose at least one or two from each type of role.

- **Academic partners:**
  - **Assistant professor:** You are in your third year in a tenure-track position in social welfare at the local university in Smithville. Although you got into academia because of your concern about social justice issues, you find that your time is increasingly spent chasing publications, in meetings, and finding grants. You come to the neighborhood meeting at the bequest of your graduate student but feel skeptical that you can commit to yet another cause, especially one that seems like it will require a lot of time without a great deal of academic payoff. *Policy preference:* You would prefer funding for the center be increased generally, at least in part because it might better facilitate a research collaboration with you.
  - **University staff member:** You are part of a community engagement unit on campus. You spend a lot of time connecting community and campus people around their shared interests. You have written grants, published papers, and been a part of every part of the research process, but your time and energy are limited, too. *Policy preference:* You would prefer funding for the center to be increased generally, at least in part to facilitate a research collaboration with one or more people from your university.
  - **Graduate student:** You are in your first year of a Ph.D. program in social welfare and are itching to do real, meaningful research with the community. However, you are a little bit at a loss as far as how to get started. You do not have funding or a CBR project you can walk into. You are also worried about how to present yourself to the community and how you can be of use, especially because you are new in the program. *Policy preference:* You would prefer funding for the center to be increased at least in part to facilitate a research collaboration with you.
- **Community partners:**
  - **Director at nonprofit organization:** Like many nonprofit directors, you are feeling a bit overwhelmed. You focus on providing services to those experiencing housing insecurity, yet you feel that the community needs a different approach to the issue. However, you do not have the time, money, or people to figure out a different solution. You are hesitant to commit to working with anyone from the university because you feel that the last time you tried to collaborate, the professor and her students were focused almost entirely on getting good data for a new book and not the long-term needs of your clients and organization. *Policy preference:* You would prefer funding for the center be increased so you can expand the number of beds you have and, therefore, the number of people you can serve.
  - **Client served by nonprofit organization:** You have been unhoused for six months after losing your job due to an untreated mental illness. You appreciate the services provided by the city and nonprofit organizations, but you also feel that you are on a hamster wheel and do not know how to get off. You know that you need to deal with your mental illness in order to change your life, but there are huge barriers to getting what you need. *Policy preference:* You would prefer funding for the center be increased so it can expand the

mental health services it offers. To this point, you and many other people in situations similar to yours have been trying to get care but have been unable to see a mental health professional. There simply are not enough of them to meet existing need.

- **Volunteer at nonprofit organization:** As a stay-at-home parent whose children recently started school, you are excited to become more involved in the organization. You are willing to put your efforts into providing these services but are leery of the talk you have heard about the nonprofit taking on an advocacy role. Your political beliefs may clash with those of others involved with the organization, and you are worried about a future conflict. You believe that the best way to reduce housing insecurity in any area is to help people pick themselves up and become economically independent. *Policy preference:* You would prefer funding for the center remain the same but more dollars be set aside for employment programs that provide training and counseling for the unhoused in Smithville.

- **Public partners:**
  - **Neighbor of nonprofit organization:** You are simply fed up with the unhoused people up and down your street. You realize they have problems, but can they just get it together and pull themselves up by their bootstraps? You are sick of it and need things to change or you are moving. *Policy preference:* You would prefer existing funds be spent to move the center to another part of town, away from your house. You have not thought about whether the total funds allocated to the center should change. You are very outspoken about your views.
  - **Board member of nonprofit organization:** You wish you could devote more time and energy to the organization, but you are limited in what you can contribute. *Policy preference:* You would prefer funding for the center be increased generally. You think they do good work and should be supported, even if you may not have time to be personally involved.
  - **City council member:** You campaigned on the promise to support unhoused people in your district, but you are also facing political backlash for recommending the building of a permanent structure for unhoused people. *Policy preference:* You are facing reelection and are conflicted between your values and staying in office. You would like to please your district population (voters) but it is not the hill you will die on.

Final Part of Role Play: Town Hall Meeting (Fifteen to Thirty Minutes, Depending on Time and Number of Participants)

The instructor/CEP acts as the meeting facilitator. The goal of the meeting is to gather feedback from community members around the housing insecurity issue. You can ask for people to contribute, but be aware that they are also acting as their roles, which may mean they are more or less vocal. Some example prompts include:

- What are your thoughts on this issue?
- What solution do you prefer?

- What do we need to do to address this issue?
- Do you have policy recommendations?
- What should the next steps be?

In our experience, we have found that students dig into their roles and the conversation flows smoothly with little support from the facilitator.

At the end, thank them for their acting and offer some space for guided reflection. We have found this is best done in a group, although it could also be done individually. Some possible reflection questions follow:

- What are your initial thoughts about this scenario?
- What did you notice about the meeting?
- How did you notice power showing up?
- Do you think any collaborations would form? Why or why not?
- How do you think the town would move forward?
- What was frustrating or challenging?
- What do you think might be different in a real-life situation?
- Did anything surprise you?

Appendix B

Additional Resources

Community engagement is incredibly context-specific work. This appendix provides an additional set of information that adds context and detail to some of the work and information we reference throughout the book.

B.1. UW–Madison's Land Acknowledgment Statement

The University of Wisconsin–Madison occupies ancestral Ho-Chunk land, a place their nation has called Teejop (day-JOPE) since time immemorial.

In an 1832 treaty, the Ho-Chunk were forced to cede this territory. Decades of ethnic cleansing followed when both the federal and state government repeatedly, but unsuccessfully, sought to forcibly remove the Ho-Chunk from Wisconsin.

This history of colonization informs our shared future of collaboration and innovation.

Today, UW–Madison respects the inherent sovereignty of the Ho-Chunk Nation, along with the eleven other First Nations of Wisconsin.

B.2. The Urban Research and Outreach-Engagement Center's Values and Guiding Principles

UROC's "Values and Guiding Principles" steer the community-university advisory committee in selecting which researchers will be allowed access to space, staff, and expertise at the center. Some include the following, excerpted from UROC's research agenda (UROC website, https://uroc.umn.edu/):

- "**Place-based:** UROC has the unique ability to leverage our place-based location in North Minneapolis and . . . the potential to leverage our human capital of established relationships. Place-based learning and research emphasizes the need to develop 'context-specific knowledge networks that support the management and planning decisions' by individuals and communities within a specific locality (Davidson-Hunt & O'Flaherty, 2007). Future research addressing priorities outlined in this Research Agenda should be place-based, aiming to leverage UROC's unique place and human capital."
- "**Collaborative:** Future research addressing priorities outlined in this Research Agenda should . . . intentionally incorporate and elevate community voices and knowledge while in the process of developing and maintaining thriving community-University partnerships and projects."
- "**Intergenerational and intragenerational:** . . . with particular attention paid to the inclusion of more youth and elderly voices in the research processes."
- "**Multiple forms of knowledge:** Honoring multiple ways of knowing calls in the importance to harness various values, beliefs, and lived experiences. That is why at UROC we find it paramount to give credit and acknowledgment to those before us . . . to build on what we have already learned and honor those whose knowledge made that learning possible."
- "**Reciprocal engagement:** Truly mutually beneficial, long-term partnerships require a commitment of time, self-examination, openness to institutional change and transformation, hard work punctuated by moments of celebration, and a commitment to stay in relationships based on shared principles in order to develop and sustain trust (Seifer, 2006)."
- "**Wholeness and intersectionality** . . . can be understood as attending to 'the whole system in the room . . . listening to everyone responsible for or affected by a change, and/or at least representatives of each group of stakeholders' (Whitney & Bloom, 2010). Future research addressing the priorities outlined in this Research Agenda, therefore, should center wholeness and intersectionality and work to minimize the dangers of a single story and/or sociopolitical lens."

B.3. Additional Recommended Readings

Foundational Reading for New CEPs

Delano-Oriaran, O., Penick-Parks, M. W., & Fondrie, S. (Eds.). (2015). *The SAGE sourcebook of service-learning and civic engagement.* Sage Publications.

Eyler, J., & Giles Jr., D. E. (1999). *Where's the learning in service-learning?* Jossey-Bass.

Gelmon, S. B., Holland, B. A., & Spring, A. (2018). *Assessing service-learning and civic engagement: Principles and techniques.* Campus Compact.

Jacoby, B. (2014). *Service-learning essentials: Questions, answers, and lessons learned.* Wiley.

Strand, K., Marullo, S., Cutforth, N., Stoecker, R., & Donohue, P. (2003). Principles of best practice for community-based research. *Michigan Journal of Community Service Learning, 9*(3).

Welch, M., & Plaxton-Moore, S. (2019). *The craft of community-engaged teaching and learning.* Stylus Publishing.

Other Good Readings

Bertrand, M., Durand, E. S., & Gonzalez, T. (2017). "We are trying to take action": Transformative agency, role re-mediation, and the complexities of youth participatory action research. *Equity & Excellence in Education, 50*(2), 142–154.

Butcher, J., Bezzina, M., & Moran, W. (2011). Transformational partnerships: A new agenda for higher education. *Innovative Higher Education, 36*(1), 29–40. https://doi .org/10.1007/s10755-010-9155-7

Cann, C. N., & McCloskey, E. (2017). The poverty pimpin' project: How whiteness profits from black and brown bodies in community service programs. *Race Ethnicity and Education, 20*(1), 72–86.

Castillo-Montoya, M. (2018). Rigor revisited: Scaffolding college student learning by incorporating their lived experiences. *New Directions for Higher Education, 181*, 37–46.

Chu, C. M. (2009). Working from within: Critical service learning as core learning in the MLIS curriculum. *Service Learning: Linking Library Education and Practice*, 105–123.

Cipolle, S. (2004). Service-learning as a counter-hegemonic practice: Evidence pro and con. *Multicultural Education, 11*(3), 12–23.

Cronley, C., Madden, E., & Davis, J. B. (2015). Making service-learning partnerships work: Listening and responding to community partners. *Journal of Community Practice, 23*(2), 274–289.

Cruz, N. I., & Giles, D. E. (2000). Where's the community in service-learning research. *Michigan Journal of Community Service Learning, 7*(1), 28–34.

Gay, G. (2018). *Culturally responsive teaching: Theory, research, and practice* (3rd ed.). Teachers College Press.

Gay, G., & Kirkland, K. (2003). Developing cultural critical consciousness and self-reflection in preservice teacher education. *Theory Into Practice, 42*(3), 181–187.

Gazley, B., Littlepage, L., & Bennett, T. A. (2012). What about the host agency? Nonprofit perspectives on community-based student learning and volunteering. *Nonprofit and Voluntary Sector Quarterly, 41*(6), 1029–1050.

Goodman, D. J. (2015). Oppression and privilege: Two sides of the same coin. *Journal of Intercultural Communication, 18*, 1–14.

Green, A. E. (2003). Difficult stories: Service learning, race, class, and whiteness. *National Council of Teachers of English, 55*(2), 276–301.

Guarasci, R. (2022). *Neighborhood democracy.* Stylus Publishing.

Hackman, H. W. (2005). Five essential components for social justice education. *Equity and Excellence in Education, 38*(2), 103–109.

Hall, B. L., Jackson, E. T., Tandon, R., Fontan, J. M., & Lall, N. L. (2013). *Knowledge, democracy and action: Community-university research partnerships in global perspectives.* Manchester University Press.

Hartman, E., Kiely, R., Boettcher, C., & Friedricks, J. (2018). *Community-based global learning.* Stylus Publishing.

Horowitz, C. R., Robinson, M., & Seifer, S. (2009). Community-based participatory research from the margin to the mainstream: Are researchers prepared? *Circulation, 119*(19), 2633–2642.

INCITE! Women of Color Against Violence. (Eds.). (1999). *The revolution will not be funded: Beyond the non-profit industrial complex.* South End Press.

Jones, S. R., & Abes, E. S. (2004). Enduring influences of service-learning on college students' identity development. *Journal of College Student Development, 45*(2), 149–166.

Kajner, T., Chovanec, D., Underwood, M., & Mian, A. (2013). Critical community service learning: Combining critical classroom pedagogy with activist community placements. *Michigan Journal of Community Service Learning, 19*(2), 36–48.

Kubal, T., Meyler, D., Stone, R. T., & Mauney, T. T. (2003). Teaching diversity and learning outcomes: Bringing lived experience into the classroom. *Teaching Sociology, 31*(4) 441–455.

Ladson-Billings, G. J. (1999). Preparing teachers for diverse student populations: A critical race theory perspective. *Review of Research in Education, 24*(1), 211–247.

Maurrasse, D. (2002). *Beyond the campus.* Routledge.

Murphy, T., Tan, J., & Allan, C. (2009). Service-learning and the development of critical reflexivity in teacher education in the United Kingdom and Republic of Ireland: Emerging paradigms. In J. Strait & M. Lima (Eds.), *The future of service learning: New solutions for sustaining and improving practice* (pp. 137–154). Stylus Publishing.

Owen, J., Tao, K. W., Drinane, J. M., Hook, J., Davis, D. E., & Kune, N. F. (2016). Client perceptions of therapists' multicultural orientation: Cultural (missed) opportunities and cultural humility. *Professional Psychology: Research and Practice, 47*(1), 30–37.

Santiago-Ortiz, A. (2019, Winter). From critical to decolonizing service-learning: Limits and possibilities of social justice-based approaches to community service-learning. *Michigan Journal of Community Service Learning, 25*(1), 43–54.

Stoecker, R. (2017). The neoliberal starfish conspiracy. *Partnerships: A Journal of Service Learning and Civic Engagement, 8*(2), 51–62.

Sullivan, M., Kone, A., Senturia, K. D., Chrisman, N. J., Ciske, S. J., & Krieger, J. W. (2001). Researcher and researched-community perspectives: Toward bridging the gap. *Health Education and Behavior, 28*(2), 130–149.

Warren, M. R., Park, S. O., & Tieken, M. C. (2016). The formation of community-engaged scholars: A collaborative approach to doctoral training in education research. *Harvard Educational Review, 86*(2), 233–260.

Yosso, T. At the coalition of urban-serving institutions.

B.4. Web Resources

Short List of Science Shop Networks Globally

CBR Canada: https://www.communityresearchcanada.ca/
C2U Expo: https://www.communityresearchcanada.ca/c2uexpo
International Living Knowledge Network: https://www.livingknowledge.net
PRIA (Participatory Research in Asia): https://www.pria.org/
GACER (Global Alliance for Community Engaged Research): https://www.uvic.ca /research/centres/cue/networks/gacer/gacer.php

Other Good Websites or Webpages

Campus Compact. (2021, October 5). *Racial inequality and community engagement knowledge hub.* https://compact.org/resources/racial-inequity-and-community-engagement-knowledge-hub?f%5B0%5D=practice_area%3A199

Coalition of Urban Serving Universities. (2020, July 27). *Leveraging students' community cultural wealth: Moving from deficit to asset-based approaches to student success.*

https://urbanuniversity.wordpress.com/2020/07/27/leveraging-students-community
-cultural-wealth-moving-from-deficit-to-asset-based-approaches-to-student-success
-by-christel-perkins-ed-d-and-andrea-rodriguez/

University of Oregon, Division of Equity and Inclusion. (n.d.). *Trainings and other activities and strategies to develop cultural humility.* https://inclusion.uoregon.edu/train ings-and-other-activities-and-strategies-Develop-cultural-humility

Humorous Videos on Global Engagement

- On stopping "humanitarian douchery," see the End Humanitarian Douchery YouTube channel, https://www.youtube.com/channel/UCXIcfjvbHJBqN44 ZQcJZQWg
- VMproductionsUK. (2010, February 24). *Gap yah* [Video]. YouTube. https:// www.youtube.com/watch?v=eKFjWR7X5dU&ab_channel=VMproductionsUK

B.5. Professional Development and Learning Opportunities

Organizations

- ACPA—College Student Educators International, Commission for Social Justice Education
- Bringing Theory to Practice
- Campus Compact
- International Association of Research on Service Learning and Community Engagement
- Place-Based Justice Network
- The Engagement Scholarship Consortium
- Outreach and Engagement Professionals Network Annual meeting
- The Research University Civic Engagement Network (TRUCEN)

Journals

- *Michigan Journal of Community Service Learning*
- *Journal of Higher Education Outreach and Engagement*
- *Journal of Community Engagement and Scholarship*
- *Collaborations: A Journal of Community Engaged Research and Practice*
- *Partnerships: A Journal of Service-Learning and Civic Engagement*
- *Gateways: International Journal of Community Research and Engagement*
- *International Journal of Research on Service-Learning and Community Engagement*
- *Journal of Community Engagement and Higher Education*
- *Journal of Public Scholarship in Higher Education*

Conferences and Institutes

- National Conference on Race and Ethnicity (NCORE)
- The Intergroup Dialogue (IGD) Institute at the University of Michigan

- Campus Compact Annual Conference
- Campus Compact Communities of Practice
- Engagement Scholarship Consortium Annual Meeting
- Outreach and Engagement Professionals Network Annual Meeting
- Coalition of Urban and Metropolitan Universities (CUMU)

References

Abimbola, S. (2019). The foreign gaze: Authorship in academic global health. *BMJ Global Health, 4*(5), 1–5. https://doi.org/10.1136/bmjgh-2019-002068

Adams, M., Bell, L. A., & Griffin, P. (Eds.). (2007). *Teaching for diversity and social justice* (2nd ed.). Routledge.

Africa Knows! Conference. (n.d.). *Creating Science Shops in Francophone Africa: Challenges, possibilities and achievements in 8 countries.* Retrieved March 21, 2023, from https://nomadit.co.uk/conference/africaknows/paper/57796

Ahad-Legardy, B., & Poon, O. A. (Eds.). (2018). *Difficult subjects: Insights and strategies for teaching about race, sexuality, and gender.* Stylus Publishing.

Al-Atiyat, I., Shaffer, T. J., Longo, N. V., Manosevitch, I., & Thomas, M. S. (2017). Tackling the "savior" complex: Teaching introduction to women's and gender studies through deliberation. In *Deliberative pedagogy: Teaching and learning for democratic engagement* (pp. 107–114).

AlShebli, B. K., Rahwan, T., & Woon, W. L. (2018). The preeminence of ethnic diversity in scientific collaboration. *Nature Communications, 9*(1), 5163. https://doi.org/10.1038/s41467-018-07634-8

American Association of University Women (n.d.). *Getting started with difficult conversations.* Retrieved March 21, 2023, from https://www.aauw.org/resources/member/governance-tools/dei-toolkit/difficult-conversations/

Andersen, B., & Fagerhaug, T. (2006). *Root cause analysis: Simplified tools and techniques.* Quality Press.

Andrade, K., Cushing, L., & Wesner, A. (2018). Science Shops and the US research university: A path for community-engaged scholarship and disruption of the power dynamics of knowledge production. In *Educating for citizenship and social justice,* Mitchell, T. D., & K. M. Soria, Eds. (pp. 149–165). Palgrave Macmillan.

Andrews, N., Kim, S. & Watanabe, J. (2018, Winter). Cultural humility as a transformative framework for librarians, tutors, and youth volunteers: Applying a lens of cultural responsiveness in training library staff and volunteers. *Young Adult Library Services*, 19–22.

Ankel, S. (2020, June 24). *30 days that shook America: Since the death of George Floyd, the Black Lives Matter movement has already changed the country.* Business Insider. https://www.businessinsider.com/13-concrete-changes-sparked-by-george-floyd -protests-so-far-2020-6

Ansari, H. (2019, March 12). A major problem: Students feel unwelcome on campus and in the classroom. *Badger Herald.* https://diversity.wisc.edu/2019/03/a-major-problem -students-of-color-feel-unwelcome-on-campus-and-in-the-classroom/

Arieli, D., Friedman, V. J., & Agbaria, K. (2009). The paradox of participation in action research. *Action Research, 7*(3), 263–290.

Association of American Colleges and Universities. (2007). *College learning for the new global century.* Association of American Colleges and Universities.

Astin, A. W., & Sax, L. J. (1998). How undergraduates are affected by service participation. *Service Participation, 39*(3), 251–263.

Bales, F. (1994). Hantavirus and the media: Double jeopardy for Native Americans. *American Indian Culture and Research Journal, 18*(3), 251–263.

Barnes, A. C., Olson, T. H., & Reynolds, D. J. (2018). Teaching power as an inconvenient but imperative dimension of critical leadership development. *New Directions for Student Leadership, 2018*(159), 77–90.

Barnhardt, C. L., Sheets, J. E., & Pasquesi, K. (2015). You expect what? Students' perceptions as resources in acquiring commitments and capacities for civic engagement. *Research in Higher Education, 56*(6), 622–644.

Basinger, N., & Bartholomew, K. (2006). Service-learning in nonprofit organizations: Motivations, expectations, and outcomes. *Michigan Journal of Community Service Learning, 12*(2), 15–26.

Bauer, T., Kniffin, L. E., & Priest, K. L. (2015). The future of service-learning and community engagement: Asset-based approaches and student learning in first-year courses. *Michigan Journal of Community Service Learning, 22*(1), 89–92.

Benenson, J., Hemer, K. M., & Trebil, K. (2017). Supporting student civic learning and development. In L. D. Dostilio (Ed.), *The community engagement professional in higher education: A competency model for an emerging field* (pp. 139–160). Campus Compact.

Bennett, J. (2020, November 19). What if instead of calling people out, we called them in? *New York Times.* https://www.nytimes.com/2020/11/19/style/loretta-ross-smith -college-cancel-culture.html?searchResultPosition=1

Besel, K., Williams, C. L., & Klak, J. (2011). Nonprofit sustainability during times of uncertainty. *Nonprofit Management and Leadership, 22*(1), 53–65.

Besley, J. C., Oh, S. H., & Nisbet, M. C. (2012). Predicting scientists' participation in public life. *Public Understanding of Science, 22*(8), 971–987. https://doi.org/10.1177/09 63662512459315

Besley, J. C., & Tanner, A. H. (2011). What science communication scholars think about training scientists to communicate. *Science Communication, 33*(2), 239–263. https:// doi.org/10.1177/1075547010386972

Bettez, S. C. (2011). Critical community building: Beyond belonging. *Educational Foundations, 25*, 3–19.

Black, K. Z., Hardy, C. Y., De Marco, M., Ammerman, A. S., Corbie-Smith, G., Council, B., Ellis, D., Eng, E., Harris, B., Jackson, M., Jean-Baptiste, J., Kearney, W., Legerton, M., Parker, D., Wynn, M., & Lightfoot, A. (2013). Beyond incentives for involvement to compensation for consultants: Increasing equity in CBPR approaches. *Progress in Community Health Partnerships: Research, Education, and Action, 7*(3), 263–270.

Block, P. (2008). *Community: The structure of belonging.* Berrett-Koehler.

Blouin, D. D., & Perry, E. M. (2009). Whom does service learning really serve? Community-based organizations' perspectives on service learning. *Teaching Sociology, 37*(2), 120–135.

Bouek, J. W. (2018). Navigating networks: How nonprofit network membership shapes response to resource scarcity. *Social Problems, 65*(1), 11–32.

Boulton, G., & Lucas, C. (2011). What are universities for? *Chinese Science Bulletin, 56,* 2506–2517. https://doi.org/10.1007/s11434-011-4608-7

Bowen, G. (2007, December). How service learning fosters synthesis and prepares students for careers. *Western Carolina University Career Journal, 5*(2). http://www.wcu .edu/WebFiles/PDFs/careerservices_cj_dec-07.pdf

Bowler, K. (2016, February 13). Death, the prosperity gospel, and me. *New York Times.* http://www.math.toronto.edu/~mpugh/Death_the_Prosperity_Gospel_and_Me _by_Kate_Bowler.pdf

Bradburd, R. M., & Mann, D. P. (1993). Wealth in higher education institutions. *Journal of Higher Education, 64*(4), 472–493.

Bringle, R. G., & Hatcher, J. A. (2000). Institutionalization of service learning in higher education. *Journal of Higher Education, 71*(3), 273–290.

Brookfield, S. D. (2005). The power of critical theory for adult learning and teaching. *Adult Learner,* 85–89.

Brossard, D., & Nisbet, M. C. (2007). Deference to scientific authority among a low information public: Understanding US opinion on agricultural biotechnology. *International Journal of Public Opinion Research, 19*(1), 24–52.

brown, a. m. (2021). *Holding change: The way of emergent strategy facilitation and mediation.* AK Press.

Brown, B. (2007). *I thought it was just me (but it isn't): Making the journey from "What will people think?" to "I am enough."* Avery.

Brown, B. (2019, November 9). The difference between guilt and shame. *Farnam Street.* https://fs.blog/brene-brown-guilt-shame/

Brown, M. K., Hershock, C., Finelli, C. J., & O'Neal, C. (2009). Teaching for retention in science, engineering, and math disciplines: A guide for faculty. *Occasional Paper, 25,* 1–12.

Burton, N. (2015, September 18). When homosexuality stopped being a mental disorder. *Psychology Today.* https://www.psychologytoday.com/us/blog/hide-and-seek/201509 /when-homosexuality-stopped-being-mental-disorder

Bury, J., & Masuzawa, Y. (2018). Non-hierarchical learning: Sharing knowledge, power and outcomes. *Journal of Pedagogic Development, 7*(1), 32–51.

Butin, D. W. (2003). Of what use is it? Multiple conceptualizations of service learning within education. *Teachers College Record, 105*(9), 1674–1692.

Butin, D. W. (2006). The limits of service-learning in higher education. *Review of Higher Education, 29*(4), 473–498.

Butin, D. W. (2007). Justice-learning: Service-learning as justice-oriented education. *Equity and Excellence in Education, 40*(2), 177–183. https://doi.org/10.1080/106656 80701246492

Butin, D. W. (2012). When engagement is not enough: Building the next generation of the engaged campus. In D. W. Butin & S. Seider (Eds.), *The engaged campus: Cer-*

tificates, minors, and majors as the new community engagement (pp. 1–11). Palgrave MacMillan.

Cahuas, M. C., & Levkoe, C. Z. (2017). Towards a critical service learning in geography education: Exploring challenges and possibilities through testimonio. *Journal of Geography in Higher Education, 41*(2), 246–263.

Campus Compact. (n.d.). *Community engagement professional credential.* Retrieved March 3, 2023, from https://compact.org/current-programs/community-engagement-professional-credential

Campus Compact National Conference website (2022, March 18). Compact 22: A better way forward. https://events.compact.org/compact22

Campbell, C. G., & Oswald, B. R. (2018). Promoting critical thinking through service learning: A home-visiting case study. *Teaching of Psychology, 45*(2), 193–199.

Capretz, L. F., & Ahmed, F. (2018). A call to promote soft skills in software engineering. *Psychology and Cognitive Sciences, Editorial, 4*(1). PsyArXiv preprint PsyArXiv:1901.01819.

Castro Atwater, S. A. (2008). Waking up to difference: Teachers, color-blindness, and the effects on students of color. *Journal of Instructional Psychology, 35*(3), 246–253.

CBS Chicago. (2013, March 22). *School closing opponents call mayor a racist liar.* https://chicago.cbslocal.com/2013/03/22/school-closing-opponents-call-mayor-a-racist-liar/

Centers for Disease Control and Prevention. (2021, April 22). *The Tuskegee timeline.* https://www.cdc.gov/tuskegee/timeline.htm

Chan, S. C., Ngai, G., & Kwan, K. P. (2019). Mandatory service learning at university: Do less-inclined students learn from it? *Active Learning in Higher Education, 20*(3), 189–202.

Chapa, J., & Valencia, R. R. (1993). Latino population growth, demographic characteristics, and educational stagnation: An examination of recent trends. *Hispanic Journal of Behavioral Sciences, 15*(2), 165–187.

Chesbrough, R. D. (2009). *College students and service: A mixed methods exploration of motivations, choices, and learning outcomes.* University of Nebraska–Lincoln.

Child, I. L. (1954). Socialization. In G. Lindzey (Ed.), *Handbook of social psychology: Vol. 2. Special fields and applications* (pp. 655–692). Addison-Wesley.

Choo, J., Tan, Y. K., Ong, F., Tiong, S. S., Nair, S., Ong, J., & Chan, A. (2019). What works in service-learning?: Achieving civic outcomes, academic connection, career preparation, and personal growth in students at Ngee Ann Polytechnic. *Michigan Journal of Community Service Learning, 25*(2), 95–132.

Chupp, M. G., & Joseph, M. L. (2010). Getting the most out of service learning: Maximizing student, university and community impact. *Journal of Community Practice, 18*(2–3), 190–212.

Clemmons, N., Blue, H., Ross-Donaldson, S., Gagliano, C., & Moore, A. (2018, November 8–11). *Root cause analysis: A community engagement process for identifying the social determinants of infant mortality.* APHA's 2018 Annual Meeting and Expo, San Diego, CA.

Clifford, J. (1988). *The predicament of culture.* Harvard University Press.

Coghlan, D., & Brydon-Miller, M. (2014). *The SAGE encyclopedia of action research* (Vols. 1–2). Sage Publications. https://doi.org/10.4135/9781446294406

Cole, T. (2012, March 21). The white savior industrial complex. *The Atlantic.* http://www.theatlantic.com/international/archive/2012/03/the-white-saviorindustrialcomplex/254843/2/

Concannon, T. W., Fuster, M., Saunders, T., Patel, K., Wong, J. B., Leslie, L. K., & Lau, J. (2014). A systematic review of stakeholder engagement in comparative effectiveness and patient-centered outcomes research. *Journal of General Internal Medicine, 29*(12), 1692–1701.

Cook, G., Pieri, E., & Robbins, P. T. (2004). "The scientists think and the public feels": Expert perceptions of the discourse of GM food. *Discourse and Society, 15*(4), 443–449. https://doi.org/10.1177/0957926504043708

Corntassel, J., & Gaudry, A. (2014). Insurgent education and Indigenous-centred research: Opening new pathways to community resurgence. In C. Etmanski, B. L. Hall, & T. Dawson (Eds.), *Learning and teaching community-based research* (pp. 167–185). University of Toronto Press.

Cousins, J. B., & Whitmore, E. (1998). Framing participatory evaluation. *New Directions for Evaluation, 1998*(80), 5–23.

COWS. (2019). *Race in the heartland: Wisconsin's extreme racial disparity.* University of Wisconsin–Madison.

Cramer, K. J. (2016). *The politics of resentment: Rural consciousness in Wisconsin and the rise of Scott Walker.* University of Chicago Press.

Crenshaw, K. (2015, September 24). Why intersectionality can't wait. *Washington Post.* https://www.washingtonpost.com/news/in-theory/wp/2015/09/24/why-intersection ality-cant-wait

Crenshaw, K. W. (1989). Demarginalizing the intersection of race and sex: A Black feminist critique of antidiscrimination doctrine. *University of Chicago Legal Forum, 1989*, 139–168.

Cronley, C., Madden, E., & Davis, J. B. (2015). Making service-learning partnerships work: Listening and responding to community partners. *Journal of Community Practice, 23*(2), 274–289.

Cruz, N. I., & Giles, D. E. (2000). Where's the community in service-learning research. *Michigan Journal of Community Service Learning, 7*(1), 28–34.

Cutforth, N. J. (1999). Presentation at Bonner Community Research Project Gathering, Morehouse College, Atlanta.

Daniels, J. R., & Gustafson, J. N. (2011). Faith-based institutions, institutional mission, and the public good. *Higher Learning Research Communications, 6*(2), 90–100.

Dantley, M. E. (2002). Uprooting and replacing positivism, the melting pot, multiculturalism, and other impotent notions in educational leadership through an African American perspective. *Education and Urban Society, 34*(3), 334–352.

Darby, A. N., Ward-Johnson, F., & Cobb, T. (2016). The unrecognized co-educator in academic service-learning: Community partners' perspectives on college students serving diverse client populations. *Partnerships: A Journal of Service-Learning and Civic Engagement, 7*(1), 3–15.

Day, K., Becerra, V., Ruiz, V. L., & Powe, M. (2012). New ways of learning, knowing, and working: Diversifying graduate student career options through community engagement. In A. Gilven, C. Martin, & G. M. Roberts (Eds.), *Collaborative futures: Critical reflections on publicly active graduate education* (pp. 163–182). Syracuse University Press.

DeCuir, J. T., & Dixson, A. D. (2004). "So when it comes out, they aren't that surprised that it is there": Using critical race theory as a tool of analysis of race and racism in education. *Educational Researcher, 33*(5), 26–31.

Delgado, R., & Stefancic, J. (2017). Critical race theory. In *Critical Race Theory* (3rd ed.). New York University Press.

DePaul, Asset-Based Community Development Institute. (n.d.). *ABCD Institute*. Retrieved March 21, 2023, from https://resources.depaul.edu/abcd-institute/Pages/default.aspx

Devine, P. G., & Ash, T. L. (2022). Diversity training goals, limitations, and promise: A review of the multidisciplinary literature. *Annual Review of Psychology, 73*, 403–429.

Dewey, J. (1938). *Experience and education*. Kappa Delta Pi.

Diaz, J. (2022, March 28). *Florida governor signs controversial law opponents dubbed "Don't Say Gay."* NPR. https://www.npr.org/2022/03/28/1089221657/dont-say-gay-florida-desantis

Dipadova-Stocks, L. N. (2005). Two major concerns about service-learning: What if we don't do it? And what if we do? *Academy of Management Learning and Education, 4*(3), 345–353.

Doberneck, D. M., Bargerstock, B. A., McNall, M., Van Egeren, L., & Zientek, R. (2017). Community engagement competencies for graduate and professional students: Michigan State University's approach to professional development. *Michigan Journal of Community Service Learning, 24*(1), 122–142.

Donahue, D. M., Fenner, D., & Mitchell, T. D. (2015). Picturing service-learning: Defining the field, setting expectations, shaping learning. *Journal of Higher Education Outreach and Engagement, 19*(4), 19–38.

Donahue, D. M., & Plaxton-Moore, S. (2018). *The student companion to community-engaged learning: What you need to know for transformative learning and real social change*. Stylus Publishing.

Doran, M., Rhinesmith, C., & Arena, S. (2021). Perspectives of community partner organizations in the development of ethical service-learning guidelines. *Michigan Journal of Community Service Learning, 27*(1), 155–180.

Dostilio, Lina D. (Ed.). (2017). *The community engagement professional in higher education: A competency model for an emerging field*. Stylus Publishing.

Dostilio, L. D., & Welch, M. (2019). *The community engagement professional's guidebook: A companion to the community engagement professional in higher education*. Stylus Publishing.

Drescher, J. (2015). Out of DSM: Depathologizing homosexuality. *Behavioral Sciences, 5*(4), 565–575.

Drexel University. (n.d.). *About Drexel*. Retrieved May 4, 2023 from https://drexel.edu/about

Droucopoulos, V. (2021, January 26). Oxford on St. Scholastica's Day, 1355: Town & gown-mitre & crown: An essay of a propositional nature. https://dx.doi.org/10.2139/ssrn.3773483

Duggleby, W., Pesut, B., Cottrell, L., Friesen, L., Sullivan, K., & Warner, G. (2018). Development, implementation, and evaluation of a curriculum to prepare volunteer navigators to support older persons living with serious illness. *American Journal of Hospice and Palliative Medicine, 35*(5), 780–787.

Duncan-Andrade, J. (2009). Note to educators: Hope required when growing roses in concrete. *Harvard Educational Review, 79*(2), 181–194.

Dunn-Kenney, M. (2010). Can service learning reinforce social and cultural bias? Exploring a popular model of family involvement for early childhood teacher candidates. *Journal of Early Childhood Teacher Education, 31*(1), 37–48.

Dweck, C. S. (2006). *Mindset: The new psychology of success*. Random House.

Easterly, W. (2006). *White man's burden: Why the West's efforts to aid the rest have done so much ill and so little good*. Penguin Press.

Eby, J. (1998, March). *Why service-learning is bad.* [Paper 27]. http://digitalcommons.unomaha.edu/slceslgen/27

Edwards, B., Mooney, L., & Heald, C. (2001). Who is being served? The impact of student volunteering on local community organizations. *Nonprofit and Voluntary Sector Quarterly, 30*(3), 444–461.

Emery, M., & Flora, C. (2006). Spiraling-up: Mapping community transformation with community capitals framework. *Community Development, 37*(1), 19–35.

Endres, D., & Gould, M. (2009). "I am also in the position to use my whiteness to help them out": The communication of whiteness in service learning. *Western Journal of Communication, 73*(4), 418–436.

European Commission. (n.d.). *Horizon 2020.* Retrieved March 21, 2023, from https://ec.europa.eu/info/research-and-innovation/funding/funding-opportunities/funding-programmes-and-open-calls/horizon-2020_en

Eyler, J., & Giles Jr., D. (2014). The importance of program quality in service-learning. In *Service-Learning,* A. S. Waterman, Ed. (pp. 75–94). Routledge.

Eyler, J., Giles, D. E., Stenson, C. M., & Gray, C. J. (2001, August 21). At a glance: What we know about the effects of service-learning on college students, faculty, institutions and communities, 1993–2000: Third edition. Retrieved April 27, 2023, from https://digitalcommons.unomaha.edu/slcehighered/139/?utm_so

Flicker, S., Travers, R., Guta, A., McDonald, S., & Meagher, A. (2007). Ethical dilemmas in community-based participatory research: Recommendations for institutional review boards. *Journal of Urban Health, 84*(4), 478–493.

Floyd, B. O. (2013). Lessons learned preparing volunteer midwives for service in Haiti: After the earthquake. *Journal of Midwifery and Women's Health, 58*(5), 558–568.

Forbes, K., Garber, L., Kensinger, L., & Slagter, J. T. (1999). Punishing pedagogy: The failings of forced volunteerism. *Women's Studies Quarterly, 3–4,* 158–168.

Francis, D. M. (2021). Using root cause analysis to help students examine social problems. *Teaching Journalism and Mass Communication, 11*(1), 61–64.

Freire, P. (1970). *Pedagogy of the oppressed.* Continuum.

Freire, P. (1985). Reading the world and reading the word: An interview with Paulo Freire. *Language Arts, 62*(1), 15–21.

Freire, P. (1994). *Pedagogy of hope.* Continuum.

Fusion Comedy. (2016, October 5). *How microaggressions are like mosquito bites: Same difference* [Video]. YouTube. https://www.youtube.com/watch?v=hDd3bzA7450

Garcia, G. A., Núñez, A. M., & Sansone, V. A. (2019). Toward a multidimensional conceptual framework for understanding "servingness" in Hispanic-serving institutions: A synthesis of the research. *Review of Educational Research, 89*(5), 745–784.

Gelmon, S. B., Jordan, C., & Seifer, S. D. (2013). Community-engaged scholarship in the academy: An action agenda. *Change: The Magazine of Higher Learning, 45*(4), 58–66.

George, M. A. (2015). The harmless psychopath: Legal debates promoting the decriminalization of sodomy in the United States. *Journal of the History of Sexuality, 24*(2), 225–261.

Global Health Education and Learning Incubator at Harvard University. (2018). *Brief introduction to the social determinants of health: Teaching guide.* http://repository.gheli.harvard.edu/repository/12238

The GLS Project. (2022, February 17). *7 targeted active listening games, exercises and activities for adults.* https://www.goodlisteningskills.org/active-listening-games-exercises-activities/

Goldberg-Freeman, C., Kass, N. E., Tracey, P., Ross, G., Bates-Hopkins, B., Purnell, L., Canniffe, B. & Farfel, M. (2007). "You've got to understand community": Community perceptions on "breaking the disconnect" between researchers and communities. *Progress in Community Health Partnerships: Research, Education, and Action, 1*(3), 231–240.

Gottlieb, M. (2021, April 19). *What is cultural humility? 3 principles for social workers.* New Social Worker. https://www.socialworker.com/feature-articles/practice/what-is -cultural-humility-3-principles-for-social-workers/

Gottman, J. M. (2008). Gottman method couple therapy. In D. K. Snyder & J. L. Lebow (Eds.), *Clinical handbook of couple therapy,* (pp. 138–164). Guilford.

Grain, K. M., & Lund, D. E. (2017). The social justice turn: Cultivating 'critical hope' in an age of despair. *Michigan Journal of Community Service Learning, 23*(1), 45–59.

Grande, S. W., Durand, M. A., Fisher, E. S., & Elwyn, G. (2014). Physicians as part of the solution? Community-based participatory research as a way to get shared decision making into practice. *Journal of General Internal Medicine, 29*(1), 219–222.

Greely, H. T., & Cho, M. K. (2013). The Henrietta Lacks legacy grows. *EMBO Reports, 14*(10), 849.

Green, A. E. (2003). Difficult stories: Service-learning, race, class, and whiteness. *College Composition and Communication, 55*(2), 276–301.

Grusky, S. (2000). International service learning: A critical guide from an impassioned advocate. *American Behavioral Scientist, 43,* 858–867.

Haas Center for Public Service. (n.d.). *Pathways of public service and civic engagement.* Stanford University. Retrieved March 21, 2023, from https://haas.stanford.edu/about /our-approach/pathways-public-service-and-civic-engagement

Haley, B., Heo, S., Wright, P., Barone, C., Rettiganti, M. R., & Anders, M. (2017). Relationships among active listening, self-awareness, empathy, and patient-centered care in associate and baccalaureate degree nursing students. *NursingPlus Open, 3,* 11–16.

Hall, B., Jackson, E., Tandon, R., Fontan, J-M., & Lall, N. (2013). *Knowledge, democracy and action: Community-university research partnerships in global perspectives.* Manchester University Press.

Hall, B., Tandon, R., & Tremblay, C. (2015). *Strengthening community university research partnerships: Global perspectives.* University of Victoria and PRIA.

Hall, E. T. (1976). *Beyond culture.* New York.

Hammersley, L. (2012). Community-based service-learning: Partnerships of reciprocal exchange? *Asia-Pacific Journal of Cooperative Education, 14*(3), 171–184.

Hammersley, L. A. (2014). Volunteer tourism: Building effective relationships of understanding. *Journal of Sustainable Tourism, 22*(6), 855–873. https://doi.org/10.1080/09 669582.2013.839691

Hardiman, R., Jackson, B., Griffin, P., Adams, M., & Bell, L. A. (1997). *Teaching for diversity and social justice.* Routledge.

Harmon, A. (2010). Indian tribe wins fight to limit research of its DNA. *New York Times.* https://www.nytimes.com/2010/04/22/us/22dna.html

Harro, B. (2013). The cycle of socialization. In M. Adams, W. J. Blumenfeld, C. Castañeda, H. W. Hacksman, M. L. Peters, & X. Zúñiga (Eds.), *Readings for diversity and social justice* (3rd ed., pp. 45–51). Routledge.

Harsh, M., Bernstein, M. J., Wetmore, J., Cozzens, S., Woodson, T., & Castillo, R. (2017). Preparing engineers for the challenges of community engagement. *European Journal of Engineering Education, 42*(6), 1154–1173. https://doi.org/10.1080/03043797.2016.1 270902

Hartley, M. (2009). Reclaiming the democratic purposes of American higher education: Tracing the trajectory of the civic engagement movement. *Learning and Teaching, 2*(3), 11–30.

Hartman, E. (2015). *A strategy for community-driven service-learning and community engagement: Fair trade learning.* Michigan Publishing, University of Michigan Library.

Hartman, E., Paris, C. M., & Blache-Cohen, B. (2014). Fair trade learning: Ethical standards for community-engaged international volunteer tourism. *Tourism and Hospitality Research, 14*(1–2), 108–116. https://doi.org/10.1177/1467358414529443

Harvey, G., Loftus-Hills, A. Rycroft-Malone, J., Titchen, A., Kitson, A., McCormack, B., & Seers, K. (2002). Getting evidence into practice: The role and function of facilitation. *Journal of Advanced Nursing, 37*(6), 577–588.

Haynes, C. (2017). Dismantling the white supremacy embedded in our classrooms: White faculty in pursuit of more equitable educational outcomes for racially minoritized students. *International Journal of Teaching and Learning in Higher Education, 29*(1), 87–107.

Heintzelman, C. A. (2003). The Tuskegee syphilis study and its implications for the 21st century. *New Social Worker, 10*(4), 4–5.

Henrich, J., Ensminger, J., McElreath, R., Barr, A., Barrett, C., Bolyanatz, A., Cardenas, J. C., Gurven, M., Gwako, E., Henrich, N. and Lesorogol, C., (2010). Markets, religion, community size, and the evolution of fairness and punishment. *Science, 327*(5972), 1480–1484.

Henry, S. E. (2005). "I can never turn my back on that": Liminality and the impact of class on service-learning experience. In D. W. Butin (Ed.), *Service-learning in higher education* (pp. 45–66). Palgrave Macmillan.

Hidayat, D., Pratsch, S., & Stoecker, R. (2009). Principles for success in service learning—The three Cs. In R. Stoecker & E. A. Tryon (Eds.), *The unheard voices: Community organizations and service learning* (pp. 147–161). Temple University Press.

Hook, J. N., Davis, D. E., Owen, J., Worthington Jr., E. L., & Utsey, S. O. (2013). Cultural humility: Measuring openness to culturally diverse clients. *Journal of Counseling Psychology, 60*(3), 353–366.

hooks, b. (2000). *Feminist theory: From margin to center.* Pluto Press.

Horowitz, C. R., Robinson, M., & Seifer, S. (2009). Community-based participatory research from the margin to the mainstream: Are researchers prepared? *Circulation, 119*(19), 2633–2642.

Howard, J. (2001). Principles of good practice for service-learning pedagogy. *Michigan Journal of Community Service Learning, 30*(1), 16–19.

Howe, C. W., Coleman, K., Hamshaw, K., & Westdijk, K. (2014). Student development and service-learning: A three-phased model for course design. *International Journal of Research on Service-Learning and Community Engagement, 2*(1), 44–62.

Hughes, V., Delva, S., Nkimbeng, M., Spaulding, E., Ruskon-Ocran, R., Cudjoe, J., Ford, A., Rushton, C., D'Aoust, R., & Han, H. (2020). Not missing the opportunity: Strategies to promote cultural humility among future nursing faculty. *Journal of Professional Nursing, 36*(1), 28–33. https://doi.org/10.1016/j.profnurs.2019.06.005

Hughey, M. W. (2010). The white savior film and reviewers' reception. *Symbolic Interaction, 33*(3), 475–496.

Hussain, M., & Jones, J. M. (2021). Discrimination, diversity, and sense of belonging: Experiences of students of color. *Journal of Diversity in Higher Education, 14*(1), 63–71.

Illich, I. (1968). To hell with good intentions. In J. C. Kendall (Ed.), *Combining service and learning: A resource book for community and public service* (Vol. 1, pp. 314–320). National Society for Internships and Experiential Education.

Inclusive Teaching at U-M. (n.d.). *Social identity wheel.* Retrieved April 1, 2022, from https://sites.lsa.umich.edu/inclusive-teaching/sample-activities/social-identity-wheel/

Ingraham, K. C., Davidson, S. J., & Yonge, O. (2018). Student-faculty relationships and its impact on academic outcomes. *Nurse Education Today*, *71*, 17–21.

Instructure. (n.d.). *The Instructure learning platform: Learning without limits*. Retrieved March 21, 2023, from https://www.instructure.com/canvas/higher-education

International Association for Public Participation. (2018). *IAP2 spectrum of public participation*. https://cdn.ymaws.com/www.iap2.org/resource/resmgr/pillars/Spectrum _8.5x11_Print.pdf

Ioannidis, J. P. (2005). Why most published research findings are false. *PLoS Medicine*, *2*(8), e124.

Israel, B., Schulz, A., Parker, E., & Becker, A. (2001). Community-based participatory research: Policy recommendations for promoting a partnership approach in health research. *Education for Health*, *14*(2), 182–197.

Iyer, D. (2018). *The map: Social change ecosystem*. Deepa Iyer. https://www.socialchange map.com/

Jacobs, M. D. (2009). *White mother to a dark race: Settler colonialism, maternalism, and the removal of Indigenous children in the American West and Australia, 1880–1940*. University of Nebraska Press.

Jacoby, B. (1996). *Service-learning in higher education: Concepts and practices*. Jossey-Bass.

Jacoby, B., & Dean, L. A. (2010). What does "quality" look like? In support of standards. *About Campus*, *15*(3), 29–32.

John Templeton Foundation. (n.d.). *Intellectual humility*. Retrieved March 21, 2022, from https://www.templeton.org/discoveries/intellectual-humility

Jolivétte, A. (Ed.). (2015). *Research justice: Methodologies for social change*. Policy Press.

Jones, K., & Okun, T. (2001). White supremacy culture. In *Dismantling racism: A workbook for social change*. ChangeWork.

Jumbam, D. T. (2020). How (not) to write about global health. *BMJ Global Health*, *5*(7), e003164. https://doi.org/10.1136/bmjgh-2020-003164

Kahne, J., & Westheimer, J. (1996). In the service of what? The politics of service learning. *Phi Delta Kappan*, *77*, 592–599.

Kajner, T., Chovanec, D., Underwood, M., & Mian, A. (2013). Critical community service learning: Combining critical classroom pedagogy with activist community placements. *Michigan Journal of Community Service Learning*, *19*(2), 36–48.

Kane, L. (2020, January 29). Bryan Stevenson: 4 steps to 'change the world.' *QCity Metro*. https://qcitymetro.com/2020/01/29/bryan-stevenson-4-steps-to-change-the-world/

Karasik, R. J. (2020). Community partners' perspectives and the faculty role in community-based learning. *Journal of Experiential Education*, *43*(2), 113–135.

Karasik, R. J., & Hafner, E. S. (2021). Community partners' satisfaction with community-based learning collaborations. *Journal of Community Engagement and Scholarship*, *14*(1). https://digitalcommons.northgeorgia.edu/jces/vol14/iss1/1

Keefe, T. (2019). Land acknowledgement: a trend in higher education and nonprofit organizations. https://doi.org/10.13140/RG.2.2.33681.0752

Kiely, R. (2004). A chameleon with a complex: Searching for transformation in international service-learning. *Michigan Journal of Community Service Learning*, *10*(2), 5–20.

Kilgo, C. A., Sheets, J.K.E., & Pascarella, E. T. (2015). The link between high-impact practices and student learning: Some longitudinal evidence. *Higher Education*, *69*(4), 509–525.

Kim, E. (2013). Reflective journaling in a college multicultural education classroom: Looking past, present, and future. In D. J. Davis & P. G. Boyer (Eds.), *Social justice issues and racism in the classroom: Perspectives from different voices* (pp. 151–169). Emerald.

Kinefuchi, E. (2010). Critical consciousness and critical service-learning at the intersection of the personal and the structural. *Journal of Applied Learning in Higher Education*, 2, 81–97.

King, P. M., Magolda, M.B.B., & Massé, J. C. (2011). Maximizing learning from engaging across difference: The role of anxiety and meaning making. *Equity and Excellence in Education*, 44(4), 468–487.

Kinsley, M. (1990, January 18). The myth of meritocracy. *Washington Post*. https://www .washingtonpost.com/archive/opinions/1990/01/18/the-myth-of-meritocracy/ff68 b614-f5bd-44e3-9c66-f1f0957a3a49/

Kirwan Institute. (2015). http://kirwaninstitute.osu.edu/research/understanding-impli cit-bias/

Klein, M. W. (2015). Settling a US senatorial debate: Understanding declines in state higher education funding. *Journal of Education Finance*, 41(1), 1–29.

Kline, M. A., Shamsudheen, R., & Broesch, T. (2018). Variation is the universal: Making cultural evolution work in developmental psychology. *Philosophical Transactions of the Royal Society B: Biological Sciences*, 373(1743), 20170059. https://doi.org/10.1098 /rstb.2017.0059

Koch, J. (2018, January 9). No college kid needs a water park to study. *New York Times*. https://www.nytimes.com/2018/01/09/opinion/trustees-tuition-lazy-rivers.html

Kolb, D. A. (1984). *Experiential learning: Experience as the source of learning and development* (Vol. 1). Prentice-Hall.

Koth, K., & Hamilton, S. (2003). *Which service is the most meaningful?* [Worksheet]. Salem, OR.

Kothari, P. (n.d.). *How to fix a microaggression you didn't mean to commit*. Ellevate. Retrieved March 22, 2023, from https://www.ellevatenetwork.com/articles/8034-how -to-fix-a-microaggression-you-didn-t-mean-to-commit

Krasny, M. E., Li, Y., Gonzales, D., & Bartel, A. S. (2021). E-Engagement: Approaches to using digital communications in student-community engagement. *Journal of Higher Education Outreach and Engagement*, 25(4), 21–38.

Kretzmann, J. P., & McKnight, J. (1993). *Building communities from the inside out: A path toward finding and mobilizing a community's assets*. Center for Urban Affairs and Policy Research, Neighborhood Innovations Network.

Kruger, J., & Dunning, D. (1999). Unskilled and unaware of it: How difficulties in recognizing one's own incompetence lead to inflated self-assessments. *Journal of Personality and Social Psychology*, 77(6), 1121–1134.

Kuh, G. D. (2008). *High-impact educational practices: What they are, who has access to them, and why they matter*. Association of American Colleges and Universities.

Ladson-Billings, G. (2007). Pushing past the achievement gap: An essay on the language of deficit. *Journal of Negro Education*, 76(3), 316–323.

Language and Culture Worldwide. (2021, January 11). *Iceberg or beacon? How the cultural iceberg guide us toward greater inclusion*. https://languageandculture.com /iceberg-or-beacon-how-the-cultural-iceberg-guide-us-toward-greater-inclusion/

Larsen, L., Harlan, S., Bolin, R., Hackett, E. J., Hope, D., Kirby, A., Nelson, A., Rex, T. R., & Wolf, S. (2004). Bonding and bridging: Understanding the relationship between social capital and civic action. *Journal of Planning Education and Research*, 24(1), 64–77.

Lather, P. (1986). Research as praxis. *Harvard Educational Review*, 56(3), 257–278.

Leana, C. (2020). Causes and remedies of overwork norms in academia. In E. Kossek & K-H. Lee (Eds.), *Fostering gender and work-life inclusion for faculty in understudied contexts: An organizational science lens* (pp. 99–102). Purdue e-Pubs. https://doi.org /10.5703/1288284317264

Leary, M. R., Diebels, K. J., Davisson, E. K., Jongman-Sereno, K. P., Isherwood, J. C., Raimi, K. T., Deffler, S. A., & Hoyle, R. H. (2017). Cognitive and interpersonal features of intellectual humility. *Personality and Social Psychology Bulletin, 43*(6), 793–813. https://doi.org/10.1177/0146167217697695

Lee, R. (2020, March). Morrill Act of 1862 Indigenous land parcels database. *High Country News.* https://www.landgrabu.org/

Leeman, J., Rabin, L., & Román-Mendoza, E. (2011). Critical pedagogy beyond the classroom walls: Community service-learning and Spanish heritage language education. *Heritage Language Journal, 8*(3), 293–313.

Leonardo, Z. (2013). *Race frameworks: A multidimensional theory of racism and education.* Teachers College Press.

Lesser, J., & Oscós-Sánchez, M. A. (2007). Community-academic research partnerships with vulnerable populations. *Annual Review of Nursing Research, 25*(1), 317–337.

Lester, D. (2002). Active listening. In *Crisis intervention and counseling by telephone* (2nd ed., pp. 92–98). Charles C. Thomas.

Leydesdorff, L., & Ward, J. (2005). Science Shops: A kaleidoscope of science–society collaborations in Europe. *Public Understanding of Science, 14*(4), 353–372.

Lin, C., Schmidt, C., Tryon, E. A., & Stoecker, R. (2009). Service learning in context: The challenge of diversity. In R. Stoecker & E. A. Tryon (Eds.), *The unheard voices: Community organizations and service learning* (pp. 116–135). Temple University Press.

Loew, P., & Thannum, J. (2011). After the storm: Ojibwe treaty rights twenty-five years after the Voigt decision. *American Indian Quarterly, 35*(2), 161–191.

Long, D. R., & Macián, J. L. (2008). Preparing Spanish majors for volunteer service: Training and simulations in an experiential course. *Hispania, 91*(1), 167–175.

Loyola University Chicago. (n.d.). *Center for Urban Research and Learning.* Retrieved March 21, 2023, from https://www.luc.edu/curl/

Loyola University Chicago. (n.d.). *The Loyola mission.* Retrieved May 4, 2023 from https://www.loyola.edu/about/mission

Lund, C. (2016). Review of: Mobilizing Labour for the Global Coffee Market: Profits from an Unfree Work Regime in Colonial Java, by Jan Breman. *Global Labour Journal, 7*(1), 108–110.

Lynch, L. (2015, July 9). *Attorney General Lynch announces federal marriage benefits available to same-sex couples nationwide.* Department of Justice. https://web.archive .org/web/20161110003040/https://www.justice.gov/opa/pr/attorney-general-lynch -announces-federal-marriage-benefits-available-same-sex-couples

Mabry, B. (1998). Pedagogical variations in service-learning and student outcomes: How time, contact, and reflection matter. *Michigan Journal of Community Service Learning, 5,* 32–47.

Marshall, J., & McLean, A. (1988). Reflection in action: Exploring organizational culture. In P. Reason (Ed.), *Human inquiry in action: Developments in new paradigm research* (pp. 199–220). Sage Publications.

Marullo, S., & Edwards, B. (2000). From charity to justice: The potential of university-community collaboration for social change. *American Behavioral Scientist, 43,* 895–912.

Mathews, D. (2014). *Ships passing in the night?* A Cousins Research Group Report on Higher Education in Democracy, Kettering Foundation. Retrieved April 28, 2023, from https://www.kettering.org/catalog/product/ships-passing-night

Matthew, S., Hockett, E., & Samek, L. (2018). Learning cultural humility through stories and global service-learning. *Journal of Christian Nursing, 35*(1), 33–37.

McBride, A. M., Sherraden, M. S., & Pritzker, S. (2006). Civic engagement among low-income and low-wealth families: In their words. *Family Relations, 55*(2), 152–162.

McClure, K. (2019). Examining the "amenities arms race" in higher education: Shifting from rhetoric to research. *College Student Affairs Journal, 37*(2), 128–142. https://files .eric.ed.gov/fulltext/EJ1255471.pdf

McIntosh, P., & Privilege, W. (1989). Unpacking the invisible knapsack. *Peace and Freedom, 49*, 10–12.

McKnight, J., Block, P., & Mosgaller, T. (2015, April 7). *Working in the gap to enhance citizen productivity*. Abundant Community. https://www.abundantcommunity.com /working-in-the-gap-to-enhance-citizen-productivity/

McLennan, S. (2014). Medical voluntourism in Honduras: 'Helping' the poor? *Progress in Development Studies, 14*(2), 163–179.

Merriam-Webster. (n.d.a). Humility. *In Merriam-Webster.com dictionary*. Retrieved from www.merriam-webster.com/dictionary/humility

Merriam-Webster. (n.d.b). Service. In *Merriam-Webster.com dictionary*. Retrieved from https://www.merriam-webster.com/dictionary/service

Metz, E., & Youniss, J. (2003). A demonstration that school-based required service does not deter—but heightens—volunteerism. *PS: Political Science and Politics, 36*(2), 281–286.

Mezirow, J. (2006). An overview on transformative learning. *Lifelong learning: Concepts and contexts*, 24–38.

Milner, H. R. (2003). Reflection, racial competence, and critical pedagogy: How do we prepare pre-service teachers to pose tough questions? *Race, Ethnicity and Education, 6*(2), 193–208.

Milner IV, H. R. (2007). Race, culture, and researcher positionality: Working through dangers seen, unseen, and unforeseen. *Educational Researcher, 36*(7), 388–400.

Mindfulness. (n.d.). *Psychology Today*. Retrieved March 21, 2022, from https://www .psychologytoday.com/us/basics/mindfulness

Minneapolis College. (n.d.). *Campus fast facts*. Retrieved April 3, 2023, from https:// minneapolis.edu/about-us/campus-fact-sheet

Mitchell, M., Leachman, M., & Masterson, K. (2016, August 15). *Funding down, tuition up: State cuts to higher education threaten quality and affordability at public colleges*. Center on Budget and Policy Priorities. https://www.cbpp.org/research/state-budget -and-tax/funding-down-tuition-up

Mitchell, T. D. (2007). Critical service-learning as social justice education: A case study of the citizen scholars program. *Equity and Excellence in Education, 40*(2), 101–112.

Mitchell, T. D. (2008). Traditional vs. critical service-learning: Engaging the literature to differentiate two models. *Michigan Journal of Community Service Learning, 14*(2), 50–65.

Mitchell, T. D. (2014). How service-learning enacts social justice sensemaking. *Journal of Critical Thought and Praxis, 2*(2), 73–95.

Mitchell, T. D. (2017). Teaching community on and off campus: An intersectional approach to community engagement. *New Directions for Student Services, 2017*(157), 35–44.

Mitchell, T. D., & Donahue, D. M. (2009). "I do more service in this class than I ever do at my site": Paying attention to the reflections of students of color in service-learning: New solutions for sustaining and improving practice. In J. Strait & M. Lima (Eds.),

The future of service-learning: New solutions for sustaining and improving practice (pp. 172–190). Stylus Publishing.

Mitchell, T. D., Donahue, D. M., & Young-Law, C. (2012). Service learning as a pedagogy of whiteness. *Equity and Excellence in Education, 45*(4), 612–629.

Mitchell, T. D., & Rost-Banik, C. (2019). How sustained service-learning experiences inform career pathways. *Michigan Journal of Community Service Learning, 25*(1), 18–29.

Mitchell, T. D., & Rost-Banik, C. (2020). Service-learning cohorts as critical communities. *Educational Studies, 46*(3), 352–367.

Morgridge Center for Public Service. (2021a, February 23). *Self-awareness in community engagement* [Video]. YouTube. https://www.youtube.com/watch?v=iX3o78PnEQM&t=10s&ab_channel=MorgridgeCenterforPublicService

Morgridge Center for Public Service. (2021b, February 23). *Words of wisdom part 2* [Video]. YouTube. https://www.youtube.com/watch?v=sR_MV7I33_w&t=8s&ab_channel=MorgridgeCenterforPublicService

Mueller, J. A., & Pickett, C. S. (2015). Politics of intersecting identities. In S. K. Watt (Ed.), *Designing transformative multicultural initiatives: Theoretical foundations, practical applications, and facilitator considerations* (pp. 193–207). Stylus Publishing.

National Equity Project. (2022, May 1). *Lens of systemic oppression.* https://www.nationalequityproject.org/frameworks/lens-of-systemic-oppression

National Science Foundation. (n.d.). *Higher education research and development survey (HERD).* Retrieved March 21, 2023, from https://www.nsf.gov/statistics/srvyherd/

Natural Resources Defense Council. (2019, July). *Definitions of equity, inclusion, equality and related terms.* https://www.broward.org/Climate/Documents/EquityHandout_082019.pdf

NPR. (2018, April 11). *Housing segregation and redlining in America: A short history* [Video]. YouTube. https://www.youtube.com/watch?v=O5FBJyqfoLM&ab_channel=NPR

Nyden, P. (2003). Academic incentives for faculty participation in community-based participatory research. *Journal of General Internal Medicine, 18*(7), 576–585. https://doi.org/10.1046/j.1525-1497.2003.20350.x

Ofir, Z., & Gallagher, L. (2021). The danger of the single story: Evaluation, ethics and the Global South. In *Ethics for evaluation* (pp. 188–210). Routledge.

Oldfield, S. (2008). Who's serving whom? Partners, process, and products in service-learning projects in South African urban geography. *Journal of Geography in Higher Education, 32*(2), 269–285.

Oliff, P., Palacios, V., Johnson, I., & Leachman, M. (2013, March 19). *Recent deep state higher education cuts may harm students and the economy for years to come.* Center on Budget and Policy Priorities. https://www.cbpp.org/research/recent-deep-state-higher-education-cuts-may-harm-students-and-the-economy-for-years-to

Organizing Committee for Assessing Meaningful Community Engagement in Health & Health Care Programs & Policies. (2022, February 14). Assessing meaningful community engagement: A conceptual model to advance health equity through transformed systems for health. *NAM Perspectives.* https://doi.org/10.31478/202202c

Orlov, A. B. (1992). Carl Rogers and contemporary humanism. *Journal of Russian and East European Psychology, 30,* 36–41.

Padmanabha, S. (2018). Indigenous methods and pedagogy: Revisiting ethics in community service-learning. *Engaged Scholar Journal: Community-Engaged Research, Teaching, and Learning, 4*(1), 143–160.

Palasz, E. (2016, February 23). In the middle of 'where they want to be': What rural students contribute to UW. *Badger Herald*. https://badgerherald.com/features/2016/02/23/in-the-middle-of-where-they-want-to-be-what-rural-students-contribute-to-uw/

Parent, M. M., & Harvey, J. (2009). Towards a management model for sport and physical activity community-based partnerships. *European Sport Management Quarterly, 9*(1), 23–45.

Pascoe, E. A., & Smart Richman, L. (2009). Perceived discrimination and health: A meta-analytic review. *Psychological Bulletin, 135*(4), 531–554.

Patton, L. D., Renn, K. A., Guido, F. M., & Quaye, S. J. (2016). *Student development in college: Theory, research, and practice.* John Wiley & Sons.

Peek, J. (2016, March 10). Young and homeless: LGBTQ+ youth are at great risk. *Isthmus.* https://isthmus.com/news/cover-story/homeless-lgbtq-youth-are-at-greatest-risk/

Penn Medicine Center for Health Equity Advancement. (2020, October 7). *Cultural humility.* https://www.chea.upenn.edu/cultural-humility/

Perkins, D. F., and Noam, G. G. (2007). Characteristics of sports-based youth development programs. *New Directions for Youth Development, 2007*(115), 75–84.

Peters-Davis, N., & Shultz, J. (2015). *Challenges of multicultural education: Teaching and taking diversity courses.* Routledge.

Peterson, T. H. (2009). Engaged scholarship: Reflections and research on the pedagogy of social change. *Teaching in Higher Education, 14*(5), 541–552.

Petty, T., & Thomas, C. (2014). Approaches to a successful adult education program. *College Student Journal, 48*(3), 473–480.

Philipsen, M. I. (2003). Race, the college classroom, and service learning: A practitioner's tale. *Journal of Negro Education, 72*(2), 230–240.

Piepzna-Samarasinha, L. L. (2018). *Care work: Dreaming disability justice.* Arsenal Pulp Press.

Pompa, L. (2002, Fall). Service-learning as crucible: Reflections on immersion, context, power, and transformation. *Michigan Journal of Community Service Learning,* 67–76.

Preece, J. (2016). Negotiating service learning through community engagement: Adaptive leadership, knowledge, dialogue and power. *Education as Change, 20*(1), 1–22.

Purzycki, B. G., Ross, C. T., Apicella, C., Atkinson, Q. D., Cohen, E., McNamara, R. A., Willard, A. K., Xygalatas, D., Norenzayan, A., & Henrich, J. (2018). Material security, life history, and moralistic religions: A cross-cultural examination. *PLOS ONE, 13*(3), e0193856. https://doi.org/10.1371/journal.pone.0193856

Racin, L., & Gordon, E. (2018). *Community academic research partnerships in digital contexts: Opportunities, limitations, and new ways to promote mutual benefit.* https://elabhome.blob.core.windows.net/resources/mou.pdf

Ratnatunga, J. (2012). Ivory towers and legal powers: Attitudes and behaviour of town and gown to the accounting research-practice gap. *Journal of Applied Management Accounting Research, 10*(2), 1–20.

Resnick, B. (2019, January 4). *Intellectual humility: The importance of knowing you might be wrong.* Vox. https://www.vox.com/science-and-health/2019/1/4/17989224/intellectual-humility-explained-psychology-replication

Reynolds, J. (2022). Notes from the icehouse: Research in theory and practice. *Global Environment, 15*(1), 177–185.

Rizzo, M. J. (2004). *A (less than) zero sum game? State funding for public education: How public higher education institutions have lost* [Doctoral dissertation, Cornell University].

Rodgers, R. F. (1990). Student development. In U. Delworth, G. R. Hanson, & Associates (Eds.), *Student services: A handbook for the profession* (2nd ed., pp. 117–164). Jossey-Bass.

Rogers, A., & Welch, B. (2009). Using standardized clients in the classroom: An evaluation of a training module to teach active listening skills to social work students. *Journal of Teaching in Social Work, 29*(2), 153–168.

Rogers, C. R. (1951). *Client-centered therapy.* Houghton-Mifflin.

RSA. (2013, December 10). *Brené Brown on empathy* [Video]. YouTube. https://www.youtube.com/watch?v=1Evwgu369Jw&t=5s&ab_channel=RSA

Rush University Medical Center. (2016, June 8). *Community snapshot: North Lawndale.* https://www.rush.edu/sites/default/files/2020-10/chna-north-lawndale.pdf

Sampson, R. J. (2012). *Great American city.* University of Chicago Press.

Sanders, M. J., Van Oss, T., & McGeary, S. (2016). Analyzing reflections in service learning to promote personal growth and community self-efficacy. *Journal of Experiential Education, 39*(1), 73–88.

Sandy, M., & Holland, B. (2006). Different worlds and common ground: Community partner perspectives on campus-community partnerships. *Michigan Journal of Community Service Learning, 13*(1), 30–43.

Santiago-Ortiz, A. (2019). From critical to decolonizing service-learning: Limits and possibilities of social justice-based approaches to community service-learning. *Michigan Journal of Community Service Learning, 25*(1), 43–54.

Satter, B. (2009). *Family properties: Race, real estate, and the exploitation of Black urban America.* Metropolitan Books.

Schechner, R. (1995). Problematizing jargon. *The Drama Review, 39*(1), 7–9. https://www.jstor.org/stable/1146396?origin=crossref

Schlake, M. R. (2015). Community engagement: Nine principles. *Cornhusker Economics, 726.* https://digitalcommons.unl.edu/agecon_cornhusker/726/

Schmitt-McQuitty, L., Smith, M. H., & Young, J. C. (2011). Preparing volunteers to meet the developmental needs of youth audiences. *Journal of Extension, 49*(1), 1IAW1.

Seattle Neighborhoods. (n.d.). *Strategies for equitable engagement.* Retrieved April 5, 2023, from https://www.seattle.gov/documents/Departments/RSJI/RacialEquity/Strategies-for-Equitable-Engagement.docx

Seifer, S. D., & Sgambelluri, A. (2008). Mobilizing partnerships for social change. *Progress in Community Health Partnerships: Research, Education, and Action, 2*(2), 81–82. https://muse.jhu.edu/article/240846/summary

Shor, R., Cattaneo, L., & Calton, J. (2017). Pathways of transformational service learning: Exploring the relationships between context, disorienting dilemmas, and student response. *Journal of Transformative Education, 15*(2), 156–173.

Simis, M. J., Madden, H., Cacciatore, M. A., & Yeo, S. K. (2016). The lure of rationality: Why does the deficit model persist in science communication? *Public Understanding of Science, 25*(4), 400–414.

Sirolli, E. (2012, August). *Want to help someone? Shut up and listen!* [Video]. TED. https://www.ted.com/talks/ernesto_sirolli_want_to_help_someone_shut_up_and_listen?lnguage=en

Skloot, R. (2017). *The immortal life of Henrietta Lacks.* Broadway Paperbacks.

Skoda, H. (2018). Collective violence in fourteenth- and fifteenth-century Oxford. In P. Dhont & E. Boran (Eds.), *Student revolt, city, and society in Europe* (pp. 222–234). Routledge.

Sleeter, C., & Carmona, J. F. (2017). *Un-standardizing curriculum: Multicultural teaching in the standards-based classroom.* Teachers College Press.

Smith, D. A. (2021). *Achieving financial equity and justice for HBCUs*. The Century Foundation. https://tcf.org/content/report/achieving-financial-equity-justice-hbcus/

Smith, L. T. (2021). *Decolonizing methodologies: Research and indigenous peoples*. Bloomsbury Publishing.

Social Sciences and Humanities Research Council. (n.d.). *About SSHRC*. Retrieved March 21, 2023, from https://www.sshrc-crsh.gc.ca/about-au_sujet/index-eng.aspx

Soukup, P. A. (1999). Service learning in communication: Why? In D. Droge & B. Murphy (Eds.), *Voices of strong democracy: Service-learning and communication studies* (pp. 7–11). American Association of Higher Education. https://scholarcommons.scu.edu/comm/85/

Standifer, A. M. (2021). *To teach, to serve: Inquiring into the impact of land-grant institutions on stakeholder perceptions of the town-gown relationship* [Unpublished doctoral dissertation, University of Georgia].

Stanford University. (n.d.). *Stanford: Our vision*. Retrieved March 21, 2022, from https://ourvision.stanford.edu/

Stephens, M. (2019, February 12). Voluntourism is self-serving, harmful to communities. *Emory Wheel*. https://emorywheel.com/voluntourism-is-self-serving-harmful-to-communities/

Stevenson, B. (2014). *Just mercy: A story of justice and redemption*. Spiegel & Grau.

Stoecker, R. (2005). *Research methods for community change: A project-based approach*. Sage Publications.

Stoecker, R. (2016). *Liberating service learning and the rest of higher education civic engagement*. Temple University Press.

Stoecker, R., Beckman, M., & Min, B. H. (2010). Evaluating the community impact of higher education civic engagement. In H. E. Fitzgerald, C. Burack, & S. D. Seifer (Eds.), *Handbook of engaged scholarship: Contemporary landscapes, future directions* (Vol. 2, pp. 177–196). Michigan State University Press.

Stoecker, R., & Tryon, E. (n.d.). *Community standards for service learning* brochure. Retrieved from https://morgridge.wisc.edu/wp-content/uploads/sites/4/2017/06/Community-Standards-for-Service-Learning_7.5.17.pdf

Stoecker, R., & Tryon, E. (2008). The unheard voices: Community organizations and service-learning. *Journal of Higher Education Outreach and Engagement, 12*(3), 47–60.

Stoecker, R., & Tryon, E. A. (Eds.) (2009). *The unheard voices: Community organizations and service learning*. Temple University Press.

Stovall, D. (2016). *Born out of struggle: Critical race theory, school creation, and the politics of interruption*. State University of New York Press.

Strand, K., Marullo, S., Cutforth, N., Stoecker, R., & Donohue, P. (2003). Principles of best practice for community-based research. *Michigan Journal of Community Service Learning, 9*(3), 5–15.

Suarez-Balcazar, Y. (2020). Meaningful engagement in research: Community residents as co-creators of knowledge. *American Journal of Community Psychology, 65*(3–4), 261–271.

Sue, D. W. (2010, November 17). Microaggressions: More than just race. *Psychology Today*. https://www.psychologytoday.com/us/blog/microaggressions-in-everyday-life/201011/microaggressions-more-just-race

Sue, D. W. (2016). *Race talk and the conspiracy of silence: Understanding and facilitating difficult dialogues on race*. John Wiley & Sons.

Sue, D. W., Capodilupo, C. M., & Holder, A. (2008). Racial microaggressions in the life experience of Black Americans. *Professional Psychology: Research and Practice, 39*(3), 329.

Sue, D. W., Lin, A. I., Torino, G. C., Capodilupo, C. M., & Rivera, D. P. (2009). Racial microaggressions and difficult dialogues on race in the classroom. *Cultural Diversity and Ethnic Minority Psychology, 15*(2), 183–190.

Swords, A. C., & Kiely, R. (2010). Beyond pedagogy: Service learning as movement building in higher education. *Journal of Community Practice, 18*(2–3), 148–170.

Taylor, G. (n.d.). *St. Scholastica Day Riot: When English people killed dozens over the taste of wine.* History Daily. Retrieved June 13, 2022, from https://historydaily.org/st-scholastica-day-riot-facts-stories-trivia

Taylor, K. B., & Baker, A. R. (2020). Examining the role of discomfort in collegiate learning and development. *Journal of College Student Development, 60*(2), 174–188.

Taylor, K. B., & Reynolds, D. J. (2019). Dissonance. In E. S. Abes, S. R. Jones, & D-L. Stewart (Eds.), *Rethinking college student development theory using critical frameworks* (pp. 94–109). Stylus Publishing.

Tchilingirian, J. S. (2018). Producing knowledge, producing credibility: British think-tank researchers and the construction of policy reports. *International Journal of Politics, Culture, and Society, 31*(2), 161–178.

Tervalon, M., & Murray-Garcia, J. (1998). Cultural humility versus cultural competence: A critical distinction in defining physician training outcomes in multicultural education. *Journal of Health Care for the Poor and Underserved, 9*(2), 117–125.

Thomas, S. B., & Quinn, S. C. (1991). Public health then and now: the Tuskegee Syphilis Study, 1932 to 1972: implications for HIV education and AIDS risk education programs in the black community. *American Journal of Public Health, 81*(11), 1498–1504.

Tinker, B. (2004). *LARA: Engaging controversy with a non-violent, transformative response* [Worksheet available on request]. Stanford University. https://sparqtools.org/lara/

Tomazos, K., & Butler, R. (2011). Volunteer tourists in the field: A question of balance? *Tourism Management, 33*, 177–187.

Trent University. (n.d.). *Trent Community Research Centre.* Retrieved March 3, 2023, from https://www.trentu.ca/community-based-research/

Tryon, E. (n.d.). *The community-university partnership: Structures for accessing resources of higher education institutions* [Unpublished master's thesis, Edgewood College].

Tryon, E., & Madden, H. (2019). Actualizing critical commitments for community engagement professionals. *Journal of Higher Education Outreach and Engagement, 23*(1), 57–80.

Tryon, E., Madden, H., & Sarmiento, C. (2016). *Executive summary: Preliminary findings of spring 2016 community-based research on UW-Madison partnerships.* Morgridge Center for Public Service. https://morgridge.wiscweb.wisc.edu/wp-content/uploads/sites/4/2017/06/CSCS-570-CBR-class-executive-summary1.pdf

Tryon, E., Slaughter, M., & Ross, J. A. (2015). The need for a paradigm shift in community-based learning partnerships to evaluate community impacts. In O. Delano-Oriaran, M. W. Penick-Parks, & S. Fondrie (Eds.), *The SAGE sourcebook of service-learning and civic engagement* (pp. 191–198). Sage Publications.

Tryon, E., Stoecker, R., Martin, A., Seblonka, K., Hilgendorf, A., & Nellis, M. (2008). The challenge of short-term service-learning. *Michigan Journal of Community Service Learning, 14*(2), 16–26.

Tuck, E., & Yang, K. (2012). Decolonization is not a metaphor. *Decolonization: Indigeneity, Education, and Society, 1*(1), 1–40.

Tuck, E., & Yang, K. W. (2014). R-words: Refusing research. *Humanizing research: Decolonizing qualitative inquiry with youth and communities, 223*, 248.

Tuhiwai Smith, L. (2012). *Decolonizing methodologies: Research and indigenous peoples.* Zed Books.

University of Connecticut. (n.d.). *Husky Sport.* Retrieved March 22, 2023, from https://huskysport.uconn.edu/

University of Michigan, Program on Intergroup Relations. (n.d.). *About the Program on Intergroup Relations.* Retrieved March 22, 2023, from https://igr.umich.edu/about

University of Minnesota, Office for Public Engagement. (n.d.). *Review Committee on Community-Engaged Scholarship.* Retrieved March 21, 2023, from https://engagement.umn.edu/faculty/review-committee-community-engaged-scholarship

University of Minnesota, UROC. (n.d.). Retrieved April 17, 2023 from https://uroc.umn.edu/news-events/living-promise

University of Texas at El Paso. (n.d.). *About UTEP.* Retrieved March 21, 2023, from https://www.utep.edu/about/?utep-home

University of Wisconsin–Madison. (n.d.-a). *Budget in brief: Budget report 2019–2020 | Board of Visitors edition.* Retrieved March 21, 2023, from https://budget.wisc.edu/content/uploads/Budget-in-Brief-2019-20_web.pdf

University of Wisconsin–Madison. (n.d.-b). *Wisconsin idea.* Retrieved March 21, 2022, from https://www.wisc.edu/wisconsin-idea/

University of Wisconsin–Madison. (2020, October). *Diversity update 2020.* https://diversity.wisc.edu/wp-content/uploads/2020/10/Diversity-Forum-2020-APIR-Diversity-Update.pdf

University of Wisconsin–Madison, Office of Data, Academic Planning and Institutional Research. (n.d.). *Distance education, state authorization, and disclosures.* Retrieved March 21, 2023, from https://apir.wisc.edu/institution/distance-education/

University of Wisconsin–Madison, Office of Inclusion Education. (2019). *Social justice 201 curriculum.*

University of Wisconsin–Madison, Office of the Chancellor. (2018, November 7). *UW's Civic Action Plan: The Wisconsin Idea at work.* https://chancellor.wisc.edu/blog/uws-civic-action-plan-the-wisconsin-idea-at-work/

Vaccarro, A. (2009). Racial identity and the ethics of service-learning as pedagogy. In S. Y. Evans, C. M. Taylor, M. R. Dunlap, & D. S. Miller (Eds.), *African Americans and community engagement in higher education: Community service, service-learning, and community based research* (pp. 119–133). University of New York Press.

Van Stekelenburg, L. H., De Ruyter, D., & Sanderse, W. (2021). 'Equipping students with an ethical compass.' What does it mean, and what does it imply? *Ethics and Education, 16*(1), 91–107.

Vaughn, L. M., Jacquez, F., & Zhen-Duan, J. (2018). Perspectives of community co-researchers about group dynamics and equitable partnership within a community–academic research team. *Health Education & Behavior, 45*(5), 682–689.

Venkatesh, M. J., Elchert, A. R., Fakoya, B., Fernandez, F., Kwong, A.c., Liu, Y. J., Lotfy, P., Lowe, D. D., Petty, C. A., Rodríguez-delaRosa, A., Seguinot, B. O., Shi, Y. & Loparao, J. J.. (2021). More than just content: Building community in the graduate classroom. *Nature Biotechnology, 39*, 1161–1165.

Vianden, J. (2018). "In all honesty, you don't learn much": White college men's perceptions of diversity courses and instructors. *International Journal of Teaching and Learning in Higher Education, 30*(3), 465–476.

Vidyasagar, A. (2016). The art of root cause analysis. *Quality Progress, 49*(1), 48.

Villalobos, J. D., Gonzalez, A. L., Núñez, G. G. & Sirin, C. V. (2022). Beyond borders: employing empathic global citizenship as a framework for enhancing critical community engagement. In W. Szmodis and S. E. Stanlick (Eds.), *Perspectives on lifelong learning and global citizenship: beyond the classroom (sustainable development goals series),* (pp. 35–55). Springer Nature. doi.org/10.1007/978-3-031-00974-7_3

Vincent, C. S., Moore, S. B., Lynch, C., Lefker, J., & Awkward, R. J. (2021). Critically engaged civic learning: A comprehensive restructuring of service-learning approaches. *Michigan Journal of Community Service Learning, 27*(2), 107–129.

Vostal, B. R., McNaughton, D., Benedek-Wood, E., & Hoffman, K. (2015). Preparing teachers for collaborative communication: Evaluation of instruction in an active listening strategy. *National Teacher Education Journal, 8*(2), 5–14.

Wallace, D. F. (n.d.). This is water by David Foster Wallace (full transcript and audio). *Farnam Street.* Retrieved March 22, 2023, from https://fs.blog/david-foster-wallace -this-is-water/

Wark, J. (2021). Land acknowledgements in the academy: Refusing the settler myth. *Curriculum Inquiry, 51*(2), 191–209.

Warren, D. L. (1976). *Town-gown conflict: Ideology, class resentment, and group interest, in the responses to an elite university* [Doctoral dissertation, University of Michigan]. ProQuest. https://www.proquest.com/openview/05d470cfaed590c000ec24d33856f1 83/1?pq-origsite=gscholar&cbl=18750&diss=

Warren, M. R., Thompson, J. P., & Saegert, S. (2001). *Social capital and poor communities* (1st papercover ed.). Russell Sage Foundation.

Weger Jr., H., Castle Bell, G., Minei, E. M., & Robinson, M. C. (2014). The relative effectiveness of active listening in initial interactions. *International Journal of Listening, 28*(1), 13–31.

Wenger, E. (1998). Communities of practice: Learning as a social system. *Systems Thinker, 9*(5), 2–3.

Whiteford, L. M., & Trotter, R.T.T. (2008). *Ethics for anthropological research and practice.* Waveland Press.

Williams, D. M. (2018). The unheard voices of dissatisfied clients: Listening to community partners as feminist praxis. In K. L. Blair & L. Nickoson (Eds.), *Composing feminist interventions: Activism, engagement, praxis* (pp. 409–426). WAC Clearinghouse, University Press of Colorado.

Wisconsin Experience. (n.d.-a). *Intellectual confidence.* University of Wisconsin–Madison. Retrieved March 23, 2022, from https://wisconsinexperience.wisc.edu/intellec tual-confidence/

Wisconsin Experience. (n.d.-b). *Purposeful action.* University of Wisconsin–Madison. Retrieved March 21, 2022, from https://wisconsinexperience.wisc.edu/purposeful -action/

Wisconsin Policy Forum. (2011, May). *UW in the 21st century: Less money, more freedom?* https://wispolicyforum.org/research/uw-in-the-21st-century-less-money-more-freedom

Wise, T. (2008). *The pathology of privilege: Racism, white denial and the costs of inequality.* Media Education Foundation. https://www.mediaed.org/transcripts/Tim-Wise -On-White-Privilege-Transcript.pdf

Witmer, D. F., Silverman, D. A., & Gaschen, D. J. (2009). Working to learn and learning to work: A profile of service-learning courses in university public relations programs. *Public Relations Review, 35*(2), 153–155.

Wolff, R., & Resnick, S. (1987). *Economics: Marxian versus neoclassical.* Johns Hopkins University Press.

Woods, F. A., & Ruscher, J. B. (2021). 'Calling-out' vs. 'calling-in' prejudice: Confrontation style affects inferred motive and expected outcomes. *British Journal of Social Psychology*, *60*(1), 50–73.

World Health Organization. (n.d.). *Social determinants of health*. Retrieved March 22, 2023, from https://www.who.int/health-topics/social-determinants-of-health#tab=tab_1

Wright, M., Caufield, C., Gray, G., & Olson, J. (2005). International research capacity-building programs for nurses to study the drug phenomenon in Latin America: Challenges and perspectives. *Revista Latino-Americana de Enfermagem*, *13*(spe2), 1095–1101. https://doi.org/10.1590/s0104-11692005000800002

Yosso, T. J. (2016). Whose culture has capital?: A critical race theory discussion of community cultural wealth. In *Critical race theory in education* (pp. 113–136). Routledge.

Zastoupil, G. J., Tryon, E., Madden, H. C., Keita, N. A., & Lipscomb, T. D. (2020). Cultural factors in preparing students for community-engaged scholarship. In A. S. Zimmerman (Ed.), *Preparing students for community-engaged scholarship in higher education* (pp. 21–42). IGI Global.

Zimmerman, A. S. (Ed.). (2020). *Preparing students for community-engaged scholarship in higher education*. IGI Global.

Contributors

Cheryl Bauer-Armstrong has designed native plantings and restorations in school-yards, parklands, neighborhoods, and home landscapes for the UW–Madison Arboretum. She has been director of Earth Partnership since 2006, leading the effort in initiatives to address environmental justice, water stewardship, nature connectedness, equitable education, culturally relevant pedagogy, and community-based conservation in twenty-two states and Puerto Rico.

Del M. N. Bharath, Ph.D., is Assistant Professor of Public Administration at Savannah State University and has a demonstrated history of professional experience in the nonprofit sector. She is the author of numerous publications, including "Strategies for Introspection and Instruction Towards Antiracism in Public Management and Administration" (*Journal of Management and Public Policy*).

Kathy Cramer is the Natalie C. Holton Chair of Letters and Science and the Virginia Sapiro Professor of Political Science at the University of Wisconsin–Madison.

James DeSota is Assistant Executive Director of UROC. He connects university researchers with community needs and oversees UROC's research agenda, scholarly affiliation process, and grant-related initiatives. Previously, James served as a community organizer, an AmeriCorps VISTA, a Peace Corps volunteer, a researcher, and a consultant.

Jamilah Ducar, Ed.D., serves as Executive Director of the Engaged Campus for the University of Pittsburgh. Ducar leads the community affairs function and establishes infrastructure necessary to mobilize the breadth of Pitt's engagement assets so that Pitt becomes a partner of choice in regional progress. She chairs the national Place-Based Justice Network.

Sandeep Dutta is a doctoral student with a concentration in sport management at the University of Connecticut whose interests lie in critically exploring programs that use sport for youth development. Sandeep has been with Husky Sport since 2021 as a member of the impact assessment team.

Kolin Ebron is an academic advisor at the University of Connecticut. He received his Ph.D. in sport management from UConn in 2021. He previously worked with the Husky Sport program as a graduate assistant and postdoctoral research associate. His research interests focus on Black males who participate in SBYD programs.

Justin Evanovich earned a Ph.D. in sport management (2011) from the University of Connecticut. A member of the leadership team with Husky Sport since 2007, he has facilitated community and campus partnerships, curriculum development, program evaluation, research, teaching, and the recruitment, development, and promotion of students, staff, and partners.

Merry Farrier-Babanovski first served as a graduate assistant helping develop the programming at the University of Wisconsin-South Madison Partnership from 2016 to 2018, and then became the Partnership's first Assistant Director until January 2023.

Dr. Azuri Gonzalez is Executive Director of the Alliance for Hispanic Serving Research Universities, Director for Institutional Policy and Practice at the Diana Natalicio Institute for Hispanic Student Success, and the former director of the Center for Community Engagement and the Center for Faculty Leadership and Development at the University of Texas at El Paso.

Bertha A. Gonzalez is a community engagement preparation graduate assistant for the Morgridge Center for Public Service, University of Wisconsin–Madison. She is a first-generation college student with a B.S. in human development and family studies and psychology and certificates in Chicano/a and Latino/a studies and criminal justice. She is currently pursuing her master's in counseling psychology.

Dr. Lena Jones is a political science instructor at Minneapolis Community College and Program Director of Race in America, a summer field study course of the Higher Education Consortium for Urban Affairs that explores past and current civil rights issues. She is also a 2022 Campus Compact Community Engagement Network Fellow.

Dr. Ruth Kassel is Associate Director at the Center for Academic Community Engagement at Siena College focusing on staff, faculty, and student development in community-engaged teaching, learning, and research. Her programs include student-faculty partnership in course design, summer interdisciplinary and participatory research, yearlong capstone mentorship, and faculty development.

Virginia Lee is a stalwart advocate for programming that fosters academic achievement and community engagement. She has over twenty years of experience developing and facilitating youth programs for nonprofit organizations and institutions of higher learning, including AmeriCorps, Reach Dane, the University of Wisconsin–Madison, and Edgewood College.

Laura Livingston, Ph.D., is Director of Sustainable Agriculture and Assistant Professor of Food Studies at Chatham University, Pittsburgh. Laura received her Ph.D. at UW–Madison studying the impacts of COVID-19 on collaborative food systems research. Prior to school, she served as a Peace Corps volunteer in Ghana.

Jennifer McGarry is a professor of sport management at the University of Connecticut. She received her Ph.D. from The Ohio State University in 2000 and started her career at UConn in 2001. She founded Husky Sport in 2003 and has been the principal investigator on a USDA grant that funds the program since 2005.

Jamie Morales is a doctoral student at the University of Connecticut. His research interests include *Latinidades* and sports, with particular interest in critically examining sports-based youth development initiatives within Latina/e/o/x communities. Jamie earned his master's degree in sport management at the University of Tennessee, Knoxville.

Maria Moreno, Ph.D., a cultural anthropologist, is a multicultural outreach specialist for the Earth Partnership program in the global health program at UW–Madison. She develops curriculum and programs centered on ecological restoration and professional development for teachers. She also designs and teaches CBL and international internships on environmental education in Mexico, Nicaragua, the Dominican Republic, Ecuador, and Puerto Rico.

Dr. Amelia Ortiz has over fifteen years of experience in various roles throughout higher education. She is specifically focusing on working with adult learners and underrepresented students to increase completion rates. Also, she volunteers to facilitate diversity, equity, and inclusion discussions on how to impact students and faculty.

Aaron Posey is an educational Workday Student consultant at Avaap and Ph.D. candidate with twenty years of experience in higher education and a passion for student development/advocacy. A leader in the student affairs division who has created initiatives that foster student success, he believes education can change the world and aims to empower students through mentorship.

John W. Zeigler Jr. is Director of the Egan Office of Urban Education and Community Partnerships (UECP) and adjunct faculty in community service studies. He provides guidance in the goal of advancing DePaul faculty and student engagement with public agencies and community-based organizations and schools in dealing with hyperlocal issues.

Makeda Zulu is University of Minnesota Robert J. Jones Urban Research and Outreach-Engagement Center's (UROC) chief executive officer with primary responsibility for securing UROC's success in all aspects of its work. She provides executive oversight of strategic planning, revenue generation, financial stewardship, organizational development, staff management, and operational activities.

Index

Elizabeth A. Tryon, M. Ed., is an emeritus of the University of Wisconsin–Madison, where she served as Assistant Director for Community-Engaged Scholarship at the Morgridge Center for Public Service. She is the coauthor of *The Unheard Voices: Community Organizations and Service Learning* (Temple).

Haley C. Madden, Ph.D., is the Assistant Director of Community-Engaged Scholarship at the Morgridge Center for Public Service at the University of Wisconsin–Madison.

Cory Sprinkel is the Community-Engaged Scholarship Specialist at the Morgridge Center for Public Service at the University of Wisconsin–Madison.